What's Next?

Igniting Change & IMPACT in Health, Fitness & Life...NOW!

28 of the World's Top Experts Divulge Their
Predictions About Optimizing Health, Vitality,
Energy & Performance!

Compiled by **Todd Durkin**, MA, CSCS
Author, Speaker, Life-Transformation Coach

ISBN: 9798352221389

The publisher disclaims responsibility for adverse effects or consequences from the misapplication or injudicious use of the information contained in this book. Mention of resources and associations does not imply an endorsement.

Table of Contents

Get Your Mind Right

Recovery Matters

Create an Experience and Build Community

Get Our Kids Fit

Sports Specialization

New Ways to Work with Unique Populations

Looking Ahead

Introduction

"What's next?"

I get this question A LOT. Honestly, from about 2015 until the pandemic, I hated this question.

I used to think, "Why does there always have to be a 'next'? Can't I just keep doing what I'm doing and let things unfold naturally? I like where I'm at."

And then the pandemic hit in March 2020, and that left ALL of us in a constant state of uncertainty. And trepidation and fear. And confusion. And fatigue. And...the list goes on and on. Let me explain.

I'd like to let you inside of my head the last couple years (since March 2020). You may not believe what I'm about to write, but it's the truth.

Here are just "10" of the hundreds of deep questions I asked myself on a regular basis throughout the pandemic...

- "How long is this going to last?"
- "Wait, are you really telling me that I have to close my business?"
- "Are you really telling me we can open after 90-days but that my team and I need to lug my equipment outside for the next 3-months so people can workout?"
- "Are our revenues really down 70%?"

- "How am I going to get through this time energetically?"
- "Why do I feel so exhausted? How am I going to continue to lead my people when I have no energy myself?"
- "Are we really going to have to teach our groups classes and sessions online for the members and clients who do not want to come back to the gym?"
- "What is the state of our fitness industry and what is the outlook for brick & mortar long-term business prosperity?"
- "Why are 'they' trying to kill the fitness industry when it's us who are the ones who are going to help keep people healthy and ALIVE with all this going on?"
- "Why do I feel so empty and broken?"
- "Can I really be burnt-out?"
- "Why is my body failing me in the midst of one of the biggest battles of my life?"
- "Maybe I should sell the business?"
- "Why do I feel like I'm in such a gap in life, despite having more success than I could have ever wished for?"
- "If I feel like this, I wonder if other people feel like this?"

OK, that's more than "10" questions. That's the 'And Then Some' I always talk about. But the point is, I had so much head chatter.

Heck, I wrote the book, *Get Your Mind Right*, and here I was battling daily to just get my OWN mind right. Seriously.

But this is real talk. These are just some of the deep, personal questions I asked myself on a daily basis.

And I must have asked myself all these questions every single day for what seemed like an eternity. It definitely was years.

Maybe you asked yourself some of these same questions also.

As the pandemic wore on and in much of 2021 and 2022, my internal questions changed, despite being tired (and even burnt-out at times).

Can anyone else relate to being completely burnt-out and shot but feeling like you have to keep going?

Those previous questions led me to ask even deeper questions as time wore on and we got through the dregs of the pandemic.

As time wore on, my questions started "shifting" a bit, going even deeper, and looking more like this...

- "Where are the opportunities in all of this?"
- "How can I use this interesting time of life to somehow get better?"
- "How can I use this pandemic as an opportunity to somehow even further pivot into some of the things that I believe I'm being led to?"
- "God, how do you want me to lead this industry, Fitness Quest 10, my team, the Mastermind and those I coach....and even me? What do you want me to focus my talents on?"
- "How can I use this pandemic as an opportunity to change into an even better version of myself?"
- "OK, I think I really am burnt out. But how do I address it?"
- "How can I rearrange my relationship with Fitness Quest 10 to not be in so much of the day-to-day operational side of things and focus even more on speaking, writing, and coaching?"
- "How can I share my experiences, pains, gains, and mindset to potentially help other trainers, coaches, and life-transformers

who genuinely want to help the world 'Be Better' and 'Do Better' and be a positive beacon of positivity and light?

- "How can I create more IMPACT in the world that so desperately needs more hope, motivation, inspiration, good health, positivity, optimism, understanding, and LOVE?"

- "In a time of such darkness in our world, how can we as a training industry deliver MORE of what the world needs right now?"

- "How can I look back in 5-years from now and not be resentful or regretful of what happened and instead look back in full-gratitude saying, 'Thank you. These last few trying years have been absolutely crucial in me becoming the man I have become. And I certainly would not have created all that I have created without it'?"

- "How can I rearrange my schedule so that I can better focus on the things that will 'move the needle' even more?

- "Where are the best opportunities that currently exist for our industry?"

OK, once again, that's more than "10" questions. But the 25+ deep thoughts and questions are so intimate to my soul, I must have asked myself many of them HUNDREDS of times in the past couple years alone.

Do you resonate with any of these questions?

I know, deep thoughts. Deep questions. And ones you have perhaps thought of yourself.

I'll never apologize for going "too deep." I definitely like to think deep, contemplate my life's purpose, and reflect on how I'm doing maximizing my gifts. I pray daily for guidance on these questions.

I also pride myself on my core values of being "authentic" and "genuine" and "loyal." And hence my reasoning for sharing my deepest and most vulnerable thoughts and questions with you today. Some of you are my most loyal of listeners, readers, fans, followers, or friends. Thank you.

Which brings us to today…

There has been a lot of pain, sweat, blood, tears, and even loss that has brought us to this book today. Congratulations for picking it up, reading it, and thinking about how it's going to "IMPACT" you!!

Today, we are still living in some crazy times. Can I get an "Amen" to that?

In a world that we have almost come to accept as "crazy," perhaps a better word is "uncertain."

Following the pandemic that disrupted and affected all of us and our businesses starting in 2020, we are now grappling with other challenges. As I write and release this book in October 2022, we are faced with…

- High inflation (currently at 8.5% as I write this).

- Increasing interest rates across the board; Heck, real-estate interest rates alone have doubled (whereas 30-year loans averaged just 3.0% 6-months ago, we are now at approximately 6.0%). But it's interest rates on all things.

- Price of oil is at $87.00 barrel (it was as high as $120 barrel recently; But was as low as $60.00 per barrel a year ago and it was almost at zero dollars at the beginning of the pandemic). These high prices affect gas and fuel prices, which is more than double what it was even a year ago.

- The price of real-estate is at a record high. Could you imagine trying to get into the market now as a first-time buyer in some parts of the country? Now that is crazy!
- A war in the Ukraine against Russia that is affecting worldwide policies.
- Supply chains for EVERYTHING are taking weeks, months, or even years longer than they should.
- A very murky economic forecast for the next 2-3 years. As we move forward, market volatility is certain to play a role and a looming recession could grip us, depending on several factors.

A couple of years ago, I attended an event and Tony Robbins presented. At that time, he said something I'll never forget: **"Winter is coming. Be prepared for winter."**

In those terms, I think "winter" is here now or it could get even a bit "colder" or more bleak economically.

Why am I sharing this?

Because, with the current economic fears and market corrections, we are living in very uncertain times.

Some people are living in fear.

Some people are stuck or stalled.

Some people are just unclear. Uncertain. Living in ambiguity and not clear on the next steps they should take.

Some people are completely burnt-out, empty, lost, or broken.

I can't help but think I've experienced ALL of these at various points in the past 3-years also. Seriously. Anyone else?

BUT, (and it's a very big BUT)…

There is also TREMENDOUS OPPORTUNITY right now... especially in the health and fitness industry or anyone in "healthcare."

And "summer" (growth) and "Fall" (harvest") seasons may be right around the corner if we keep going and are focused on doing the "right" things.

But you gotta make it through winter first.

With every great adversity, challenge, or setback, there is opportunity on the other side.

We compiled this book because this worldwide shift is creating a moment for us to re-define our industry. It's giving us a perfect opportunity to address the needs of people in new, exciting and more effective ways, and it is giving us a chance to help even more people get fit and healthy when the world so desperately needs it.

Think about this...

- The more uncertain and out of control life seems to be, the more certainty and stability are needed. I remind people all the time that they need to "Control The Controllables," especially when it comes to one's health!

- The higher the stress...the MORE people will need us. Those of us who are in the health and fitness industry understand that exercise, fitness, nutrition, and mindset are tools that mitigate and alleviate stress!

- The more people have NOT been able to "touch" each other in the past 3 years, the MORE people are going to need compassion, love, relationships, community, and TOUCH THERAPY as part of their healing, happiness, and fulfillment.

- The more that fear surrounds us...the more that we must ignite gratitude, positivity, hope, optimism, love, compassion, and sound body and mind habits.

- The more UNHEALTHY people have become physically and mentally, the MORE healthy they are going to want and NEED to be. There is just way too much "sickness" and "ill-health" out there, and that's no way to live life.

I guess what I'm trying to say is that if there was ever a time that the world needs us...it's NOW.

If there was ever a time that we were called to serve EVEN MORE... it's NOW.

If there was ever a time to double-down on your gifts and serve people in EVEN greater ways...it's NOW.

If there was ever a time to help people get out of pain (physically, mentally, emotionally, or spiritually)...it's NOW.

If there was ever a time to step into your best and deepest SELF... it's NOW!

If you've been following me for a while, then you know that I am all about creating IMPACT.

I.M.P.A.C.T. stands for:

I = Live Inspired

M= Master Your Craft

P= Play at World Class

A= Take Action

C= Condition for Greatness

T= Be Tenacious

And if there was ever a time to 10x your IMPACT, it's right NOW!

Are you ready to do that?

Then turn the page and keep reading.

This book is not just filled with prophecies and prognostications from me, it's also filled with tons of wisdom from 27 other leaders and experts in the health, fitness, healing, and wellness world. It's people like them…and people like YOU…who will be driving the trends and capitalizing on this moment.

These 27 people are part of my Tribe in some way. They have been with me through the "thick and thin" of the last few years. Some for over a decade. I trust them. I respect them. And I'm really excited for you to "meet" them, hear their extraordinary predictions on "**What's Next**" and see what they are doing to make ripples in the world and create some IMPACT as well.

I do believe that one of the trends of the future is collaboration. Collaboration is going to be mission critical to get things done. This supports the notion of "surrounding yourself with the right people," "Iron Sharpens Iron…who sharpens you?" and "If you want to see yourself in 5 years, look at the books you will read and the people you will surround yourself with."

Well, my friend, in your hands is a "collaborative" book that welcomes 27 fire-breathing dragons (28 if you count me 😊) into your head that will fill you up with wisdom, heart, soul, and intellect to help YOU tap into your best self…and share their thoughts on "**What's Next.**"

Some of the predictions will come true. Some may not. Some of them will come out too late. Others may be too early. But every single one of the predictions is worth considering. These are some of the top thought-leaders in our field, and I admire the work they are doing. Because I believe in them and the great work they are doing, I've asked them to be part of this project. And I take great pride in what you are going to read in each and every chapter.

You may agree with some of it. Some of it you may not. My hope is that you get one, two, or three ideas, confirmations, affirmations, or new connections with an "expert" that may even change the trajectory of your career.

This collaborative book was written to help YOU "live a life worth telling a story about."

Now it's time to reflect on your story. Be grateful for your story. And ultimately get fired-up for **WHAT'S NEXT** with your story.

You ready to go? Dive in and let's get ready to send massive positive shock waves across this world right now because it NEEDS it. It needs us. And it needs YOU! We need an army of men and women committed to be their best and rise up to meet the demands of today's world.

Ready? Let's GOOO!!! I now present to you, *What's Next!*

Much love…and a ton of IMPACT (x28)

Todd Durkin, MA, CSCS
Founder, Fitness Quest 10 & Todd Durkin Enterprises
Author, Speaker, Podcaster…COACH!
The Todd Durkin IMPACT Show Podcast

LOOKING
BACK

Chapter I

Fitness Looks Back To the Future

By Kirk Lawrence

I'm 66 now, and began my fitness journey as a Kenpo Karate student in March of 1972. Surprisingly, it helped me stumble upon the elements of a good early morning routine. My routine included stances, forms, punches, breathing, perspiration, and relaxation – a positive habit that started 50 years ago! Whether involved in fitness, personal training, management, construction, sales, or other business, I kept to an early morning routine, and it was a lifesaver. Will anything in the future equal the benefits gained from a routine performed over a lifetime?

While researching past, current, and future trends in health and fitness, I was drawn to the visionaries and fitness leaders who motivated me through their real-life examples of overcoming the odds, gaining vitality, and becoming beacons of inspiration. My top mentors in the fitness industry give me confidence that the best days for health and wellness are ahead. How do my choices compare with your heroes and mentors?

My Top Titans

It seems like America woke up to the possibilities for health and fitness in the late '60s and early '70s. With the help of television and other media sources, many celebrities and athletes began to spread a message about the importance of fitness for everyone.

✥ **Jack LaLanne** was the first physical fitness mass communicator. For more than a generation, he provided the most effective fitness information available on television. He was a man of legendary fitness stunts – for example, he towed 70 boats in the Long Beach Harbor, over One mile, on his 70th birthday! I first met Jack in the Green Room of the *Today Show* in 1984. My fiancée at the time, Joanie Greggains, was on the show with Jack for a fitness leadership segment. He was a nice guy, and his wife, Elaine, was right by his side.

The funniest story I recall about Jack LaLanne is when he was giving his amazing motivational life story to a standing room only crowd of Fit Pros at the 1987 IDEA Awards ceremony. During his talk he suddenly turned to the side and says, "Look at these buns!" The crowd roared in applause and agreement.

✥ **Bob Bowerman and Phil Knight** showed that jogging could be an effective and enjoyable fitness routine on its own, aside from the competitive sports of track and cross country. Bowerman continued to coach many Olympic and world-class athletes, and along with Phil Knight, were the founders of Nike, Inc. in Beaverton, Oregon. Bowerman's 1966 book, *Jogging*, sold over a million copies, and even helped to create a new category for athletic competition, the Master's Division. Jogging became a popular vigorous activity for personal health and recreation, and early fitness pioneers helped create the '70s jogging craze as a forerunner to the full-blown fitness revolution years later.

✿ **Dr. Kenneth Cooper** is known as the Father of Aerobics. He coined the term "aerobics" in 1966, and his 1968 book, *Aerobics*, included a points system for acquiring improved cardiovascular fitness. In addition, Cooper would be first to speak of the "training effect," as he was testing thousands of both healthy individuals and cardiac rehab patients years before anyone else. Other physicians complained that there was no such thing as preventative exercise, and that Cooper was a quack. However, through the hard work of The Cooper Institute, the validity and benefits of aerobic conditioning were proven over time. More than just the Father of Aerobics, he was a tough and determined Texan, both a visionary and early believer in the benefits of regular exercise. I first became certified as both a personal fitness specialist and a group exercise leader in 1984 at The Cooper Institute. With his wife, Millie, Cooper delivered daily lectures, coaching, and encouraging us to improve the health of Americans, young and old, with programs for aerobic exercise and muscular conditioning. He had a nickname for me, "The Frisco Kid," because I was a 49ers fan.

✿ **Jim Fixx** was a well-known runner and author of the best seller, *The Complete Book of Running*. However, part of his legacy is the fact that he died at 52, ironically while running. His death in 1984 was a wake-up call to not overdo it, and this helped teachers and coaches improve fitness practices to include activities for heart health, muscular activities for strength, endurance, and flexibility, and mental relaxation exercises for optimal health.

✿ When **Jane Fonda** released the "Jane Fonda Workout" videotape in 1982, it created an entire new industry for millions of primarily young urban women in the US. Her Jane Fonda videos, books, and workout studios in Los Angeles and San Francisco revolutionized the concept of indoor group workouts. I first met Fonda in 1982, at one of her early master classes for teachers in the budding new aerobics industry. What a great coach and source of fitness inspiration! Her influence on fitness was global.

✤ **Arnold Schwarzenegger** - Another huge leader in the growing American health and fitness movement was the young Austrian bodybuilder nicknamed "the Austrian Oak." Schwarzenegger won his first Mr. Olympia title in 1977 at the age of 20, then went on to become a popular action star in movies before serving as Chairman of the President's Council on Physical Fitness and Sports from 1989-1992. He helped popularize bodybuilding and weight training for men, women, and physical fitness for kids. He was also a famous, high-profile actor known to millions, and a passionate advocate for improving youth fitness. You should have heard him speak to school students. In his speeches to kids, he recalled that as a child, he would have to "earn" his breakfast with morning activity and exercises before breakfast.

Arnold endorsed "Raisin Youth Fitness.", the youth fitness program my ex-partner and I created and taught. He made it available to every public elementary school in the country in 1991 and 1992. It was a 12-week fitness-related physical education curriculum designed to both prepare American public elementary students for the President's Council physical fitness tests and prepare kids with motivational messages. Over 1,000,000 students practiced Raisin Youth Fitness.

✤ **Bob Anderson** wrote his modern-day Bible on flexibility in 1975 with his book, *Stretching*. It was a godsend for me. I wore out the pages of this book, both as a young Black Belt teacher, and later, in 1979, when I started a career as a personal trainer. When I was asked by a busy, hardworking neurosurgeon if I would be his personal trainer, Anderson's book helped me with the functional benefits of stretching in warm up and cooldown. It also provided specific stretching routines for a wide variety of sports and activities. In 1981, I was hired by a pro football player to help him get in the best shape of his life. A combination of martial arts, running, dance, ballet, yoga and stretching using Bob Anderson's methods, helped this athlete, **Charle Young**, get in terrific condition. He led his teammates by example and then took his team, the 1981 San Francisco 49ers, to a Super Bowl XVI victory.

❦ **Charle Young, Bill Ring, Joe Montana, and Bill Walsh** were all instrumental in encouraging me to develop my own career, and also in the way they embraced innovation in fitness and sports performance. Charle hired me as his personal trainer in Feb of 1981. A month later he encouraged me to "help the other players" because he said they needed what I knew! I followed him down to the 49ers headquarters in Redwood City, California. Bill Ring was a free agent hoping to make the team. Joe Montana was a young promising QB coming from his legendary Notre Dame career. He was determined and hardworking, low key and friendly, always sporting a baseball cap. Bill Walsh asked to meet with me to discuss stretching and its contribution to overall football conditioning… and asked if it could help his tennis game! I kept his phone message to me on a little cassette for 20 years.

❦ **Joanie Greggains** started a 1982 early morning TV exercise show in San Francisco for the CBS affiliate, KPIX. In July of 1983 I met and was hired by Joanie to help her get stronger as an athlete, to share my aerobics knowledge and to help her engage with IDEA and the fitness and aerobics industry. Essentially, my job was to keep Joanie on the cutting edge of the fitness trends so she could mass communicate that message on her daily network syndicated show. This was about 15 years before the birth of the internet, and she already had a daily audience of almost one million viewers. We were also asked to do a TV show filmed at San Quentin for the benefit of the prison population after a deadly riot. That was an unforgettable experience. We worked hard on Morning

Stretch and watched her show grow from five markets to over 100 in syndication!

⭐ **Peter and Kathie Davis** were the pioneering couple who started the IDEA organization in 1982 in San Diego, CA. Thousands of fitness professionals are lucky they did. For almost 40 years IDEA, the association for fitness professionals, has led the way with education, business coaching and fitness inspiration. I was in Osaka, Japan in 1986 leading over 1,000 aerobics competitors in a national aerobics championship known as The Dole Cup. It was an unreal experience, and Peter and Kathie were in the stands cheering. They were instrumental in creating universal appeal for fitness, aerobics and health.

⭐ ⭐ **Todd Durkin** is, in my opinion, at the leading edge of fitness and real health, the current state-of-the-art in coaching greatness, personal fitness training, functional fitness, fun group style workouts, human performance, bodywork/touch, and developing a positive mindset. He and his team train weekend warriors to world champions in a multitude of sports, young and old, and coach the mind, body, spiritual mindset that combine to form a healthy, fit, positive and humble person.

The Future of Fitness
Obesity or Opportunity: The Unmotivated Masses

While these truly iconic American fitness leaders helped pave the way for the health and wellness movement we benefit from today, the limits of the fitness industry can't be ignored. We can all agree that there are more fitness options, information, services, variety and training programs than ever before. At the same time, the stress and pressures of our modern lifestyle have more Americans than ever suffering from the effects of too little movement and too many calories. Excess calories are available faster than you can click "Door Dash" or "Uber Eats."

Without the energy needed to make a change, no action takes place and "stinkin' thinkin'" creeps in to fill the void. There is more youth and adult obesity now than ever before, and the Covid pandemic, now in its early endemic stage, has only increased inactivity as more Americans spend extra time isolated and alone at home. Still, it's a **lack of motivation** to start and continue an exercise regimen that is still the biggest barrier to improving fitness and health outcomes looking ahead.

This challenge is also our greatest health and wellness opportunity. It is through the 12 years of public-school instruction that school students can learn the life-time nutrition and activity practices that can keep our future society healthier and well. Nevertheless, new ways of encouraging people to adopt the "movement is medicine" practice are needed. That is what this book is all about. As we learned from these titans, who created a strong foundation, let's "move" into the future, remembering that our health is precious. Our health is our wealth!

Kirk Lawrence
2021 California Senior Fitness Games 5-time Gold Medalist
Author, *Zero's Heroes*
zeroonceheroforever.com
Motivational Public Speaker
klaw49@icloud.com

Kirk has enjoyed an amazing fitness career, first certified by Dr Kenneth Cooper in 1984 as a personal fitness specialist and group exercise leader in Dallas, TX. Kirk's goal is to help others develop fitness skills and positive mindset that can last a lifetime.

Kirk's story is told in his book, *Zero's Heroes*, and includes growing up in a divorced family, fighting his father, running away at 17, almost murdered hitchhiking, yet unwilling to become a statistic.

In 1981, Kirk became the first personal trainer in the NFL, working with the San Francisco 49ers when he was hired by Charle Young, a

49ers tight end. The positive experience changed both of their lives for the better. Career highlights include earning a Black Belt in Kenpo in 1975 and becoming the first Men's National Champion in FitAerobics in 1984. Kirk was hired by Joanie Greggains and appeared on the Morning Stretch TV show between 1983-1988. During that time, Kirk worked with inmates at San Quentin and filmed a TV show in the prison in 1985. He gave the Opening Keynote Address at the 1st World Aerobics Championships in Chiba, Japan in 1990.

He is also a co-author of *Raisin Youth Fitness*, endorsed by Chairman Arnold Schwarzenegger of the President's Council and offered FREE to public schools in the USA. One million students practiced Raisin Youth Fitness! Kirk was hired by UCSF to develop the training protocol for the landmark, published NIH-funded study on using exercise to build bone mineral density and prevent osteoporosis.

Thirty years later, on September 19, 2021, Kirk competed in 8 events in the California Senior Games (65-69 Men's' Division), and won 8 medals, including 5 gold.

Kirk coaches men, women and children on fitness and healthy living, in mind, body and mental attitude. Today Kirk lives happily in Indianapolis with his wife, Dianna, their kids, dogs, cats, and chickens. He is a recurring fitness expert on the TV show, Indy Now, and leads the morning fitness warmups at FedEx. Kirk loves to present his "Zero's Heroes Plus" presentation to students, teams and business for maximum impact.

"Rest if you must, but just don't quit."

Kirk Lawrence

Age: 66 Ht: 5'8" Wt: 152
Resting HR: 45 bpm BP: 107/62

Sept 19, 2021 California Senior Fitness Games
Masters Division, 65-69 years
8 events, 🏅🏅🏅🏅🏅🏅🏅🏅
Event Scores, 9/19/2021:

🥇 Jump rope: 180 jumps in 60 seconds
🥇 Rowing Machine: 1 minute, 50 seconds (500 m)
🥇 15 lb Slamball: 48 in 60 seconds
🥇 Kettlebell Squats: 101 with 35 lb.
🥇 Farmers Carry: 21 min 5 sec w 2 40 lb. Kettlebells
🥈 Dead Arm Hang: 2 min 42 secs
🥈 300 yd shuttle run: 1 min 10 sec
🥉 Keg Toss: 27 feet

CHAPTER 2

5 Winning Secrets from 5 Great Champions

by Sarah Sneider

1. Arnold Schwarzenegger, Mr. Universe, Actor, Governor of California

My husband Harry and I joined the huge crowd gathered at the entrance to the Los Angeles Coliseum. Arnold Schwarzenegger, then-Governor of California, was promoting the Olympic Games in LA. Many Olympic athletes packed the stands just behind Arnold, and television crews were there to capture the news.

After Arnold's speech concluded, Harry wanted to say "Hello" to his long-time friend. As he started to make his way through the crowd to see Arnold, the Secret Service pushed him back. He told them, "But I know Arnold!"

They said, "Sure, everyone says that!"

So, Harry shouted loudly, "ARNOLD!"

Arnold, recognizing the voice, turned and shouted: "HARRY! COME ON OVER HERE!"

23

Harry met Arnold shortly after he came to America. Arnold invited him to be a part of the film *Pumping Iron*. At the time, Arnold told Harry he wanted to be the best bodybuilder, he wanted to be a great actor, and he wanted to get into politics. As an immigrant, he attained all three goals, and so much more!

On another occasion, we arrived at Arnold's office complex, and were welcomed with a firm handshake and friendly greeting. Arnold proudly showed us photos from *Conan the Barbarian,* which currently was being filmed. We were excited for him, and enjoyed seeing some previews of the coming film.

Arnold invited us there so we could show him the new fitness system Harry and I had created called "The Perfect Workout, Aerobic Resistive Rebounding." This new revolutionary system is even more popular today as rebounders/mini-trampolines became extremely popular during the pandemic.

Arnold was very gracious and interested in what Harry had to say. Pictures were taken. After talking for some time, we returned home, and the photos were developed; remember, this was before digital cameras. We sent several photos to Arnold, and he approved one he liked to be included in our book, *Harry and Sarah Sneiders' Olympic Trainer.* The new 40th anniversary edition of this classic best-selling book was published in 2021 and, of course, it contains that original photo of Harry, myself on a rebounder with the soft hand weights, and Arnold.

As Chairman of the President's Council on Physical Fitness and Sports, Arnold championed after-school sports programs to keep children and youth healthy and safe. He continues to promote fitness and health through his Arnold Sports Festivals, an annual multi-sport event in the United States, Spain, Brazil, Australia, South Africa, and England.

#1 Winning Secret: "Dream Big, Take Action, and Stay Hungry."

Harry and Sarah Sneider with Arnold Schwarzenegger.

2. Jack LaLanne, The Godfather of Fitness

It was a beautiful day in Southern California. Harry and I were driving to Hollywood to meet Jack LaLanne. It was 1974, and Jack had invited us to be on his famous *Jack LaLanne Show* after Harry wrote him a letter. Harry wrote that he was disabled in his right leg due to a childhood injury, but he could squat 490 pounds on his left leg.

We were super excited to be invited! Arriving at the studios, we parked the car, entered the building, and an assistant led us to Jack's studio. Jack had a warm, friendly smile as he reached out his hand to greet us. He explained to us what we would be doing.

I had prepared to be on the show, but being shy and seeing the large cameras in the studio, I suddenly became fearful, declined to appear on camera, and watched from the sidelines as the show beamed into homes all across America with Jack and Harry demonstrating lunges, dips with chairs, squats, and other exercises. Jack was the original virtual fitness trainer!

During the show, Jack turned to the audience and remarked, "For someone to squat that kind of weight on one leg, it's remarkable. What about you out there? Why are you guys laying on the couch? ...Get up!"

After the show, we talked for a while with Jack, thanked him for the opportunity, and told him what a great service he was doing to help those at home to keep fit. As we were driving home, I realized something: *shy people who are afraid miss out on a lot of things in life!*

Harry and I had an invitation to be on the *Body Buddies* television show a couple years later. This time I made sure to participate and enjoy the opportunity! As Franklin D. Roosevelt said, "The only thing to fear is fear itself."

In 1980, Jack invited our family to his beautiful home in the Hollywood Hills, with a large statue of Jack at the entrance. After going into his spacious gym, we shared the system Harry and I developed using a mini-trampoline and soft hand weights. Jack not only endorsed this new system of exercise but even allowed us to include photos of him in our book, *Olympic Trainer*. We had brought along an Olympic medalist in the high jump, Dwight Stones. Jack enjoyed competing with Dwight, doing pull-ups, leg extensions, and more. And, of course, Jack always won those friendly competitions, even though he was much older.

After the entertaining gym workout, Jack brought us upstairs to his large kitchen to meet beautiful Elaine. Soon Jack was throwing carrots, a banana, spinach, and other fruits and vegetables along with vitamins and supplements into their blender. I can still hear the loud grinding sound of vitamins hitting the glass as it was all mixing together. He had a huge smile on his face as he drank the nutritious fresh juice that included his vitamins and supplements. Jack's energy and enthusiasm for life was so evident and amazing.

When Ambassador College in Pasadena, California, our employer, closed in 1990, Jack again gave us encouragement and direction. Harry had been on the AC faculty and was men's fitness director for 23 years. He was almost 50 years old. I had been the women's fitness director for 14 years. We both suddenly lost our jobs with only six months' severance. What do we do next? How do we support our family?

Inspired by Jack LaLanne's home gym, we created a gym, and opened Sneiders Family Fitness in our home. It was the perfect solution with Harry's limited mobility from his childhood injury, where we could continue to train athletes and celebrities, and serve those in the community.

Jack LaLanne was a personal inspiration as a mentor and friend who motivated, inspired, and encouraged us to reach out and inspire others to better health and fitness. He told us, "Anything in life is possible, and you can make it happen." He would encourage you in such a way that made you feel you can do anything – that you can stay fit, and that you can help others to stay fit.

#2 Winning Secret: "Anything in Life is Possible, and YOU Can Make it Happen."

To learn more about Jack LaLanne, read Elaine LaLanne's book with Jaime Brenkus, *If You Want to Live, Move!* and Elaine LaLanne's book with Greg Justice, *Pride & Discipline: The Legacy of Jack LaLanne.*

The Sneider family and Olympic medalist Dwight Stones visit Jack LaLanne at his home.

3. Bobby Fischer, World Chess Champion

"Are you a weightlifter? I want arms like yours! Can I train with you?" The voice was coming from Bobby Fischer, world chess champion! Bobby was visiting the Ambassador College campus in Pasadena, California, where Harry was teaching physical education classes in weightlifting, racquetball, basketball, softball, and other sports.

This conversation became the start of a 36-year friendship between Harry and Bobby, whom many consider the greatest chess player of all time! Bobby made headlines around the world when he beat Boris Spassky in 1972 during the Cold War between the United States and the Soviet Union. Did you know Bobby had studied chess up to 16 hours a day for years leading up to the World Chess Championship match? Day after day, year after year, he studied night and day before he won the championship. Bobby had a goal of being the best ever.

Before meeting Harry, Bobby enjoyed watching Jack LaLanne and his daily fitness program on television. One of Bobby's winning strategies – one that's important to chess players as well as everyday people in order to stay healthy – is working out. One must have a program that works the heart and strengthens the muscles and bones. This requires daily effort.

He told Harry that chess players had to get into better shape. There is a mind-body connection that is self-evident and that begins to make a difference in long, exhausting tournaments. Working with Harry, Bobby was in great shape. His abs were flat, his resting pulse rate was at a low athletic rate, his muscles were firm, and his confidence was brimming over.

Harry's training program for Bobby is included in his book about his 36 years of friendship with Bobby. Due to be published in 2022, the book was dictated to me shortly before my beloved Harry's passing.

One of the rules Bobby had was to not take a photo of him and definitely not talk about him to the media. When our *Olympic Trainer* book was first published, Bobby looked through the entire book and later said to Harry, "Good man, Harry! You didn't mention me in your book!"

Don't tell anyone, but I did sneak in a photo of Bobby at his finest in the latest *Olympic Trainer, 40th Anniversary Edition*. The photo was taken at our home. Harry's dad was visiting from Minnesota and quickly snapped a photo of the world chess champion!

Bobby's fear and paranoia in his later years unfortunately prevented him from capitalizing on his great success as the world champion in chess. Much more is discussed in Harry's book about Bobby.

#3 Winning Secret: "Prepare, Study and Train Day After Day, Year after Year, But Balance is Important."

4. Bob Wieland, "Mr. Inspiration," "Most Courageous Man in America"

Driving my Volkswagen van up Santa Anita Drive, I was nearing the top when I glanced at the grassy median in the center of the street. There was Bob, without legs, walking on his knuckles up the hill wearing a weighted vest. Bob was preparing for his Walk Across America on one of the steepest hills in Arcadia. It was a hot day in sunny California. I waved, and he motioned me to stop. I stopped the van, slid the side door open, and Bob propelled himself inside with his arms.

Bob Wieland was a combat medic in Vietnam. While rushing to save a fallen comrade, he stepped on a mortar mine and, as he says, "My legs went one direction, my life another." He was placed in a body bag and declared DOA (dead on arrival). Then someone noticed a movement, and realized he was still alive.

Bob wrote a letter to his parents from the hospital:

> *"Dear Mom and Dad,*
>
> *I'm in the hospital. Everything is going to be O.K. The people here are taking good care of me. It won't be that much of an adjustment. Please don't worry about me. Maybe I'll help you out in real estate.*
>
> *Love, Bob.*
>
> *P.S. I think I lost my legs!" One Step at a Time, Bob Wieland. Zondervan, 1990. p. 23.*

Bob's dream from childhood was to be a professional baseball player. Before going to Vietnam, he was ready to sign a contract with the Philadelphia Phillies.

We first met Bob when he came to the Ambassador College track in a wheelchair. Bob writes, "I met with Harry Sneider, a celebrity-athlete trainer at Ambassador College in Pasadena… Running on the track was Mike Mentzer, body builder, Mr. Universe 1978; Dwight Stones, world record holder in the high jump; and James Butts, silver medalist in the triple jump. Harry was coaching some of these athletes for the 1984 Olympics."

As they were watching the athletes train, Harry kept talking. "Have you ever tried walking on your hands and your stumps? Why don't you get out of that chair, and let's give it a shot." The training began, day after day, Bob walking on his hands and stumps, often bouncing on a rebounder. *One Step at a Time, Bob Wieland.* Zondervan, 1990. p. 63, 64

Bob walked on his knuckles from California to Washington, D.C., and was greeted by President Ronald Reagan at the White House! It took him three years, eight months, and six days. You can read his amazing story in his book, *One Step at a Time.*

Bob's a champion powerlifter, the only double amputee to complete the Ironman Triathlon without a wheelchair, and he has completed many marathons, including the NYC Marathon and the LA Marathon! His message: "Through faith in God, determination and dedication, a person can achieve anything." Bob has changed the lives of thousands of people through his motivational program, "Strive for Success."

#4 Winning Secret: "Through Faith in God, Determination and Dedication, a Person Can Achieve Anything."

Bob Wieland walks across the U.S. on his knuckles.

5. Harry Sneider, World Powerlifting Champion

At 2 ½ years old, Harry fled Latvia in a cattle car with his mother and 4-year-old brother during World War II. His father had been taken by the Germans and forced to join their military. The Russians were about to invade Latvia. Harry, his mother, and his brother had to leave quickly.

They eventually made it to a displaced person's camp in Germany, where at age 6, Harry was injured, developed osteomyelitis, lost his right hip joint, and almost died. He would never run or ride a bike like other children. One moment that stuck in Harry's memory was the time an American soldier gave him a Hershey bar.

That one act of kindness had a profound effect on Harry, and resulted in a lifetime of giving small gifts to his family, students, clients, friends, and others he met over the years. A small treat, a memento from a trip, a handwritten note – there were many unique surprises.

Harry and I served as Directors of the Ambassador Health Club. One day, a client brought in a small round unit called a rebounder. She said,

"I'll leave this here for you." Harry at first thought, "This probably isn't very useful. Compared to the other equipment in the Health Club, it seems insignificant." But, he said, "Thanks. I'll try it."

Little did we know at the time, that rebounder a lady left in the Ambassador Health Club would change our life for the better – writing the bestselling *Olympic Trainer* book, participating in The Great American Workout on the White House Lawn, Harry speaking at the World Congress on Fitness, coaching at the Goodwill Games in Moscow in 1986, being on the Governor's Council on Physical Fitness and Sports, and much more.

One act of kindness can make a huge difference in someone's life. As fitness professionals, we can look for ways to make that difference in our clients, friends, and those we reach with a message of how to live a healthier, happier life. The soldier who gave a Hershey bar to Harry as a small boy in a displaced person's camp during World War II, the lady who put a rebounder in our Ambassador Health Club... You can make a difference in the trajectory of someone's life with a simple act of kindness.

It was an honor and pleasure to work side by side with Harry, my best friend and soul mate, for 45-plus years. You can read more about Harry's remarkable life in our classic bestselling *Olympic Trainer* book. It's the most complete book on rebound exercise ever written, and contains specific programs for all ages from toddlers to seniors, plus programs for 17 different sports. It's a fun way to stay fit and fabulous, gets the feel-good endorphins flowing, and benefits both mind and body. Try it! You'll like it!

Finally, I offer this from my youngest grandson, who is my inspiration. Julian is so much like his late grandfather, Harry. Recently, after having fun bouncing together, we started to play a board game. I read the directions, "Youngest person goes first." Apparently feeling real grown up, he said, "Grandma, I'm eight! I'm older than you! You go first!" This kid sure knows how to make someone feel good!

Perhaps as fitness professionals, it's all about making others feel good in life – by motivating them to keep working out regularly, eating healthy, being grateful, and making the most of their God-given talents in service to others!

By taking every opportunity and realizing anything is possible and you can make it happen, staying hungry for your dreams, working hard, being prepared, and never giving up, you are all WINNERS! You CAN make this world a healthier, happier place!

#5 Winning Secret: "Go For It! You Can Do It! You're a WINNER!"

Harry Sneider bench pressing at age 61.

7 Trendy Ways to Stay Fit at Any Age!!

1. Hybrid Classes

Trends in fitness will include fun ways to keep fit. With the pandemic, people realized even more than ever how important it is to stay healthy, exercise, eat healthy, boost the immune system, and be physically and mentally strong and flexible. People will enjoy workouts with hybrid classes – at home via the internet and also in person at their fitness facility.

2. Outdoor Activities and Tech Wear

Outdoor group activities such as walking, running, cycling, hiking, and mountain biking will continue to be popular. The use of wearable tech and smart watches to compete and compare results virtually via the internet with others through apps such as Strava will increase. Wearable tech can measure steps taken, calories burned, heart rate, sleep, and much more. Technology has certainly revolutionized fitness.

3. Meditation and Yoga

Meditation and yoga will continue to grow in popularity for stress reduction and mental well-being. There will be partnering with nutritionists, chiropractors, and physical therapists. Wellness will be emphasized for both mind and body.

4. Games and Competitions

Games and competitions such as Masters Meets and Senior Games will also be very popular. After being isolated during the pandemic, people are eager to socialize and enjoy participating in group activities and friendly competitions. To learn more about Masters Track & Field for anyone at age 35 and older, go to: *usatf.org*. There are also Masters Meets in swimming and other sports. Senior Games with multiple sports are for anyone 50 years of age and older. Find out more at: *nsga.com*. Also, check out Huntsman World Senior Games for anyone over 50 at: *seniorgames. net*.

Training for these events is a great motivation for clients to work out consistently. The competition motivates you to work out and working out keeps you in the competition. It's a WIN-WIN for all!

5. Home Gyms and Mini-Workouts

Home gyms with minimal equipment that became popular during the pandemic will remain important for convenience and saving time. Treadmills, bikes, trampolines, dumbbells, and other cardio and strength equipment to furnish home gyms were in high demand during the pandemic when public gyms and fitness centers were closed.

Working out at home became a habit for many and is especially convenient for those who can continue to work from home. It saves time and money. Mini-workouts for 3-5 minutes spread throughout the day help busy people find time for exercise.

6. Mini-Trampolines

Bouncing on trampolines will continue to grow in popularity in both the club and home markets. It's one of the best exercises to boost the immune system, improve balance, reduce stress, and increase energy. It's easy on the joints, fun, convenient, and effective. The Daily Dozen program described in our *Olympic Trainer* book is the perfect mini-workout for the home or office. See programs for any age from toddlers to seniors in the *Olympic Trainer*!

Among those enjoying bouncing are humanitarian and motivational guru Tony Robbins, 90-year-old actress Rita Moreno (*West Side Story*),

Olympians, professional athletes, celebrities, and even a former president of the United States.

Tony Robbins writes: "But one of the best all-weather aerobic exercises is trampolining, which is easily accessible and puts minimal stress on your body…Please take the time to pursue this life-enhancing form of exercise. You'll be glad you did." *Unlimited Power*, Anthony Robbins. Fireside edition, 1997. p. 172.

Currently, Tony Robbins has a mini-trampoline embedded on his stage platform for his live virtual events. He reaches multiple thousands around the world from this stage virtually, which has been extremely helpful during the pandemic.

Tony's most recent book, *Life Force*, contains very helpful information about the latest technology for making exercise fun and addictive, new advanced technology for muscle and bone strength, and more. *Life Force*, Tony Robbins. Simon & Schuster, 2022. p. 320-347.

7. Fitness Professionals (and those who wish to be)

For fitness professionals, may I recommend attending the annual IDEA World Fitness Convention, where you will be introduced to the latest trends in fitness from excellent leaders. I've attended IDEA World's great conventions since 1990. For more info go to: *ideafit.com*. IHRSA, Club Industry, and Fit Expo conventions are also great sources for the latest information on fitness. Harry and I have attended many of these over the years. You meet wonderful people, can take classes, and see the latest trends.

Fitness professionals, you are valuable! You are important! You are needed for the health of this nation and the world!

Sarah and Harry Sneider

Sarah Sneider is the wife of Harry Sneider, Ph.D., "Dr. Fit," a world-renowned authority in fitness education, Olympic coaching, and a world powerlifting champion. They co-authored the bestselling *Olympic Trainer*, 40th Anniversary edition published in 2021, and in 1981, founded Sneiders Family Fitness, Inc. Together they developed a simple system involving a mini-trampoline and a set of graduated hand-held soft weights called "The Perfect Workout." They've demonstrated in their own fitness center – with world famous athletes, businessmen and women, housewives, children, retirees, and the disabled – that the system works! They created *Sneiders Perfect Rebounding Workout* DVD and with son Rob, *Sneiders Resistance Rebounding* DVD.

Harry and Sarah participated in The Great American Workout on the White House Lawn. They represented the U.S. at the World Congress on Fitness in Chicago, where Harry spoke to representatives from 75 nations. At the Goodwill Games in Moscow in 1986, they were able to "go behind the scenes" as U.S. coach and official photographer. Harry was placed on the California Governor's Council on Physical Fitness and Sports.

The Sneiders have hosted California and Pasadena Senior Games Powerlifting for 27 years. Having never competed in sports through high school or college, Sarah began competing at age 50 in Senior Games, starting with powerlifting and later adding track & field, cycling, and rope climb. She also competes in Masters Track & Field and Huntsman World Senior Games.

Along with son Rob, Sarah continues to personally train athletes, couples, and anyone wishing to get in the best shape of their life.

Sarah credits exercise for helping her get through the unexpected loss of the love of her life, her best friend, soul mate, motivator and encourager – her beloved Harry. They were married over 45 years and have three children and four grandchildren.

The Sneiders are featured in the film *Impossible Dreamers* by three-time Emmy winner Eric Goldfarb. Harry's interviews are included in two documentaries, *Bobby Fischer Against the World* and *Bobby Fischer – Anything to Win*. The Sneiders, especially Harry, have appeared in articles in various newspapers including *The New York Times*, *The Los Angeles Times*, and *USA Today*, and magazines including *Shape* and *Sports Illustrated* as well as on television, including ABC News, NBC News, and CBS.

Website: www.DrFit.net
FB: Sarah Sneider
IG: @sneidersfamilyfitness

THE VALUE OF COACHING

CHAPTER 3

Time to Expand

By Adrian and Linda Parsons

"The wise investment of having a coach helps us do better and be better human beings."

CoACH FRANK PUCHER

Over the past couple of years, most of us have experienced loss one way or another, but on the 9th of January 2015, we experienced a loss like no other. Our little boy, Joshua, was stillborn, which was the hardest thing that we have ever had to endure. Anyone who is a parent understands that the loss of a child is the worst thing to experience. We were not sure how we were going to get through it, but we both trusted in God's big plan for us.

When we lost Josh, there was period of numbness and a dissociation from others. It was tough to get out of bed. It was a challenge just to take care of ourselves, and our nutrition suffered. It was even difficult to go to the gym. The feelings that we have in our body when we have been hurt or have experienced a loss cause us to go inward. During times like this, it becomes virtually impossible to think about growth, connection, or expansion.

During that time, what we knew is that we had to focus on the positive emotions and spend less time on the negative feelings connected with the emotion of loss! We also knew we couldn't do it alone. We called on each other, our family, our pastor, and our team members for their support. They were all awesome and helped us immensely, but it still wasn't enough! We desperately needed a coach to help us work through the negative emotions that we were clinging to.

That's where Todd Durkin came in. When we met Todd, it was a turning point in our lives. He brought the energy shift we needed.

We first saw Todd at a live event in Melbourne, Australia. The energy he brought to the room was captivating. His passion to serve everyone in the room was truly inspirational. We both immediately thought to ourselves, "Who is this guy? We've never met anyone like this before." We had come to the conference to learn more about fitness and running our business, but Todd left us thinking about our purpose and mission. He made us think deeper about *why* we were running our business and how we could create a greater impact on our community.

We kept in contact with him, and in 2019, we decided to attend his 3.5 Day Mentorship program in San Diego. At the program, Todd found out that Adrian was very uncomfortable with public speaking. During one of the sessions, he asked him to stand up in front of a room full of fitness professionals from all over the world and talk for a few minutes. He encouraged him to step out of his comfort zone. This was nerve racking, to say the least, but Todd knew that it would elevate him and make him more confident to live out his dream of public speaking. He still can't believe he got up there! But we know, for sure, that he wouldn't have done it without Todd's coaching and support.

Not long after that, we joined the Todd Durkin Mastermind Group (TDMM). A mastermind group is where like-minded individuals come together, network, build strong communities, craft their skills, fuel their passion, and learn from those who have been there before. A mastermind group will elevate you by doing anything they can to support your dreams and your journey. The TDMM became like a family for us. It gave us an opportunity to network with some of the best coaches in the world and to receive the coaching we needed to build our business and to build back our life.

Most people think of coaching in association with sports. However, we'd like to change that train of thought and open your eyes to the great benefit of having your own coach. A good coach is dedicated to supporting you and giving you the skills needed to help you fight the challenges you face in life. A coach will keep you accountable and help you to become more resilient. They will work shoulder-to-shoulder in the trenches with you when life knocks you down. Coaching is for anyone who is serious about growing and developing their passion and purpose in life, nutrition, sports, business, and so much more.

We believe coaching is more important now than it ever has been. As the world has experienced a worldwide pandemic for the past few years, we have all endured some challenging times. Here in Australia, kids were not allowed to attend school, sports stopped, and our kids were at home 24/7. As a result, parents were suddenly expected to wear all the hats of being parents and teachers while continuing to work. We can honestly say that there many times where we were exhausted and at our wit's end, and most of you can probably relate to that feeling.

During the first lockdown, which here in Australia went from the 23rd of March to the 19th of August 2020, the physical, mental, and spiritual drain the pandemic had on us was devastating. Even though it was nice to be working from home, spending more time with our children and doing some of the things we wanted to do with the extra time we had on our hands, we felt the pressures of home schooling, work deadlines, and leading our family through a time of such uncertainty. The news kept feeding the fear and negativity. It was so toxic, and we didn't know what to believe anymore.

There was a shining light in all the dark and gloominess, though, and that was when our coach, Todd Durkin, turned up online every day with what he called "The Good News Network." To get us to focus on what was going well and to be more positive, he shared good news each day. This really lifted our spirits, helped us to focus, and always inspired us to shift or focus on the things we could control.

Todd also inspired another idea for us during the pandemic. After listening to Todd interview Kelli Watson on his *IMPACT Show* podcast, we had an idea that we thought might help our kids. We thought it would be a great project to have our son, Noah, and some of his school friends write about the feelings they experienced during the first lockdown. Writing about what it was like to be away from their school mates, how they found home schooling to be, what they felt about not being able to play sports, and also not being able to see many of their extended family members seemed like a great way to express some of their feelings.

We immediately reached out to Kelli, who co-owns Scriptor Publishing Group, and asked how we could create a strategy for the book project to happen. Together with Scriptor, we were able to work with the school community and create a book titled *Quarantime Down Under*. It features drawings from all the students in Noah's grade as well as a Foreword by the students in the 5th and 6th year classes. The power of networking enabled us to take this dream and make it a reality.

The impact of the pandemic has changed us in so many ways. People are burnt out, and many have come to us with the feeling that they have lost their identity. Working in the trenches with our clients to transform their attitudes, we help them to understand that they are worthy of greatness and that the pain that they have experienced is only temporary. Just like we are held accountable by coaches in the TDMM, we have held our Smashing Calories family accountable, continuing to love them and elevating them to greatness.

The Given vs. The Construction is a methodology Linda developed during a time where growth has been difficult. "The Given" are situations, events, and circumstances in our lives that we can't change. For example, we can't change how old we are. "The Construction" refers to building strategies, ways of networking, and the ability to connect virtually to find ways to grow in any situation. Our vision coming out of lockdown and moving forward was to be conditioned and ready, and to have a construction foundation to tackle whatever situation is thrown at us.

Growth is definitely not a word most of us felt during 2021-2022, but now, more than ever, we need to tap into a growth mindset. We have to let go of the past, the self-limiting thoughts, fear, and judgement of what people may think or say. Whatever it is that has held you back in the past, do not allow that to rob you! It's time to stop worrying and to get on with it. It's time to "construct" a new foundation.

The world has changed, and it's time to learn new skills, grow your business, and get better in your life. Whether it's joining a mastermind group or getting a coach to help with an aspect in your life, don't be scared to grow and expand. It doesn't matter who you are. Even the most successful people have coaches and understand the power of networking.

Are you ready to ask for help?

Are you ready to grow and expand?

Then it's time to get a coach!

Linda and Adrian Parsons

Linda is a coach, co-founder, and co-owner of Smashing Calories. She has been working in the fitness industry for over 15 years, and has worked with "Australia's Biggest Looser" contestants. Linda has built Smashing Calories on the foundation of serving and inspiring those who have faced adversity. As a qualified personal trainer, Linda is passionate about sharing her life experiences to help others, especially women and mothers. Linda has a deep passion to also serve and educate our young, to dream big, to break old molds, and to create powerful habits that serve the mind, body, and soul.

Linda has been through three pregnancies. She is mother to two beautiful kids, Noah and Emilia. She has experienced loss and pain in the stillborn death of her first son, Joshua, and through the loss, has developed resilience and strength to share her story and help others.

Linda's love of kids is expressed through the youth programs at Smashing Calories, built to help kids with their confidence, which is dear to her heart having struggled with confidence as a child growing up. Linda loves her two children and her husband, Adrian. They fill her heart with so much joy and support her with all the light she spreads through the world.

Website: www.smashingcalories.com.au
FB: @smashingcalories
IG: @smashingcalories
Personal FB: @lindaparsons

Adrian is the co-founder of Smashing Calories **and** has been the head of training for the past 10 years. Today, Smashing Calories specializes in personal wellness and small-group training for children and their everyday mums and dads. Adrian holds a diploma in Fitness *and* has held fitness trainer certification for over 10 years. Adrian also holds qualifications in youth training and TRX.

Adrian had worked on another book project, bringing together the idea of kids sharing their experience during the early stages of the pandemic, *Quarantime Down Under.*

Adrian's life purpose is to change the way that people live their lives so that they can believe in themselves and live a life where they fulfill their full potential. He wants people to love themselves rather than comparing themselves to others. However, his greatest joy is the time spent with his family – Linda, Noah, and Emilia.

FB: @smashingcalories
IG: @smashingcalories
Personal FB: @adrianparsons

CHAPTER 4

Trauma-Informed Coaching

By Alex Garzaro

As we move into the future, the fitness industry will need more specialization. Already there is a big demand as clients want coaches who specialize in everything from nutrition to pain management. Becoming a specialist in your field is a crucial next step for anyone looking to grow in this industry.

If you're not sure what to specialize in, consider what you have experienced and overcome. What is a topic that is easy for you to speak about? Perhaps it is muscle-building, or maybe it's weight loss. When you dive into your niche, you increase your authority and impact and, as a result, your income.

One specialty I want to highlight is trauma-informed coaching. As trainers, we have a unique position with our clients. We see them regularly, we help them feel better, and in the process, we earn their trust. Because they trust us, clients often confide in us about different aspects of their lives. Although we must stay within our scope of practice, we do have the potential to help our clients even more if we learn some specific techniques. If we can connect with our clients on a different level by helping them understand their behaviors, we can create transformation that will cultivate a new experience for their future.

Oftentimes, clients come to us because they feel like they've lost control, and it is natural for someone who feels like they need control to look for external solutions first. That is why they choose to go to a gym. They seek to regain control of their behaviors by working out and eating better. Trainers help them stay accountable and teach them how to do it properly, and as the clients change their behavior, they begin to feel better. Those improved habits can continue for a long time until something triggers them. When the client ends up triggered, they revert to what brought them comfort from that original trauma.

When I say trauma, that doesn't necessarily mean something extreme. There's extreme trauma, and then there is generational trauma and experiential trauma. This could be as simple as your parents wanting you to get straight A's and then being disappointed when you got a B. Dealing with that disappointment can be traumatic for a young child. They cope with it by creating behaviors that get stored in their neuro system. These cycled habits and behaviors are simply conditioned programming in our subconscious minds. When something happens later on that triggers a similar emotion, the subconscious remembers it and reacts with the same pattern of behavior.

An example of this concept happened with one of my clients, whom I will call Sue. Sue's trauma was that she hadn't been validated, supported, or seen by the significant people in her life. So, to overcome that loss and trauma, she found comfort in something she was able to control – food. Even though she didn't realize she consciously chose to overeat to make herself feel better, it was still her external solution. As her trainer, I could see that she had this pattern, and I was able to provide her with a path

52

to connect her present-moment behaviors to the past. That past trauma was the root cause of why she was in an unhappy place with her body.

The ability to discover the pattern and root causes of behaviors isn't difficult to do, but it does require that we become investigators. We need to question our clients about their patterns and their behaviors, by asking them who, what, where, when, and why, we discover clues that will help our clients realize their triggers.

It can play out like this in Sue's example:

Question 1: Who are you with when you engage in this behavior?

Answer: In Sue's case, she told me that she engaged in poor eating habits when she was with her husband.

Question 2: What is the behavior you are engaging in?

Answer: Sue told me that her husband smokes. So, when he has a cigarette, she eats a candy bar.

Question 3: Where do you behave this way?

Answer: In Sue's example, she said she had recently been at the store when her husband bought cigarettes, and that's when she bought the candy bar.

Question 4: When does it happen?

Answer: For Sue, this wasn't the first time. She said she often buys food when her husband buys cigarettes.

Question 5: Why do you engage in that behavior?

Answer: Sue said that she wanted to have a candy bar because she could share it with her husband.

As I asked her these questions, I realized that her need to share was an indicator that she was trying to make a connection with her husband. Further questioning revealed other instances where Sue engaged in behaviors that indicated she was trying to be included and connected with people. My questions allowed her to begin to see the pattern herself, and she started realizing that she was using food to fulfill a need to connect and be seen by others.

The reason all of this is important is that if we really want to create transformation for our clients, we have to go beyond just giving them a meal plan and a program to follow. If we don't dive deeper to find out the root causes of their patterns, then our clients will just revert to previous behavior. When we allow a safe space for our clients to come in and provide confidential information, having tools to assist them to transform and heal from the inside out is imperative.

And, of course, it's definitely a work in progress. Any behavioral change will depend on how far back the behavior started, and it will take just about the same amount of time to rewire and transform the neuro system effectively. It is also important to note that it is not our job as trainers to do this work for our clients. Rather, by going one step further and asking questions, we have an opportunity to help them discover the answers for themselves. Then it is up to that individual to take a courageous step forward to heal the traumas and change their behavior.

The secret to your clients having long-term results is to help them recognize their habits and discover and understand their behavior patterns. Gaining this skill is the new evolution for fitness trainers. When trainers understand how to get these results, they will be specialists in their field. Inevitably, they will elevate above the rest because they will create a long-lasting impact on their clients.

Alex Garzaro

Alex Garzrao is a speaker, wellness educator, certified fitness professional, holistic nutritionist, and mental health expert. Using science, psychology, and energetics to assist people in removing subconscious beliefs to redefine their narratives and redesign their bodies. She has spent the last decade in the fitness industry, coaching hundreds of people both in-person and online. She has studied various forms of training styles such as; functional training, kettlebell, bodybuilding, powerlifting, circuit, and running to name a few. She has taken all her training knowledge and not only applied it to her own personal transformation but developed her own specialty training style, her F.A.S.T. (**F**unctional **A**thletic **S**tyle **T**raining) method. As a holistic nutritionist who personally understood the effects of genetic and generational unhealthy nutrition, she is dedicated to not only providing healthy and delicious food alternatives but teaching people how to scientifically understand food to fuel their bodies in an easy and fun way.

Physical transformation is just the beginning of a lifelong transformation. This is why Alex developed her **Neuro Mapping Method** to assist people in understanding and healing the deep-rooted causes that developed the unhealthy habits and food relationships they desire to change. Health setbacks are not accidental, they are either a conscious or subconscious reaction to an experience.

Alex also spends her time working with a fitness professional in developing their SHIFT (Stop Hiding In False Truths). Assisting them in understanding the reasons behind the self-doubt, hesitation, procrastination, and limiting success, as well as external and internal programming for their clients.

She is also a wife, a mother to two amazing little gentlemen, Sebastian and Zavier Garzaro, and everyone's health hype woman. Her mission is to help a million people break their unhealthy generational health inheritances both externally and internally.

A Note From Alex

There are two ways to begin a transformation: one is external, and the other is internal. Understanding the process of which to start with and which to transition into is a crucial part in developing a lifelong transformation for clients. Some need a physical (external) transformation to gain the strength to begin their internal healing and transformation. At the same time, others need to work on their internal transformation before becoming ready to tackle their physical transformation. I have found that the most optimal route for a transformation is to start with one, either internal or external, and then when the client is ready to begin introducing the other. This single focus gradual process will reduce the Acute Stress Response, allowing you to work with clients long-term.

For more information on Alex,
visit her website at www.alexgarzaro.com
Instagram: alexgarzaro

CHAPTER 5

The Value of Silence

By Vincent Catteruccia, PhD

Shhh, don't say anything; watch how the person sits. Oh, look, they're getting up. Let's see how they get out of the chair. Did you see how they used their arms to assist themselves? Did you see how they leaned forward to rise from sitting? The key here is to realize the assessment begins when you first set eyes on your client or patient. Understanding the value of unspoken clues derived from observation will immeasurably amplify your ability to help the person.

Try it yourself. Go for a walk during your lunch break and see what happens when you focus on the sounds and sights surrounding you. The body warms up as you walk, your mind relaxes, and you begin to feel better generally – not just physically. Realize the essence of this experience, the power of using hearing and sight to capture everything in your intrinsic and extrinsic world. Don't just focus on the loudest sounds or the most vibrant colors – pay attention to everything.

For some, allowing yourself to come to a level of awareness that gifts you the experience of hearing and seeing all things surrounding you will be challenging. Now let's point this energy toward your ability to observe a person's posture or movements. Again, not just their hair, shoes, or the clothes they have on. Let's focus on the person's stance, how they present themselves according to vertical and horizontal gravity lines, and how they sound when they speak. Are they exuberant, sad, mellow, or life-loving? There is so much to our interaction with everyone we meet. Each element is significant for your ability to drill down and understand why they hurt or perform sub-optimally (physically or emotionally). Nonverbals, the things people aren't saying or the things that exist between the words they are saying, are as important, if not more important, than extensive movement tests or measurement methods we use traditionally in fitness or rehabilitation. This isn't to say testing is less valuable in solving body trouble or understanding a client's baseline. However, both instruments of assessment should be considered equally as a level of priority.

Nowadays our clients are more intelligent than ever before. Today's client is far more thoughtful about what they need and how they want it than five years ago. As professionals, we have to be on top of our game. We have to be super-educated, or should I say super-informed. We have to be on our toes and ready for that client walking through our door today. We have to be prepared to answer more complex questions, to ebb and flow with the client's physical and emotional needs. The new-era client can choose between professionals who have advanced degrees or certifications and those who can take their academic knowledge and fold it into an emotionally intelligent package. If you – the coach, the trainer, the therapist – cannot meet that expectation, you will not survive in this new era..

Let's look at this from a business perspective. What differentiates you now? What makes you better than the trainer down the road, or what makes you stand apart from that online offer? What separates you from all the rest? If we were standing toe to toe, the one differentiator for us is the ability to quickly and effectively understand the nonverbals: the ability to observe and understand the client or patient within seconds of meeting them; your ability to pick up on what they aren't saying or how they are saying it; your ability to observe and understand how the person moves, how their emotions and psyche impact their posture. Being good at movement or exercise is no longer the only thing to excel in. We as care professionals have to be on top of the game when it comes to our emotional intelligence.

This chapter isn't going to get into the details of emotional intelligence, but there is a specific aspect of this skill set I selectively consider very important. To begin, care professionals must embrace their instincts. And to do that, I think one must spend time in silence watching people, observing how they move or stand – noticing asymmetries in foot position, arm swing, or stride length. What doesn't look right? As you have conversations or consultations, watch the posture, how emotions affect a person's standing posture or how they walk. Watch how the good feelings, happiness, and joy changes how they look or move. Compare this to the stance of someone sad or existing in depression. Those postures will present entirely different from one another. What does this mean, and how do we help?

The answer lies within my experience with Emotional Quotient (EQ) nd how it has shaped my success as a care provider. Years ago, as a young aspiring clinician, I was blessed with great learning opportunities. I had opportunities that most would never have. Directly learning from the men and women who wrote the books that our profession relies on has been invaluable throughout my career. Authorities like Dr. McGill, Dr. Butler, Dr. Perry, Dr. Liebenson, Poliquin, Verstegen, Dr. Bajusz, Clark, Dr. Skaggs, Pavel Tsatsouline, Dr. Janda, and Dr. Lewit provided me with practical knowledge. Aside from the practical, I was also able to study their mannerisms and methods of execution and presentation. As you can imagine, each one of these "gurus" had unique ways of delivering the knowledge, explaining, demonstrating, and connecting. On one occasion that stands out, I had the luxury of meeting two neurologists from Prague, Czechoslovakia. Their home base was the Department of Rehabilitation and Sports Medicine, 2nd Faculty of Medicine, Charles University in Prague, and Motol University Hospital. For decades, these men provided the world with fantastic knowledge of locomotion (human movement), spine rehabilitation, and developmental neuroscience. These two amazing men have influenced how we think about the human experience with pain or dysfunction. Their teachings about motor development allow us to help our clients and patients physically perform in life and sport. As practitioners, our knowledge in some form or fashion was born in Prague at Motol Hospital. Their work flows through various allopathic medicine, fitness, and complementary alternative medicine concentrations. Every day, in some way or another, we are using the information from these two men, Vladimir Janda, MD, and Karl Lewit, MD. Over eight years, spending in-person time with these men and their colleagues at Motol University Hospital changed how I think and care for my clients. I consider myself a purist, using their teachings daily to help people out of trouble, maintaining the exact methods they taught. Of all this remarkable knowledge from Dr. Janda and Dr. Lewit, the most impactful has been how to see (observe) dysfunction and quickly know what to do about it.

During the summer of 2002, I had my first learning experience with Dr. Janda. I had the opportunity to travel to the Hamptons, at the east end of Long Island. I spent four intensive days with a small, hands-on group learning and Dr. Janda as the keynote instructor. It was an extraordinary time to see this master perform a patient exam from start to finish. It's hard to explain how rare this opportunity was;

it was like seeing a unicorn. The guest patient was in terrible physical trouble. Selected to be a part of our learning experience, the patient had spent years searching for an answer to his cascading decline in physical health. As I stood amongst the top providers in the nation, observing Dr. Janda perform his evaluation, I was ready to learn the "secret sauce." The students (from all over the country) wanted to learn something special from this Yoda of human movement and rehabilitation. We were all looking for better, faster, and more efficient ways to help clients suffering from unusual physical circumstances, and we were expecting to learn something about the physical nature of this patient's trouble. We anticipated seeing posture and gait assessments, different movement tests, and provocative testing. We were all hoping to leave New York with a great goody-bag of tests or maneuvers that we could apply to our day-to-day clinical practices (which we did). Surprisingly, those mentioned above were inconsequential compared to what we learned about factors driving the objective physical findings. We discovered it's not just about the material being.

If you think about it, this makes sense. As my father would say, "You need to step out of the woods to see all the trees." You have to account for the intricacies of the whole human system. For example, the influence of the nervous system and how it plugs into the musculoskeletal system is critical to how we move. At the end of the day, if our body's electrical system is unhappy or overloaded, our muscle system – our extensive moving system – works dysfunctionally. All humans demonstrate body (physical) dysfunction in different ways. The nervous system will affect parts of the body for various reasons. We are body- and mind-unique, and how we express and experience body dysfunction is autonomous to the person. If the nervous system is unhappy for too long, it can have a global or whole-body effect. In medical terms, this whole-body impact is called central sensitization, better known as fibromyalgia. This example is precisely why we mustn't be myopic in attaining just physical expertise. We must understand behavior and psyche correlated with the body to remain sustainably viable in our professions.

The formal diagnosis of fibromyalgia is the perfect example of the disconnect in modern-day medicine. I won't get too deep into this for time and interest. When a person is in trouble for too long, this is the damning diagnosis received in the U.S. Our medical system traditionally medicates this condition because the thought is that the pain is strictly manifested and experienced through nerves and skin. However, this myopic perspective only considers the physical parameters of the complaint. I propose that pain, in this case, is a symptom of a much more significant player, the mind.

I recall when Dr. Janda sat next to a patient, simply sitting very close to them, asking questions about their feelings, why they were hurting, and why they were feeling that way, because pain is what a person says it is, not what we think it might be. The students observed the whole assessment as Dr. Janda discussed the history of injury, all of the pragmatic things we would generally ask as clinicians: history of injury, illness, disease, current, and experience with pain, medications, and relief strategies. But he went further by asking about how they felt about the injury. How does it affect their life? What activities can and can't they do? How is this affecting their family? How about the family? Is the family happy? How about friends? Money? He discussed the socioeconomics that factor into why a person doesn't move right or feel good when moving. Long story short, Dr. Janda spent an hour just talking and watching this person's responses. Did you catch that? He was watching the patient's responses.

It is mind-blowing to me. Think about how a healthy person sits. They might change their position once in a while because they get stiff in that position; your body has an innate reflex to change posture to stay comfortable. People in pain move a lot. They don't like to be in one spot for very long. During this conversation, Dr. Janda took account of all the different positions the person was assuming to stay put in that chair. Every once in a while, Dr. Janda would reach over, touch their hand or arm, and watch how the person would respond. At one point, he'd extend his hand very gently, place it on top of their head, and monitor their response. We were all just sitting and watching, waiting for Dr. Janda to point out some miraculous, physical dysfunction that we were missing.

After about an hour, the doctor looked at the students and asked, "What do you see?

What's happening?" We all looked at each other; what do you mean? What do we see? You haven't done anything yet. We haven't moved or done any testing; we are only consulting – having a conversation. We're waiting. One of the students said, "The conversation has been great. We have great insights into the person's injury. We understand his family. We know his hobbies. We know all the activities this person enjoys or wishes to participate in but can't because he's hurt."

Dr. Janda shook his head and said, "... You're missing it. You're missing all of the key points that we just discovered during this hour-long conversation."

Looking at him inquisitively, we thought, "What do you mean we missed something?"

He began to point out the clues we overlooked. Dr. Janda explained, "...Did you see how many times the person changed position? When I reached out to touch his leg, did you see that he moved away from me? And then, at one point, I reached over to touch his arm and he quickly moved away from me. When I went to touch his head, he flinched and ducked his head away. And when I made contact with his scalp, he cringed; he wanted to escape."

Dr. Janda explained that when a person hurts for a sustained amount of time, the electrical system becomes overloaded. The pain has existed for so long that the wiring system inside of that body (much like a home, those wires get hot, and the walls of that home start to heat up – that's like the skin), becomes hypersensitive, and you begin to function in fear of any movement or any touch. This patient moved away from any physical connection with Dr. Janda. It all started to make sense. Wow, this person has been in trouble for so long that the whole house is on fire. And so what do we do about this? What do we do when a person ends up at this level of trouble?

What can we do as practitioners, as providers accustomed to putting our hands on people, or as trainers who have a person move to improve their level of performance or level of activity? This would all be too much with a patient or client like this. What do we do?

Understanding the space that exists between the mind and the body is critical. This space, called the limbic system, is like a bridge between two different continents. One continent is the psyche, the brain, the mind. The other is the body, the physical, the muscles, the skeleton. When a person is in trouble for an extended period, the bridge's limbic system becomes shaky. It becomes overloaded, in jeopardy of crumbling. So, what do you do about this? You have to focus on behaviors, coping skills, and mind-setting. You have to focus on the psyche. Help that person by getting their head wrapped around the significant value in their perception and experience they're having with the trouble they exist in.

The early stages of taking care of a person in trouble are about observing and communicating to understand the complexities of what the person faces. It's about getting the client or patient to trust that you get it and understand how expansive the trouble is. All that it affects – communicating your understanding of how their system experiences pain or dysfunction – gives them hope. What is hope? Hope is that notion that they're going to get better because, finally, there is someone who gets it. Remember, frequently, this is a client or patient that's resigned themselves to feeling crummy forever. Nothing they've done or tried has worked – medications, exercise, surgeries, injections – nothing has worked. Until now, nobody has spent time understanding the breadth and depth of their troubles.

When the central system, the brain, spinal cord, and all the connecting nerves are overloaded, there has to be a methodology that backs the person out of this trouble from the top down – in other words, from the brain out. We have to figure out how to down-regulate or turn down the amount of electricity that flows through that system. How are we going to do that? Through education. We have to teach this client, this patient, about themselves and their problems. They need to understand why and how the problem won't just go away with corrective exercise or nutrition modification. The complete strategy is to back themselves out of the problem. They have to learn how to breathe again, sparingly tie their shoes, stoop or squat correctly, and they need to learn the value of meditation. They have to know the importance of positive talk or positively speaking to themselves. They need to understand symmetry, how to rest or recover from activity. Their nutrition and sleep hygiene have to be in check. It all needs to be understood and implemented – consistently.

I've spent considerable time in this chapter highlighting the importance of our relationship as a physical being with the mind and our emotions. On the same level, I have just as much appreciation for the physical nature of who we are. People ask me, "How do you know…, or see what you see?" It doesn't make sense to many folks how I see all the intricacies of a person's posture or their aberrant movements while they walk. The best way to explain this is to have a snapshot of what perfect movement or posture looks like in my brain. And with that, I have a standard of comparison. I'm able to see abnormalities in posture or gait very quickly. The key is the many years I've spent practicing this skill – all of the gait and posture analyses, the consults, and conversations I've had. I learn from every interaction. I can very quickly, in seconds, understand a person's tightness or weakness profile. Couple this with learning about their mental-emotional state or socioeconomic position; it's a recipe for success.

In other words, when the body isn't moving correctly or standing appropriately, many factors are at play, intrinsic and extrinsic. There's a tightness or a weakness in the musculoskeletal chain, but why? This is the ultimate question. Understanding a problem quickly and then correlating to specific muscles, tensions, or deficiencies within the kinetic chain, coupled with mood and emotional stressors, can very quickly explain the cause of an issue and, therefore, provide an effective solution to the problem soon. It's about observing the whole person. Observation is a skill unlike that acquired from a book. You can't just read about it, learn it, and apply it. You must practice observation through thousands of consultations, and gait and postural analyses.

I would go to the mall or airport and sit and watch people walk early on. At one point, I even created copies of my evaluation forms with my contact information. I would give it to a person after doing their gait analysis. Of course, this was before 9/11, when the TSA closed the gates to non-travelers. Fifty percent of the people were very accepting of what I offered, and 50 percent of the people were offended, probably because they didn't understand the value of what I was doing. But at the end of the day, I did thousands of gait analyses and thousands of posture analyses to refine the observation skill. It's the only way to get good at it.

Once you have realized the power of observation, it changes you and how you care for people. That client or patient becomes more than just a body that moves. The responsibility you have changed. Your level of care becomes more profound and more detailed. It will force you to spend more time in your evaluative process to attain all the information needed to create a strategy to meet the goals. Being a proficient observer slows the process down, but the new approaches to client care results are dramatically improved and long-lasting.

Go for that walk and listen for the less obvious. Take a deep breath and feel the energy that surrounds you. Bring yourself to the next level of awareness for the people in your care. Anyone can build a fitness program, lead a workout, or perform therapy. The differentiator, the element that separates the skilled from the mechanic, is your ability to see, hear, and understand the nuances that aren't so obvious.

Dr. Vince Catteruccia

Dr. Vince Catteruccia is an internationally known musculoskeletal rehabilitation expert recognized for uncovering hidden sources of physical pain and producing lasting solutions for his patients – without medication or surgery. His natural approach to solving pain is guided by his unique combination of professional credentials, including a PhD in Behavior, a Master of Science in Kinesiotherapy, and a Master of Science in Human Performance. Dr. Vince is also a licensed neuromuscular therapist.

He's learned from the best in the world, traveling the globe to uncover natural solutions to nagging pain, including time in Prague at the renowned Motol Hospital of Rehabilitation and Manual Medicine. During his 30-year career, Dr. Vince is proud to have helped thousands of people end their battles with chronic pain. Today, he lives in Arizona with his wife, Jennifer, and his son, Gabriel, where he works with patients worldwide virtually and in person.

A Note From Dr. Vince

It pains me to see people like you suffering. The truth is your body is built to heal naturally. My mission is simple: encourage healing, without pills and procedures. Over the past 30 years, I've helped people from all walks of life eliminate pain, including loving parents, busy executives, and professional athletes. My natural healing methods work – no matter your age, gender, or genetics. That's why doctors, physical therapists, and other medical professionals confidently refer patients to me. I look forward to working with you and personally crafting a custom plan to end your pain once and for all.

The Patient Experience

Dr. Vince refers to his patients as partners. And he refers to himself as a problem-solver. Your pain is unique to you, as is Dr. Vince's approach to solving it. After an in-depth evaluation, Dr. Vince will pinpoint the source of your pain and develop a personalized plan to alleviate it as fast as possible. Dr. Vince has the ability to work with you virtually, so you can experience relief from anywhere around the world.

What Others Are Saying

"Dr. V heals in a way no one else does. I have my life back thanks to him." – Jason Perkins

"He's solved my issues many times over. He's a godsend to me." – Mark Brodhagen

"I recommend Dr. Vince to everyone I know. His methods change my life and they can change yours too." – Jennifer Pierce

"I tried everything to get out of pain … in just a few minutes, Dr. V started fixing me up. I feel like I'm 20 years old again." – Todd Dessell

"I call him my body whisperer." – Bradley Berndt

Get in Touch

Email: Drvince@lpfmethod.com
Phone: 480-462-9894
Website: www.drvincecatteruccia.com

CHAPTER 6

Beyond Body Image
Changing the Way People See Fitness
By Heather Deffenbaugh

Why do you work out? What is your motive behind it, and how is it benefiting you? This is an essential question for both the client and the trainer alike. Is it to achieve an aesthetic outcome like six-pack abs, buns of steel, or brawny biceps? Perhaps you have been encouraged by your health practitioner to get to the gym, not so much for your physique as for you to reduce your risk of developing a chronic health condition or metabolic disease. These are the typical reasons for many of our clients who come seeking guidance and motivation to achieve these goals. The internet is saturated with influencers showing off their chiseled bodies and offering quick workouts and solutions on how to look as good as them. The options are endless for those seeking to conquer their hamster-mill progress and yo-yo dieting and attain that perfect body, yet studies are showing people are more depressed, unmotivated, hurting, and desperate for authentic connection and support. Mental health issues are on the rise, and those of us in the fitness business have an opportunity to rethink how we service our clients.

The pandemic has exacerbated the looming problems and struggles that people are having with personal wellness. Self-medicating with food, alcohol, and Netflix binges brought comfort in a time of lockdowns, quarantine, and stress. For many, it has wreaked havoc on far more than their waistline; it has taken its toll on their mental well-being. The vast majority have experienced intense fear, bereavement, financial hardship, isolation, deprivation, and disruption of daily routines. All of us have endured difficulty on some level, and we have been denied the simple joys and freedoms that were once at our fingertips. Those of us who love to work out in the gym or studio longed for the days we could gather in person again. Even those people who saw their workouts as a punishment for overindulging began to view the opportunity to work out as a privilege. While we all adapted and offered online classes to the gratitude of many participants, and we saw a surge in the wide-spread use of virtual programming during the pandemic closures, many people are eager to connect with community in person now that restrictions are lifting.

Fitness facilities are open for business, and mask mandates are becoming a thing of the past. Working out at home is losing its luster. What was once convenient, safe, and cost effective is no longer the driving motive for home workouts. There will always be a demand for online fitness, but realizing that the explosion of participants in the past two years was due to people temporarily being forced to exercise at home, we now have an opportunity to reevaluate the needs of the consumers coming through our doors and shift our attitudes and awareness outside of the box of just physique. Now more than ever, it is crucial that we address overall wellness: mental, emotional, spiritual, and physiological health, in addition to physical health. Consider this excerpt from a November 12, 2021 *Time* magazine article:

"The fallout of the pandemic highlighted the need for self-care, and Americans have become more attuned to messaging around that. Exercise has become a priority — wherever people prefer to do it. But the uptick in gym visits and memberships resonates even more. 'I'll tell you what makes me hopeful regarding people's mental health,' says [Alison Phillips, associate professor of psychology at Iowa State University]. 'If people are very depressed, they don't take action to get out there and exercise. You have to be mentally healthy enough to take that action and get out there and start doing something. So to me it also reflect [sic] positively on people being resilient. And not only coming out of their homes, but out of their shells.'" Gregory, S. (2021, November 12). America's Going to the Gym Again. That's Bad News for Peloton, But Great News for Mental Health. *Time.* https://time.com/6116651/gyms-peloton-planet-fitness/)

Fitness trends tend to evolve as consumer behavior changes and with so many people emotionally and mentally affected by the aftermath of the pandemic, this is an opportunity for fitness professionals to be innovative on how they train, motivate, and guide consumers in their quest to feel great, both inside and out.

People feed off the energy in the room and desire to cultivate relationships that keep them coming back to the facility they call their fitness home. This connection boosts consistency. Although physical fitness is a key component to health, it is only part of what develops "wholeness" in a person. What our bodies look like should not be the definition of success, but a part of the success. Wholeness is where true contentment, peace, fulfillment, and gratitude are birthed, and it is from this space that we operate out of our best self. When all the areas of wellness are given adequate attention and balance out, wholeness is achieved. Developing wholeness within ourselves is a lifelong process. We are constantly evolving, and we experience setbacks, hardships, roadblocks, and hurdles. The COVID-19 pandemic has been a monumental hardship for many, and left several people in survival mode. We have the opportunity to move our clients into thriving mode. In July of 2021, ideafit.com featured an article titled *Sell Mental Health and Wellness, Not Exercise,* that shed light on this very need.

> *"More and more people are seeking relief from chronic stress, anxiety and depression, even if it does not rise to clinical levels. While older adults have borne the greatest physical health risks from the pandemic, younger adults and women, in particular, have suffered higher mental health risks, according to research in The Lancet (Pierce et al. 2020). The American Psychological Association's Stress in America™ poll revealed that parents, essential workers and people from communities of color were all more likely to report mental and physical health consequences, and that Gen Z adults (ages 18–24) were the most likely to report a worsening of their mental health and wellness compared with pre-pandemic times (APA 2021). Fitness professionals possess important skills and knowledge to address this crisis, but promoting physical training while also uplifting minds and spirits requires clear understanding and intention. Across the spectrum, from business owners to trainers, fit-pros can promote exercise not only for its penchant to improve physical health but also for its powerful ability to serve the entire person — to provide mental health and wellness benefits without any of the side effects of pharmaceutical treatments."*

(https://www.ideafit.com/mind-body-recovery/sell-mental-health-and-wellness-not-exercise)

I have been a fitness professional for 32 years, training thousands of clients, teaching countless group exercise classes, and coaching many transformation programs throughout my career, and it wasn't until I began to integrate "wholeness" into my life that I realized how profoundly it enhanced my overall well-being. Wellness leads to wholeness and it is a holistic approach that includes the whole person – engaging the mind and body while nurturing the spirit. The focus is more on authenticity, living life fully, having grace for yourself, and striving for optimum health. Physical fitness alone can focus too much on what you should be eating and what you should be doing, and when people fall off the wagon or can't stick to the program, they feel defeated and frustrated.

Wellness is about the journey and giving time and attention to all the essential areas in one's life that allow a person to thrive. These areas can be categorized into five essential pillars: physical, physiological, mental, emotional, and spiritual. I personally have been incorporating all five into my own wellness journey over the past few years, and it has been life-changing. So how do we help our clients integrate this into their lives? We encourage them to take a personal inventory in these five key areas, and offer them strategies on how to create a change in their behavior patterns. Behavior change is the driving force to achieving overall wellness. Let's take a closer look at each pillar and the vital role they play in developing wholeness.

Physical: Typically, clients fall into two categories when it comes to working out. Either they are creatures of habit who have a routine and love to do the same classes repeatedly, or they like the fitness buffet that offers a variety of classes, and they mix it up with HIIT, barre, indoor cycling, weight lifting, and Pilates. There can be perks to both, but workouts that are balanced with variety as well as with proper recovery, such as myofascial release and proper stretching, will reap the most benefits. Challenging the body in new ways can also improve confidence and keep the body from adapting. Obviously if you are training for a marathon or race of some sort, repetition is necessary, but for overall longevity and sustainability of joints, a balanced workout will benefit the person in the long run. Staying with one genre because the client is hooked results in imbalance and can even cause injuries. Cardio, strength training, flexibility, core development, and meditation are all important, and can be incorporated in creative ways in every fitness setting. Educating our clients on this as well as guiding their form will set them up for long-term success.

Physiological: What you put in your body matters. The food supply in America is littered with toxicities and is wreaking havoc on many peoples' gut health and immune systems. Most people, including some in the fitness industry, are not abreast on how conventional food has taken its toll on the health of millions of Americans. Just because you appear fit on the outside, does not mean that you are fit on the inside.

When it comes to eating plans, there is so much conflicting and confusing information floating around that it's become impossible to know the right one. Knowing some basic information on this in order to guide our clients on where to look for sound advice will not only enhance their success and trust in the trainer, it will also separate you from the masses as a competent and credible professional who offers a little bit more than the workout. We want to point people in the right direction of food that will lead to good health, vitality, and longevity, not just a lean body. And with so many eating plans claiming to be the holy grail for shedding weight and improving health (keto, intermittent fasting, carb cycling, paleo, vegan), our clients are confused and overwhelmed. These eating plans are not bad in and of themselves, but they are not one size fits all, and it is a good reminder to give our clients. It may have worked well for one person, leading everyone to think that is THE way, but we know it's only one way. Some may not achieve the same results, and there is hope knowing that there are other options for them.

Mental: This is probably the most pressing and critical issue for so many people and can be overlooked in the fitness field. When the brain is under distress, it becomes distorted, and sometimes even damaged as a result of trauma, stress, substance abuse, head injury, or a debilitating illness such as bipolar, anxiety, or depression. This affects decision-making, perception, and motivation. Simply being aware that a client may be affected in this way, offering our patience and encouragement, and being intentional with them, can make a big impact. Mental wellness has become a top priority for people across the nation. In a recent article published, www.mindbodyonline.com, and written by market research lead analyst Margot Badzioc, mental health was ranked the most important dimension of wellness by the greatest number of Americans.

"Half of America (49%) agreed that the pandemic has negatively affected their mental wellbeing — with women more likely to feel this than men. The pandemic appears to have had a more significant impact on Gen Z and millennials than older generations — as 57% of Gen Z and 53% of millennials reported the pandemic negatively affected their mental health versus 37% of younger boomers. More than half of Americans (59%) said they are focused on their health and wellbeing because they want to reduce stress. Millennials are the most stressed generational group while younger boomers are the least stressed.

But how can fitness, beauty and integrative health services support mental wellness? The leading reason that consumers exercise is to feel better mentally (43% reported this). Over three-quarters of Americans believe being physically active helps their mental health. In the past year, 37% of Americans have incorporated physical fitness into their routine to help support their mental wellbeing while 14% have added yoga, and 9% have added wellness treatments like acupuncture to their routines."

(https://www.mindbodyonline.com/business/education/blog/
wi/7-wellness-trends-watch-2022Emotional)

Emotional: Meeting people where they are emotionally goes a long way. Many have put their workouts on hiatus and have a poor self-image. The inner-critic can be harsh, and they can feel defeated before they even enter the gym. Just coming alongside them and asking simple questions about how they feel, what they fear, and how we can be helpful may give them the assurance that they are seen and they matter. Building trust and forming a bond will ensure a good experience for both the fitness coach and the client.

"Fitness instructors have the training, the skills and a powerful tool — safe and effective movement — to boost health and wellness; they just need to let the public know. "When trainers understand the power of their tools in helping people deal with emotional distress, sometimes even more directly than medication or psychiatric treatment, and take the time to learn how to approach and properly communicate with those who are emotionally distressed, a training session will bring far more health than another set of crunches will ever do," says Michael Mantell, PhD, a transformational behavior and leadership coach in San Diego. "Personal trainers are not doing psychotherapy or counseling. They use fitness to boost healthy mood. They [can] use the tool they have — fitness — to help emotional functioning."

Shirley Archer-Eichenberger, JD, MA. 2021. Sell Mental Health and Wellness, Not Exercise.

(https://www.ideafit.com/mind-body-recovery/sell-mental-health-and-wellness-not-exercise/)

Spiritual: Gratitude, faith, prayer, and meditation all have a significant role in developing wholeness as well as peace of mind. Learning to quiet the noise in our head and be fully present can yield considerable gains when participating in fitness classes and training sessions. It also boosts mood and contributes to making better choices, especially when it comes to comfort eating. There are simple tools we can steer people toward in order to enhance their spiritual life, such as journaling, creating gratitude boards, spending time outdoors in nature while taking in all the sights and sounds, soaking in a bubble bath, practicing mindfulness, and more.

Incorporating these five pillars into the way we coach, think, and behave will have a profound and sustainable impact on our clients and ourselves. They are the key to a successful and ongoing fitness/wellness journey. Creating small goals along the way will pay off and lead to fulfillment. We can assist our clients in setting realistic goals by providing a template on what that looks like. The American Council on Exercise has laid out a SMART goal system where the acronym steers the course to success.

"Having a goal is important, but making sure it is a SMART goal — specific, measurable, attainable, relevant, and time-bound — has been shown to lead to greater success.

Try this: Create a SMART oal. If you want to become a faster, more fit walker, for example, consider signing up for a walking event. This goal is specific (how many miles you'll walk), attainable (start with a realistic mileage, depending on your current fitness level), relevant (walking is something most people find enjoyable, and training for this event will help make progress toward the goal), and time-bound (the date of the event gives you a set target to aim for when training). This same process can be used with a wide range of goals, including losing weight, increasing strength or improving your diet. The key is to make sure that your goal includes all the elements of a SMART goal so you end up with a specific plan, rather than a vague idea of what you need to do to achieve it. Change is not easy and it takes time. Don't underestimate the power of a good mindset, be curious about this process and have fun with your journey."

Shelby Spears, April 29, 2021. Change Your Behavior, Change Your Life.

(https://www.acefitness.org/education-and-resources/lifestyle/blog/7849/change-your-behavior-change-your-life/?authorScope=183)

Achieving wholeness is the goal. Living an active and balanced lifestyle in all five pillars is a journey, and we fitness professionals have the privilege to come alongside people who have been stuck in unhealthy patterns and guide them to living their best life. Now that people have survived the pandemic, they are looking to thrive. We can help them do just that while living it out ourselves. The old fitness phrases, such as "No pain no gain. Shut up and train," have expired. Hard work, discipline, owning excuses, and facing fears are still high-priority, but it is how we deliver the motivational package that makes a difference. It's healthy to embrace one's imperfections and limitations and treat the body both with kindness and care. This is what society is desperately seeking, and it is time to rewrite the narrative regarding what fitness looks like. This is an opportunity for the fitness industry to pivot toward that need. Improving overall wellness is the ultimate goal.

Heather Deffenbaugh

Heather is a bestselling author, speaker, wellness educator, fitness professional, holistic nutritionist, and mental health advocate who aims to help people overcome strongholds and become the very best version of themselves. She has been in the fitness industry for over 30 years, teaching many genres of group exercise such as indoor cycling, strength training, step classes, TRX classes, boot camps, and Pilates mat... just to name a few. In addition, she has coached hundreds of people through personal training and transformation programs, and has helped them to achieve higher levels of fitness, confidence, knowledge, and change. As a certified holistic nutritionist, she has guided and taught people how to infuse healthy and delicious food into their daily routine in order to achieve optimum health, while educating them on understanding what is in our food supply and what foods and are critical for thriving. She is passionate about "wholeness" in one's life, and teaches others how to thrive by achieving overall wellness in five key areas: physical health, mental health, spiritual health, physiological health, and emotional health.

Heather released her new book and memoir, *From Ashes to Beauty: How a Child of Two Mentally Ill Parents Went From Surviving to Thriving*, in May 2022, in hopes of helping many people who suffer from trauma and mental health issues go from surviving to thriving. Her book has become a bestseller and is available for purchase on Amazon.

She just celebrated 31 years of marriage with her husband, Dan, and they have two amazing children, Dylan and Megan, who are now thriving adults. Heather loves to travel the world with her husband and friends, develop her own healthy versions of comfort food and cook for others, share the love of Jesus, constantly educate herself, and listen to music incessantly.

For more information on Heather and her five pillars of wellness, visit her website at www.heatherdeffenbaugh.com

Instagram: heather_deffenbaugh

GET YOUR MIND RIGHT

CHAPTER 7

Fun, Adaptability, and Mindfulness

By Heather Fahrenkrog

As a child, I had a front row seat for the first wave of fitness. My dad was a bodybuilder, and I was the free child labor tasked with cleaning his gym. My dad won the title of "Mr. New Jersey" when I was a kid, so I've grown up alongside the fitness industry, both of us evolving with each passing decade.

My vision for the future of fitness is strongly influenced by what I've experienced over the years. I've witnessed a lifetime of fitness fads and realized some enduring truths along the way that have shaped my love of fitness. Our recent global pandemic brought a few new lessons and forced most business owners to reevaluate their business models and reinvent themselves in some way. The upside of that was many of us discovered deeper meaning and purpose in our work. Fitness professionals now have an unprecedented opportunity to serve more people than ever before, and in a much more holistic, interconnected way.

When I think about what's next, I know we must continue to motivate our communities toward a healthy lifestyle by making fitness fun, encouraging adaptability, and, now more than ever, teaching our clients to embrace mindfulness. Fun and a willingness to reinvent as circumstances and life change are imbedded in my DNA, but more recently I have learned the importance of *inner* fitness, or mindfulness. The mental, emotional, and spiritual skills and practices that foster resilience are also a vital aspect of wellness. Our communities need all three – fun, adaptability, and mindfulness to truly feel good and live their best lives. I learned these important lessons throughout my own fitness journey.

My roots, just like those of the fitness industry, took hold in the hardcore bodybuilding gyms of the 1970s. In the '70s, the fitness industry consisted of small bodybuilding gyms like my dad's and the YMCA, that was it. It was a scrappy beginning; I can still remember how my dad's gym looked and smelled. Imprinted in my mind are the huge barbells and weight racks, stacks of black plates, and the giant men who lifted them. The men wore tiny shorts and tank tops with wide leather weightlifting belts, and they survived on handfuls of vitamins and supplements that were washed down with raw eggs from a blender. Steroids were common, and most bodybuilders (including my dad) took them regularly as an unquestioned aspect of "fitness."

The 1980s brought the emergence of group exercise, back then called "aerobics." The cardio craze was just beginning, and what I remember most is the sense of freewheeling fun. Fitness in the '80s was not so much a discipline, but rather one big party. With his bodybuilding days behind him, my dad blazed a career path that was unheard of at that time. He took over a failing tennis club, and for a brief period, he created the fitness trifecta of Nautilus, aerobics, and racquetball. Dad endlessly dreamed up new fitness events: fashion shows, concerts, boxing matches, limbo contests, pool parties, and themed racquetball tournaments. Creativity was the main ingredient in my dad's approach to this new business model and I soaked it in.

My love of group fitness can be traced back to these early days of aerobics. My mom and her best friend taught the first aerobics classes: Jane Fonda look-alikes with a boom box on a tennis court doing high knees in high top sneakers. By age 15, I was teaching my own aerobics classes. Over the years, I created my own style of fitness fusion, combining formats with aspects of dance and various equipment in my own creative way. To this day I love combining strength and fun, those same themes from the '70s and '80s.

But there was a dark side to the emerging fitness culture. The flip side of the '80s fun was a toxic culture of physical perfectionism. At that time, fitness was all about how you looked, not how you felt. There were many extremes, an absence of balance, and zero talk of mental health, personal growth, or the mind-body connection. I had no example of a growth mindset growing up in the '80s; instead, I learned loss. My dad's business ultimately failed, and our family lost everything. I learned a painful lesson, a passion for fitness is not enough. Entrepreneurs must be constantly learning and evolving. We must invest in ourselves and our teams to run successful businesses and to grow them. Then, we must teach and mentor self-growth to our clients. I did not understand these basic truths until many years later.

For many years teaching group fitness was a fun side hustle. Throughout many decades I saw the fads come and go, and I enjoyed teaching them all. My evolution in fitness continued into my 40s when I started "Kettlebell in the Park" in the summer of 2014. I was working part-time as a prosecutor in Chicago and teaching a variety of group fitness classes in a large downtown gym, but I wanted to take my fusion thing out on my own in the town where I lived with my family. I learned something very important about myself with this experiment - I am not afraid of risk. Pretty surprising considering what happened with my dad's business. It turns out that I am a natural entrepreneur with both passion and a yearning for personal growth. I also luckily suffer from chronic over-confidence. If you consider yourself to be a natural entrepreneur, do a gut check and be honest with yourself about your willingness to work and risk to serve others. The skill set required to build your vision into a successful business requires far more than passion. You need a strong work ethic, a stomach for risk, a willingness to learn as you grow, and a love of people.

Kettlebell in the Park was a hit – I took 80 people and created a community by the end of that summer, and it was indeed fun. I decided to move indoors and sublet a small dance studio. Within weeks, I needed a larger studio and a method for people to register that didn't involve legal pads and collecting paper checks. I found a larger dance studio and sublet during off hours. I purchased a branded app, even though I didn't yet have a website or a sign on the door. To open my own brick-and-mortar studio, I knew I needed to build an autopay membership base while subletting at a low cost. I encourage all fitness entrepreneurs to first create a strong following with low overhead before taking on the expenses that come with a brick-and-mortar studio. Take your time building your brand first – you need a community!

Within one year of Kettlebell in the Park, I had 100 autopay members using my branded app. I hired several instructors, and I was ready for my brick-and-mortar studio. My husband had created a file on our desktop with my member lists called "Heather's Gym." I thought it had a nice ring to it. My sister-in-law created a beautiful logo, and the name stuck. Heather's Gym is a brand that continues to grow and has evolved into "HG Studios," now encompassing three separate studios. I did not see that coming.

I'm not sure why it took me so long to admit I was in the business of fitness, and to accept that it was inevitably going to be my full-time job. I wanted to serve others in some positive way, I thought I would best serve as a lawyer. Instead, I decided to leave my 19-year career as a prosecutor so that I could grow my fitness business. Looking back, when I went out on my own that first summer, there was some nostalgia for me that my young daughters would see firsthand, like I had as a child, that fitness is fun. It's a twist of fate that what began as a six-week summer program in the park became my life's passion and purpose. I had found what I was meant to do, but before I retired as a lawyer, I made sure I had a vision for what I wanted to create in my life.

Whether you tend to be overconfident or risk-averse, it's never too late to reinvent yourself. There is so much to be gained by evolving who you are and who you serve. It doesn't happen overnight, and it will absolutely involve struggle. Who *you* are (your influences, your career paths, your passions, your losses) will shape your growth. The sooner you understand who you are and what has shaped you, for better or worse, the sooner you can play to your strengths and improve your areas of weakness. Reinvention cannot happen without self-reflection and self-awareness. Once you understand your story, share it! Your story should become synonymous with your name and your business. People relate to your story first. Your brand *is* your story.

Those of you wondering if you can, or should, begin to build a business in fitness while keeping your day job, I say absolutely, yes. Let your brand and confidence grow without depending on the revenue. Start with a little risk and adjust. Once you take the initial leap and start to do what you love, don't stop there. You must continually invest in yourself and in your team to learn and grow. It is not possible to navigate growing pains without a strong team who are also growing and supporting the mission.

One year after opening Heather's Gym, I opened HG Cycle. Looking back, I made a lot of miscalculations. I had the cash to invest in 21 bikes, so I found a space to build this new studio, but many members were slow to adopt cycling into their fitness routine, and others didn't want to go to two different locations. Even worse, the building where the studio was located was falling apart. It was a bad choice in location and a significant investment, it was a struggle for over a year before it began to generate profit.

In 2019, I added hot yoga classes to my original studio. I felt my members needed more recovery and mind-body connection. I knew I had to lead the way, so I convinced several instructors on my team to become yoga-certified along with me. While I worked on my certification, I researched hot yoga and the logistics involved in offering that type of class. I had been looking for a separate studio for hot yoga but couldn't find a good location or a space large enough. I also feared my members wouldn't want another location. It was a risk, but I decided to purchase 26 heat panels and add them to my original studio – we led the way into this new frontier of yoga, and it worked. By February of 2020, my members were enjoying hot yoga and cycling, and both studios were making a profit. Then February turned into March 2020 and, well, we all know what happened next.

It's hard to put into words the toll that the pandemic years took on me. Like many fitness professionals, I had a very strong community heading into the pandemic, and yet it took everything I had to keep them committed to their health and moving forward for those two years. I lost many members to online training, and many others gave up because they had to wear masks. I somehow held my team together, and we did everything we could to lift our community up, adapt, and survive. What we learned along the way through the various technologies, the virtual classes, the non-stop re-designing of classes and schedules, the logistics in the studios, teaching in various PPE, teaching outside and in garages, renting out most of our equipment, and then ultimately closing the cycling studio, was the importance of adaptability and *inner* fitness. I am a better business owner and coach today because of the pandemic, and my community is stronger and more connected because of what we went through together. I did not see that coming.

After enduring a two-year struggle for survival, I see a big lesson for all of us who coach others. I return to what made an impression on me growing up. People now need, more than ever, a variety of wellness experiences to feel good. People need to enjoy themselves while doing whatever they are doing for their health, or they simply won't continue. We must embrace that freewheeling '80s vibe, without forgetting the importance of making people strong that began in the '70s, and the lesson from the pandemic years – adaptability and community are everything. Today's fitness innovators should be creative in planning experiences that draw people to a fun atmosphere with a strong community ambiance that also includes mindfulness.

I encourage fitness professionals to create a calendar of campaigns. Give each campaign a name, create a challenge, a reward, and a clear plan for your members. Each campaign should have the fun baked right in. I often buy matching headbands and wristbands (circa 1980), as well as silly props and costumes to use in our marketing and challenges. People want to feel like they are part of something bigger and they like to see how they are doing in relation to others. It's amazing what a few matching headbands can do for collective morale, it's truly powerful to experience a community-oriented fitness campaign.

The purpose of every campaign is to make your community feel healthy and connected. Every business has its own style and brand, so think about how you can uniquely reach people with the campaigns you launch. How can you weave mindset awareness into physical activity? How can we foster a strong sense of community as a constant reminder that community *itself* boosts our health? I try to find campaign names that are fun: The Beat Goes On, Spring it On, and March MATness, just to name a few. Gamify your campaigns. We've done sticker charts and MyZone challenges, all with fun team names, team captains, and prizes. Create the community vibe and the magic happens.

In an ever-evolving field, the future of the fitness industry also requires input from the very people we serve. Ask and listen. Bring the best of what you know and leave behind ego and perfection. Your clients and members appreciate a say in the vision as it evolves. I now conduct focus groups before I expand or launch a new idea. Before I opened my new cycle studio in March of 2021, I conducted focus groups and listened to people who didn't completely see or agree with my concept for the studio or the new technology I was investing in. Through listening, I gained a clearer picture of how to message and market my ideas, and those who were involved felt valued because they had a voice. The new cycle studio, complete with new technology, is now thriving. I conducted focus groups a second time before raising my membership cost following the pandemic. I wanted to know where I was failing to deliver value to my clients. In 2022, I opened a hot yoga and meditation studio, again after conducting a round of focus groups. If you want to know people's honest feelings about your business, your brand, or your ideas, get them talking. Focus groups will give competing perceptions. The hard work is what you do with that information.

Growing my business now, compared to pre-pandemic, is far more member centered. I listen more and use the objections and suggestions to tweak the vision. I attribute these changes to my personal growth and evolution in this business, and I thank my coaches and the people I surround myself with for helping to keep me in a growth mindset. It's not easy to hear competing opinions or critiques of your ideas, but the ability to do so will make you a far better leader and business owner.

The future of fitness must not be about physical perfection, or *any* kind of perfection. Fitness professionals must lead by example encouraging mindfulness and self-growth as part of every fitness experience. I am proud to be part of a new era of leaders who demonstrate balanced, holistic health. The future of wellness must embrace mental health, real food, recovery, and love for our bodies. We must address our client's *inner* fitness. A lack of inner fitness – mental, emotional, and spiritual balance – leaves people struggling. I watched my dad struggle his entire life because he lacked this inner fitness. I vowed to do better for my clients.

As I scale my business post-pandemic, I try to approach my members from a holistic perspective. I try to meet people where they are. I ask myself: how can I create a more holistic approach to this client's pain points? How can I grow my business to meet these new demands and create a more integrated wellness experience for each client?

I believe that our communities yearn for authentic leaders who are not afraid to be honest about the mental and physical struggles that make us human. We must connect with each client, lead with passion, and let our story, what we have learned through experience, be the foundation upon which we build those relationships. Be the leader they can trust, by showing through example that self-growth is a way of life. We are playing the long game so show your members how to evolve. To do that consider hiring your own coach, join a mastermind group, read business and mindset books, and listen to self-growth podcasts. Draw from your experiences, the ups, and the downs, utilize all of this in your marketing, coaching, and speaking. Your self-growth is your spark, and it will create a true bond between you and your community.

It's a tall order to put so many pieces together to offer a more holistic wellness experience for our clients, but I believe today's fitness leaders are up for the task. I am so grateful for the perspective I gained from evolving over the years along with the fitness industry. My journey taught me that our calling is to build community, facilitate connection, and encourage our clients to evolve right along with us. With fun, adaptability, and mindfulness we can truly make an impact and help others to live their best lives. I am no longer in the front row observing, now I lead the way. Let's go!

Heather Fahrenkrog

Heather Fahrenkrog is a lawyer-turned-fitness studio owner. Heather is a longtime runner and triathlete, but her true passion has always been group fitness. In 2014 she opened her first studio, Heather's Gym. Her fitness business has expanded to include two additional studios: RPM Cycle & Bootcamp and Zen Yoga & Meditation – together they comprise HG Studios. Heather has been teaching group fitness for over 30 years, she is ACE certified, RYT 200 certified, she is a Platinum member of the Todd Durkin Mastermind Group, a certified Impact coach, a motivational speaker, and an outspoken advocate in her community for living a balanced, healthy life. Heather lives in Libertyville, Illinois with her family.

Website: www.hgstudios.club.
Social Media: @heathersgym.club
@zen.libertyville
@rpm.libertyville

CHAPTER 8

Becoming Resilient

By Ken McCullough MA CPT, PN1

Resilience doesn't come from a weekend certification or from reading a book. It comes from having the knowledge to adapt and the perseverance to get back up when life knocks you down, something I have become a bit of an expert on. I struggled with mental health issues and alcohol abuse a lot during my life, including two DWIs that shifted my life's plans and essentially knocked me down when I was desperately trying to elevate myself. But we have two options when we get knocked down: stay down or get back up and use life's struggles as a positive turning point in life and stepping stones to greater things.

It can be challenging to imagine positive outcomes when a flurry of negative things are occurring in life. There are strategies you can use to flip the internal switch, turning difficult moments into something positive and moving forward stronger and wiser. One of the things I used to regularly tell myself is that if something bad happened to start my day, it meant more bad was coming my way. Ever caught yourself saying things like, "I spilled my coffee; it's going to be a bad day"? These types of thoughts can lead to a self-fulfilling prophecy of having a "bad" day. Events during the day don't happen to you, they happen FOR you. Once a perceived "bad" event happens, you have to sit down and look at the event with a wider perspective, seeking out the potential silver linings, and then simply moving forward. Resilience consists of the strength to get up when life knocks you down and having an adequate toolbox of knowledge to help you to get back up.

March 16, 2020 was a day that left many of us feeling confused, afraid, and utterly knocked down. I remember that day vividly. By 9 a.m., before the state of New Jersey announced the shutdown of all gyms, I had already experienced client after client contacting me to cancel. At 11 a.m., we ushered everyone out of our fitness facility for what would be the final time. It probably would have been easier to go home and just sit and wait, but instead I went right to the local sporting goods store and bought as much fitness equipment as I could possibly afford. The plan was to train and hold classes in the park. It was March, so it wasn't unreasonably cold by midday. I was able to hold one class before the parks were closed a few days later. It was time to open up my toolbox again and pivot in a new direction.

I decided to focus on the power of social media and various online possibilities. I had plenty of experience coaching people online, so I jumped right into creating a one-month online program (because who could have imagined a shutdown lasting longer than that). Having an online trainer certification from the Online Trainer Academy founded by Jonathan Goodman was a vital tool in my toolbox. Thankfully I was used to posting online for marketing purposes on a daily basis, so I began using my platform to go live on Facebook every day to get people moving.

As summer rolled around, parks opened up, and I put my original plan to train outdoors back into action. I was ready to rock and roll and get back to what I loved. My clients were thriving, and the outdoor classes were going great until the cold weather returned to New Jersey.

Working outside was no longer an option, so I was able to precure a spot in an off-the-radar private studio on a local farm and teach small classes indoors as well as on Zoom for those who preferred to stay remote. Things were moving along: classes were thriving inside the barn while heavy weightlifting classes were held in small sheds. During the summer of 2021, just as things were opening back up, COVID-19 reared its ugly head again, this time close to home. Within my small group of ladies, a few got breakthrough cases of COVID-19, scaring everyone else away from class for about a month.

It was a precarious time for everyone, and I was no exception to the fear of the unknown. I was witnessing the dissolution of my career as I had known it. No one wanted to come to class out of fear. In-person, one-on-one training was about to take a further hit as my snowbirds were flocking south and past clients were disinterested in training at home or the barn. I began to realize I was spinning my tires and getting nowhere marketing exclusively to older adults, who had been my primary niche, both online and in person. I now had an abundance of free time, feeling despair and wondering constantly where to go and what the future would hold.

Just because you might have resilience, it doesn't mean everything is always going to be sunshine and rainbows. I have faced many obstacles in my life, so much so that I made a hobby out of overcoming obstacles by competing in obstacle course races. Although obstacle course races are essentially for fun, there is a sense of resilience in the heat of a race. In 2021, I ran an 18-mile obstacle course race, on one of the hottest days in New Jersey. As sweat dripped down my face, fatigue set in. There were plenty of times I thought about packing it in, to stop before I hurt myself, my energy levels waning. But it was another moment in time to practice utilizing my toolbox to face the obstacles in front of me. Having access to fuel, electrolytes, and food, as well as the inner drive to see myself accomplish the goal of finishing, helped pick me up. Similarly, when the obstacles of COVID-19 began to unfold, it was that same muscle of resilience I needed to flex to meet the challenges ahead.

I had to sit back and think about my life, about my past experiences and how I could wield them to help me reach more people. It was after talking to my online business coach, Ren, that I realized I didn't have to be married to my in-person niche of helping older adults, that I could in fact pursue other areas of focus online. As someone who is eight years sober, I am in a couple of Facebook groups for non-alcoholic beer enthusiasts who are mostly sober. It was there that I started talking to, and offering fitness/mindset/nutrition help to, people struggling with their sobriety. I decided to switch up my niche by using my life experiences and my strength in sobriety, to show others how fitness, nutrition, and mindset coaching could help them on their journey of staying clear of substance abuse. Alcohol abuse is on the rise because of the pandemic, so I recognized a ballooning need to offer support for those who were struggling.

In the fall of 2020, I participated in a day-long IMPACT Life coaching certification hosted by Todd Durkin and Kelli Watson. It was an amazing day of connecting with like-minded people while working on an exceptional certification. At the time of the training, I wasn't completely clear on how I would implement what I gained, but as time moved on and the rollercoaster of COVID-19 dragged on, I recognized it was the perfect time to use some of my new tools. Having this new training in my toolbox helped me move in the direction of helping people with substance abuse issues to use fitness, nutrition, and mindset coaching to maintain sobriety.

In a world where fitness has never been more accessible through apps, YouTube videos, and free online programs, fitness professionals must find a way to stand out. Helping improve people's mindsets and connecting with clients on a deeper level helps set coaches apart from the pack. Individuals struggling to maintain sobriety can find exercise and dietary recommendations anywhere. My intention was to help them address their obstacles by addressing their mindsets and helping them cultivate resilience.

We can't make it all about numbers on a scale or pounds lifted. When we help strengthen minds and improve attitudes, we help individuals to become more well-rounded, and in my case, help those in sobriety cultivate the mindsets that keep them on track and bolster a level of fitness that helps them feel resilient from the inside out.

Resilience is a quality of character that springs forth when our inner and outer toolboxes are well stocked. But the will to open that toolbox and utilize its contents starts from the inside, your mind. Feeding your mind, building upon your life experiences and the lessons learned, is just as important for us in the health and wellness fields as it is for clientele. Try listening to podcasts from professionals like Todd Durkin, Jay Shetty, Jon Gordon, Ed Mylett, and Lewis Howes, just to name a few, and let yourself be inspired and lifted up by the positive voices in the fitness/health industry. Commit yourself to reading and learning beyond what's "required" to keep up your certification or licensure. Remain a student of life.

Obstacles, challenges, and unprecedented times offer us an opportunity to dig into our inner resources and meet life with strength and creativity. This is resilience: the capacity to recover quickly from difficulties. It would have been easier when the world shut down to sit around, collect pandemic money, and hope for things to improve.

If you're reading this, chances are you're in this business of changing lives, so perhaps you agree that doing nothing was never an option. We never know what life is going to throw at us next, but wherever we are, whatever the obstacle, we can trust in the contents of our unique set of tools and our ability to add more tools when push comes to shove. Nothing is impossible when we use our inner strengths.

Ken McCullough

Ken McCullough is a fitness, nutrition, and mindset coach and speaker. In 2021, Ken founded Healthy Fit Sober Life, an organization aimed at helping those with alcohol abuse issues to use fitness, nutrition, and mindset coaching to aid in their sobriety.

Ken holds a Master's degree in Exercise Science and has been a certified personal trainer through the American Council of Exercise for close to 14 years. He also holds certifications in nutrition coaching, TRX suspension training, online coaching, and behavior change.

Ken's purpose is to leave the world a healthier place than when people entered it, both inside and out.

FB @Kmccullough514
IG @SOBERFITKEN

CHAPTER 9

Unknown Bravery

Finding the Sense of New Self During Grief

By Tracy L. Markley

It began in February 2020 when I traveled to southern California to teach my Stroke Recovery Training course for the first time live to fitness professionals at UC Irvine, and to speak at a stroke support group. I also visited my father in Long Beach. At that time, he was not at his best health, but he was not extremely ill either. I remember sitting at the event in Irvine on the last day and out of the blue I started to cry. I felt a strong urge to go see my father one more time before I flew out on the plane back to Oregon. I felt like I might never see him again, even though I had a trip already set up to come back in July for the IDEA Fitness Convention, and to visit my father for his 80th birthday.

It is important for me to always listen to my gut feelings, or as I also call it, my intuition. I left the event immediately and brought lunch over for us to eat together at his home. I knew when I hugged him goodbye that day that it might be the last time I see him. I thought it was because he would become more ill. Once I was back in Oregon and saw my clients the next day, I began hearing about COVID-19. It was still new and very confusing for everyone to understand. Within a few weeks, my studio was closed down and I could not see clients, like many of us experienced in the fitness industry. A few weeks later, my stepfather, Lee, who lived near me in Oregon, was diagnosed with prostate cancer that quickly metastasized into bone cancer. Although I did not welcome COVID-19 into the world, I welcomed the time off from seeing clients in person so I could be with my stepfather. He was a part of my life for 45 years, and we were very close. I taught a few group training classes and a couple of private clients on Zoom, and spent the rest of my time with him.

Like most of us in the industry, I had to learn immediately how to use Zoom for business, be insured properly for it, and learn how to have legal music access to continue training clients via the internet. All this was going on as I watched my stepfather in pain and declining. I was not sleeping much those days. When I was not with my stepfather and mom, I had to keep my mind busy, so I focused on writing. During the last couple weeks of his life, my stepfather spent 11 days in a row in the hospital. Due to the COVID-19 restrictions in hospitals, only my mom could visit him. She drove over an hour to and from the hospital every day for those 11 days to be with him. My mom arranged an ambulance for him to come home for his last few days. We took care of him through hospice, and it was very sad. He passed away July 30, 2020.

My stepfather walked two to three times a day for all the years I knew him. I always had in my mindset that he would outlive all my parents. I train clients who are in their 80s, 90s, and over 100 years old. I always had in my mind and beliefs that my stepfather would live to be 100. When he turned 80, I thought that was still young. Wow, did my sense of belief and faith get altered.

Somehow in the time frame between the time my studio was closed down due to COVID-19 and a week or so after he passed, I had published three books. I look back and it doesn't seem possible that I could do such a thing. Also, during this time, thousands of fitness businesses were closing permanently.

I'm in a private Pilates studio owners' group on Facebook. Everyone was supporting one another as shutdowns and closures were happening. Some professionals were on there trying to sell all the Pilates equipment they had in their studios. It was a difficult time for the fitness industry for sure. Everyone was making forced changes created by circumstances out of their control. One day as I was interacting within this Facebook group I remembered a great scene in the movie *You've got Mail* when Meg Ryan was forced to close her bookstore. Her aunt in the movie said, *"Closing the store is a brave thing to do. You are daring to imagine you can have a different life. I know it doesn't feel that way and you feel like a big fat failure now but you're not. You are marching into the unknown, armed with... nothing."*

I always thought that was a powerful scene. It's true, many of us were forced to make changes, and it took true bravery in our hearts and souls to take on the unplanned and unpredictable journey put upon us. I think we need to continue to remind ourselves and our clients of how strong and brave we were, and still are.

A part in this journey I faced was not seeing my regular clients two to three days a week. My dog, Wasabi, worked with me. We both missed these people. He would sit in the window and wait for clients to show up and no one would. At one point the vet diagnosed him with sadness and grief because he also lost my stepfather and all the daily people he worked with. This was another sense of loss I endured, like most fitness professionals also did, by not seeing the community of clients that we all created.

I believe there may be a lot of people, including professionals, that endure this sense of loss and grief but do not realize it is happening within themselves. Loss and grief make us feel different. It can be physically exhausting, and we can fatigue quicker in our activities.

We know and teach our clients daily how important moving the body and exercise is for mental and emotional health. The emotions I have been sharing in this chapter can cause a person to feel unmovable and/or emotionally paralyzed. I would try to continue my daily walks, but I would tire out quickly. When I did my resistance and functional training, I would do a few minutes and just stop. I had no energy to continue, and just wanted to rest.

Many clients that have come back or will be coming back during and after the pandemic may have this fatigue and loss at some level and not understand it. It's important for us to keep a good communication line open with them on their mindsets, because many people may be different from who they were before the pandemic. They may not connect to the realization that their physical fatigue could be the outcome of the mental and emotional experiences they have had since the start of the pandemic.

I think it is important to understand that studies have shown that some people who had COVID-19 have had aftereffects of neurological issues and heart problems. In the beginning months of the pandemic, a fitness professional shared on social media that she was feeling off after having COVID-19. She shared that she would stop at stop signs and forget to continue driving after she stopped. If someone tells us in training or classes that they feel off or dizzy, it may not be a food or hydration situation, it may be related to COVID-19. We need to understand that we may have to suggest to our clients that they consult their physicians regarding their symptoms.

Less than a month after my stepfather passed, I got a call from the Medical Alert company that my father in California had fallen. I was still in Oregon, and I could not travel due to COVID-19 safety. Los Angeles county was extremely high in hospitalizations at that time. My dad told me not to come and risk getting COVID-19, plus he could not have visitors. He fell down on August 24th and he never returned home. He had a lot of health issues, was on dialysis for over five years, and had just turned 80 in July. He spent the last four months of his life going back and forth between nursing facilities and the hospital. He ended up in the ICU on a breathing machine for a few weeks and then passed right before Christmas.

The hospital was great during that time because they always had an iPad available for visiting. I visited with my dad through Zoom. If I had not been forced to master Zoom for business during the pandemic, I may not have understood I could use Zoom to visit with him. For those few weeks I would sit at home on my computer in Oregon and play his favorite music and talk to him while he laid there unconscious. My dog, who my dad enjoyed howling with, also howled and sang for him. The doctor called me one day and said that he was in an ICU unit that now had 30 COVID-19 patients, and he needed to move dad into a private ICU facility. While those plans were being made, the doctor called again and said that my dad was near the end of his life and that he could stay on the breathing machine for a few more days, or we could just let him go. I had to make the decision knowing my father would want to go, so I did. I was with him via Zoom when he passed.

There were no services for my stepfather or father because of the pandemic. What I also found difficult for them was that they both had to spend their last months and weeks of their lives only seeing people wearing face masks. I was able to visit my dad with no mask and he could see my face because of the iPad and Zoom. I liked that for us both. I wrote a thank letter to Zoom for being there to use so I could visit my dad and make that time with him possible.

I share my story with you because as hard as it was and is, it is not such an uncommon occurrence of what people have gone through in the pandemic. My best friend's sister, who used to babysit me, also died from COVID-19 a month after my father passed. Then a few months later my dog, Wasabi, passed. I have experienced so much loss. I know how brave I am to get up every day and try to find joy and feel good, somehow. I read cards from my dad that he used to send me telling me how proud he was of me. One even said he was proud of me for the woman I turned out to be because I proved that I could face many trials in life and come out OK on the other end, and still be a good person. That touches my heart and helps me get through the grieving days I have been facing. I think many of our clients will need to be reminded of things like this. Encourage them to be proud of themselves for getting through what the pandemic time and changes brought them through, as well as getting back to, or even beginning, their fitness programs.

By mid-2022 as we are publishing this book, over six million people worldwide have passed away from COVID-19. That is a lot of loss and grief worldwide in the hearts of people. People also dealt with losses that had nothing to do with COVID-19.

I confirmed with a psychologist, a nurse practitioner, and other healing professionals that some people have become complacent or comfortable in their new "depressed" version of themselves. They need to get moving, exercise, and switch things up in their lives to recreate the new version of themselves by moving out of depression. In fact, that may be a great slogan for getting clients now.

"Have you become comfortable with sadness or depression during the pandemic? Come join us and let's exercise it away together." Or something like that.

Millions of people had to be brave and move through their personal and work journeys with an unknown vision. Many are not only experiencing and trying to heal from grief, many also have developed post-traumatic stress from all the losses, changes, fears, and the ups and downs of the continued times when the number of cases were decreasing, then increasing, time and again, and then with new variants, etc. This alone has caused many to fall into deep depression, the sense of giving up hope, and some even giving up on themselves.

As fitness professionals, like many other businesses, we were shut down temporarily a few different times, with some having closed permanently. There is a sense of grief and loss that we have felt in the industry, as well as our healthy and unhealthy clients losing their time in the gyms and training.

As the pandemic fades away and the fitness communities and gym facilities of all exercise modalities proceed to run their businesses as they normally did before the pandemic, some may find it more challenging. Not only have most of us developed a virtual side of our businesses that will always be with us in the future of fitness, we will meet new people who suffered loss and are carrying grief much like myself.

I mentioned previously that some people don't realize they are in a state of grief. Some also have experienced a level of shock. They have been in fight-or-flight mode for a long time. People have developed post-traumatic stress disorder, PTSD. Many felt traumatized. These mental and emotional stages are not something that positive thoughts can just snap someone out of. It takes love, care, understanding, people, companions, laughter, positive thoughts, feeling the grief, self-care, and time.

I believe understanding that our mindsets are not the same as before the pandemic, will help us with our clients and businesses. Many were scared, and some experienced great isolation and loneliness. It will take great inner strength, and being brave, for many to come to the fitness community and feel safe again. We need to continue to root them on for showing up each time we see them, probably now more than ever.

Fitness professionals can develop a level of loss and grief from things, such as:

- Closing a fitness studio. If you are like me, I loved the energy, vibe, and equipment I provided and created in my fitness studio. I loved just being in the studio, as it is a part of who I am. It hurt and left a void when that was gone and changed drastically.

- Not seeing the same clients that we were used to seeing once or a few days a week.

- Hugging our clients and the many daily person-to-person interactions we created for our workspace.

- The income.

- The joy and energy for pumping up our clients, seeing their results, and being proud of them.

- The human connection we have with clients when they share with us about the good and bad things they go through.

- The list can go on and on. We all have our own personal connections and losses.

As fitness professionals, many of us are going back into the work we love full-time again with a different mindset and possibly a different inner vibe. What we used to feel going to work may feel different now.

I work with many stroke survivors, and they long to feel like they did before their stroke. I tell them, "You're going to find a comfort in the new you. You won't feel who you were before because you are different now." Many people, including us as fitness professionals, may feel the same. We have to find our new sense of who we are, like the stroke survivors.

I had three major losses in less than a year during the high times of the pandemic. Each loss left me feeling a sense of emptiness, sadness, and being alone. Wasabi was also a therapy dog. He was my best friend. He worked with all my different clients and came with me to group classes since 2009. My dog loved my clients and they loved him. When my business was first shut down in March of 2020, Wasabi would sit in the window and wait for clients to come. In fact, he just knew what time specific clients came, and a few minutes before that time he would sit in front of the window and wait. He would also wait for my stepfather to come over because they were best buddies. My stepdad would walk him on my busy days working with clients. The vet even diagnosed my dog with grief during this time.

Now I am in the world without my two fathers, my dog, and closure of a fitness studio. I moved back to California and reopened a studio. I feel like a totally different person now. I know as my grief continues to get lighter, I will be a different person from who I was two years ago.

It is so important for kindness to take place and to create our training environments to be as professional and caring as we can. Our clients need a physical, emotional, and mental safe space to go and exercise now more than ever. We all need a sense of belonging with a family or group. The isolation we've experienced has taken that away from millions of people of all ages. I do think the senior community felt it differently.

For example, my mother lost her husband of 45 years, the father of her children, and moved from her home she shared with my stepfather in Oregon. She stayed home to be safe, due to her health, even though she has been vaccinated and had her booster. She has been in remission from a rare case of Vasculitis that she was diagnosed with in 2015 that almost took her life. In 2021, she was told by a doctor that she is probably clear from it, and it will likely never come back. The fear that if she caught COVID-19, it could be too much on her body is something that so many seniors and people with different health ailments experienced. They are healthy fears, but they have left many feeling isolated.

I have interacted with some older people who have isolated themselves, and they are different now. Their communication and talking skills are weakened. The isolation has been unhealthy for their brains.

I strongly see more development of brain care and having a healthy brain as a necessary future fitness trend. That includes eating well and staying properly hydrated, as we all know, but also kindness, laughter, a sense of community and gatherings, and losing the isolation habit some are stuck in.

When clients feel they can just be themselves in their healing time around us, the better we can help them and the better chance they will stay and become a long-term client.

Have kindness, and don't judge them or label their grief or fear as a negative thing.

Tracy L. Markley

Tracy L. Markley was the 2021 IDEA World Personal Trainer of the Year. She is the owner of Tracy's Personal Training, Pilates, and Yoga Studio and has been working in the fitness industry for over 25 years. She is a certified Fitness and Biomechanics Specialist, BOSU® Master Trainer, personal trainer, dance & group exercise leader, AFAA Group Exercise, FiTOUR pro-trainer, Reiki master-teacher, as well as a Pilates instructor and RYT 200-hour yoga instructor.

She is an educator and has authored and created two CEC courses for fitness and therapist professionals: *Stroke Recovery Training* and *Functional Anatomy 101*. Links to these courses can be found at her website.

Tracy is the author of 10 books, four of which are on stroke recovery. She created and manages a stroke support Facebook group with over 5,200 members. She personally trains clients worldwide via Zoom. Her books and videos have helped many people, including hundreds of stroke survivors and caregivers worldwide. In 2020, Tracy was awarded the Second Place Medical Fitness Professional of the Year Award with the

Medift Foundation, and she was also one of the three finalists for the 2020 IDEA World Personal Trainer of the Year Award. She has been in several magazine articles and has written fitness articles for newspapers. She writes a monthly health and fitness article for the *Live, Love and Eat Magazine*. Tracy is the host of the radio show, *The Health and Fitness Show with Tracy*, on KXCR FM radio on the Oregon coast. Her show can also be heard at her podcast channel that is found on several podcast platforms.

Tracy is available for speaking events, book signings, and training. She can be reached through her website and social media. Her books are available at her website and on Amazon:

www.amazon.com/author/tracymarkley
www.tracymarkley.com

Chapter 10

The Art Of 1% – Getting Back to the Basics

By Jenna Mango

I am no mathematician, but I do know that when you strive to get 1 percent better every day, it will add up. Small actions and small habits over time will pay off. Let me take you back to March 2020, in the middle of lockdown. I felt lost, just like many people in their profession. COVID-19 not only took lives but it also took jobs, sanity, and passions. It just so happened that my job was (and still is) my passion. At the time, I was a personal trainer at Equinox, and my entire business had to switch to being virtual. I questioned if I was in the right profession, and watched people around me on social media start to crumble. I watched them fall out of a health and fitness routine, and felt like I was doing the world a disservice. I started to feel myself slipping, and was interacting with people who kept me in a comfort zone. I missed having social interaction, and I hated seeing my friends on FaceTime and not being able to physically be in the same room as them. I felt afraid to go to Target, and with a mask shortage, I needed to make them out of hair ties and bandanas. Then one day I woke up and looked at all the signs I had on my dresser at my parents' house. One said "RISE," one said "Do More of What Makes You Happy," and the last one said "It's a Great Day to Have a Great Day." It was then that I decided to use quarantine as a chance to get back to the basics. I felt like I was living the scene in *Rocky IV* where Rocky and Drago are training for their fight. Drago had all the high-end technology, and I felt like that's where I was at Equinox before lockdown. Rocky had nature, house-made items, and a small collection of workout equipment. That's where I was during lockdown.

I knew it was challenging to get any workout equipment online because everything was out of stock, backordered, or would take months to get to me. I had a very small collection of equipment, but I also had a massive hill in my backyard, household items I could use, and a creative brain for programming workouts. I got to work and felt an improvement in myself, not only physically, but also mentally, emotionally, spiritually, and socially. I became the leanest I'd ever been because I had the time to focus on my health and fitness. I got creative with easy meal-prep ideas, and spent time diving deeper into programming, human anatomy, postural restoration, and biomechanics. I started to see who my true friends were, I developed a closer relationship with God, and I started going to therapy to work on myself so I could become a better version of myself in order to help others. Before I knew it, April 2020 came, and I felt called to do more.

I put out social media posts that I was creating a free quarantine fitness Facebook group. I was hoping I could get at least 5-10 people, knowing that my closest friends and my mom would join. It wasn't long until the messages started coming in, and before I knew it I had 20+ women wanting to be a part of my group. These women joined for different reasons, weight loss being the biggest reason. Another reason was having support from like-minded people, and improving their mental state. I had women from Connecticut, New York, Pennsylvania, New Hampshire, Florida, California, and the Netherlands. All of these women I personally knew, and before I knew it they all started to interact within the Facebook group. They started following each other on social media, hyping each other up on posts, and all eager to learn more from me. The group received a weekly workout plan every week, daily motivation, a live workout with me every Sunday, meal-prep ideas, Q&A segments, weekly education on fitness/health/nutrition, and a group of like-minded people to be authentically themselves. I created this group because I felt called to do more, needed accountability for myself, and wanted to make an impact.

As the group went on, I started to see massive positive changes in these women, and I felt my confidence growing at the same time. I was on this journey with them, and seeing them feeling physically confident and having that confidence trickle to other parts of their lives put a smile on my face from ear to ear; all this because I made the decision to take charge of my life and go back to the basics.

When the world opened back up, I made sure I always had time carved out for me in order to get back to basics and take the time to slow down. If the pandemic taught me anything, it's that small actions and habits add up over time. We as human beings make life so complicated for ourselves when it doesn't have to be. There is always one small action that you can take today in order to be one step closer to where you want to be tomorrow.

Going back to the basics looks different for everyone, but here's how I did it...

I implemented what I call the 10/10. I discuss the 10/10 on page 122 of my book *Choose to RISE*. I start by writing down 10 things I am grateful for and then 10 things I need to accomplish before the day is over. Sometimes things get repeated, but it can be as big or as small as I'd like them to be. From being grateful for my family to being grateful for a sweatshirt on a chilly day, I just know I can control that part of my day. I need to control the controllable, and I can control what I write down every day.

I'm sure you've heard many experts say you need to write your goals down, and to that you might roll your eyes… but it actually does work. Why is it that every leading expert in your industry or those you may admire say you need to write things down? No, not using a notes section in your phone, no, not typing it into your iPad, no, not speaking it into a voice memo… you need to physically take a pen to a piece of paper. Why? Writing things down has two levels to it, encoding and external storage. Encoding is the deeper process that occurs. It's what we think that travels to our hippocampus in our brain to be analyzed. The hippocampus is responsible for learning and memory – that's the role it plays. So, the encoding process is a decision about what will be stored in our long-term memory, and what gets thrown out. External storage is simple – it's something to easily access and review at any time you would like. So basically… it's a piece of paper that you can store in an easily accessible location – maybe in your room, maybe taped to the mirror like Rocky's next opponent, etc. Like I said, I'm no mathematician, and I'm also not a neuroscientist. But it doesn't take someone like that to know that a visual cue you stare at as a reminder every day will force you to remember. So basically, bringing it full circle, when you write something down… it has a much greater chance to not only be remembered but also… be accomplished.

So now, let's circle back to the 10/10. These are more than goals – these are daily things you need to accomplish while also showing gratitude every day. Just like writing goals down, this is something you need to write down at the start of every day. It doesn't matter how big or small it is, just write it down. It doesn't matter if something is repeated the next day, just write it down. When you wake up and start your day with something as simple as the 10/10, you start your day with a full grateful heart while also seeing what you need to get done before the day is over. A grateful heart, and a drive to get 1 percent better every day, will continue your progression as a person, will hold you accountable, will give you that drive to succeed, and accomplishments will happen.

In the fitness world, let's use athletes as an example. If you watch them on television or at the stadium, you may see athletes reverting back to basics or the fundamentals. It is important to lay the groundwork in order to be successful as an individual and as a team. A lot of times, regardless of the level you play at, you probably will hit a funk. A key factor to getting out of that is… say it with me… going back to the basics! Don't skip ahead, especially when you aren't ready to. Because the big plays, the big wins, come from laying down the groundwork… they come from the basics.

As a former collegiate field hockey coach, we would spend a majority of our time on the basics, because if you're not great at the basics then you will always fall behind. We would have players become very frustrated that we weren't doing complex skills, and that we were always focusing more on stickwork, passing routes, shots, short and long corners. We pulled them all in one day for film, and discussed why the basics were so important and why we focused on them so much. I used this time to whip out a famous saying that my father would tell our team when he was my travel softball coach. He said, "Games are won and lost by a fraction of a second." Let that sink in for a moment, and let me say it again… "Games are won and lost by a fraction of a second."

All of the plays, decisions, and reactions play a role in whether you win or lose, like the fraction of time where you could have hustled to the ball rolling out of play but you didn't because you were frustrated about a play before. You could have gotten it, but you didn't. That could have resulted in moving the ball up field, a breakaway, a foul and return of possession, or maybe… a goal. You don't know what could have come of the situation. The fraction of time between moving on to the next play, or recovering, vs. throwing your stick or smashing equipment on the ground plays a role. If a stranger were to come to the field and look at you, not the scoreboard, they should not be able to tell if you are having a good or bad game. So, when we discussed this as a team, we realized we needed to embrace the basics. There were a lot of games that we won because of the basics. Goals, touchdowns, shots, knockouts, etc., don't need to be fancy. Does it make for great entertainment? Sure. But what makes for greater entertainment? A hard-fought win. I was the assistant field hockey coach at Western Connecticut State University from July 2016-2020. During my four seasons coaching at WestConn, we experienced a major shift in our program. In 2016, we were 5-13 overall, 2-9 in conference. In 2017, we were 6-13 overall, 5-6 in conference. In 2018, another strong team joined our conference, and we knew we needed something to give us an edge. This is when we dialed in on what needed to change and realized we had neglected the basics. By getting back to the basics, we improved to 11-7 overall, 9-3 in conference. In 2019, we achieved the greatest success in WestConn field hockey history. After embracing the basics and having our whole team on board, we went 15-5 overall, 10-2 in conference. I'll let that sink in for you… and by the way, let me add this: In 2016, we almost didn't have a team. We started with 15 players. My final season, through extensive recruiting efforts and finding players who aligned with what we were working toward, we had 26 players. We were working toward getting 1 percent better every day in every aspect of our lives, not just on the pitch. The basics to us meant making sure we held each other accountable, every member of the team made sure their job got done, our locker room was always clean, we took care of all our equipment, etc.

Small actions and small habits will add up over time. Getting back to the basics is an integral part of that in order to get 1 percent better every day. The little things we do every day become the big things over time. This can be done by getting back in touch with ourselves and renewing our love, compassion, empathy, vulnerability, and values. When people say that they lose or lack motivation to do something, think deeper. Does motivation help? Sure. Let me ask you this, though – are you motivated to brush your teeth every morning? No. That right there is discipline. Every discipline relies on fundamentals.

So how does getting back to the basics on an everyday basis look for you?

To start, know your "why" and your vision. Why do you do what you do? Write down your "why," then write down your short- and long-term goals. Then when you're done with that, start implementing the 10/10 into your morning routine. If you don't have a morning routine… start one now, and while you're at it come up with a nighttime routine as well. Yes, start powering down those electronics early.

Next, take care of your mental state. You can get physical repetitions done in the gym all you want, but if you don't get in your mental repetitions, you'll continue to struggle. Take care of your mental state, come to be extremely mindful of your time, stop comparing yourself to others, and learn to say "no." If it costs your mental health, it costs too much. Shift your mindset to a more growth mindset over fixed, and take time to yourself in order to decompress and reflect.

Lastly, clean. Yes, clean. Clean your car, your bedroom, your kitchen, everything. This will reduce any feelings of anxiety, minimize procrastination and avoidance, help reduce stress, and increase the ability to focus as well. When you have a clean home and a made bed, you've already achieved something in your day and have a driving factor to be more productive. So, no matter how the day goes, you achieved something.

Ask yourself this question: Are your current habits putting you on the right path in order to succeed?

A slight change in your daily habits and striving to get 1 percent better every day can guide you to where you want to be. We think that small changes don't matter over time, and we think that massive change needs some serious massive action, when in reality that can leave us defeated, burnt out, and frustrated. Don't neglect the small stuff, the fundamentals, the basics.

I challenge you to start today. Put into action the small stuff I have stated above. Even if you don't feel like they're working, stick to it. Nothing great has ever happened overnight. Getting 1 percent better every day will, in time, pay off. That is a promise I can guarantee because it worked, and still works, for me.

I am currently a performance coach and personal trainer at Fitness Quest 10 in San Diego, California. Before that I was a personal trainer at Equinox in Connecticut. I loved my job, but I didn't necessarily love where I was in my life. The plan after graduation was never to stay in Connecticut, but things kept happening that caused me to stay. I knew that nothing great ever came from a comfort zone, but I also knew that my dreams wouldn't be achieved overnight. I worked extremely hard and continued to get 1 percent better every day in all aspects of my life. By doing the small things, I found that in time my confidence grew to then put me in a position to take a risk and email Todd Durkin and Jeff Bristol about a possible job opportunity at FQ10, even though they weren't actively hiring. It paid off, because here I am. If I didn't stay consistent and believe fully that my small actions would eventually pay off, I wouldn't be where I am today.

You can do anything that you set your mind to. I'm sure you've heard that time and time again, but it's true. However, your life's journey is a marathon, it's not a sprint. Climb the mountains in life with an exclamation point, not a question mark. Be intentional, be consistent, be disciplined, be present, be 1 percent better.

Jenna Mango

Jenna Mango is the bestselling author of *Choose To RISE* and currently works at Fitness Quest 10 in San Diego, California as a certified personal trainer and performance coach. She is originally from Bethel, Connecticut and her passion for the fitness industry started early on when she began playing elite sports at the age of 8. In field hockey and softball, she was always the smallest on the team, and it was instilled in her very early on that you don't get what you wish for, you get what you work for.

Jenna has a Master's Degree in Applied Behavior Analysis from Western Connecticut State University and a Bachelor's degree in Psychology from Eastern Connecticut State University. She was a former collegiate field hockey player and upon graduation, she accepted the position of assistant field hockey coach at WestConn and spent four seasons with the team.

Jenna has a passion for helping people break through limitations they set on themselves, or that other people may set on them. She is also currently a WTBA (World Thai Boxing Association) coach and NLP

(Neuro-Linguistic Programming) master practitioner. Jenna continues to train in Hawaiian Kempo, Muay Thai, Brazilian Jiu-Jitsu, Kickboxing, and Boxing.

Follow Jenna:
FB: @jennamango
IG: @jmanggg13

CHAPTER 11

Keeping "It" Simple

By David Pohorence

Anyone operating in the fitness industry during COVID-19 has faced many obstacles and challenges. I think the same can be said for most working professionals in all industries. Challenges often become fertile ground for reevaluation, change, growth, and asking ourselves some important questions. My goal throughout this chapter is to offer some basic tips, strategies, thoughts, and action items that will help you navigate through the many questions you might be asking yourself. We all face tests in our career and in our lives at some point along the way, and often it will happen more than once. Challenge holds the potential for extraordinary growth, and need not be viewed exclusively through a negative lens. As you take in this chapter, I invite you to relax and take a breath. Get yourself a pen and paper and be ready to take notes!

After everything we've gone through in the past two plus years, I believe this pandemic has had a far greater impact on people's lives than most of us could have ever imagined or could have seen coming. What it's done is force many of us to stop, take a step back, and evaluate where we are now. We've been forced to ask ourselves some tough questions about our futures, questions that I believe many were not prepared to answer, including myself! What are some of those questions? Let me first start by saying that no matter what the question is, I firmly believe there is always an answer. The answer might not always be the one we hope for, but in the end, whatever "it" is that brought us to where we are today, I believe it is the path meant for us to follow in both business and in life.

The first question I asked myself was simple, yet it's one I believe we don't ask ourselves or our teams enough as business professionals: what are the basic principles that led me to have success in my business or profession? Go back and look at your original business plan. Does it still align with how you are operating today? Do you know how those principles have helped you or are you so far away from them that you can't identify with them anymore? Do you need to adjust your current business to your original business principles, or do you need to adjust your principles to the current state of the business? Don't worry if you don't have an existing business plan – there are ample software packages you can purchase for a small fee that will help you create the plan now.

I suggest that you use the activity below to help you identify the key points you want to focus on in your business plan and how they apply to the service you would like to offer. This is a great exercise to do at any point in your business or career. In the activity below, write down your top five business principles that you feel will lead you to success. Keep it simple. As you think about your principles, ask yourself, what was the initial reason you got into the business or profession you are in today? Use this activity to identify if that reason still applies today, or if it has changed over time. If it is the same and you still identify with this, that's wonderful. If not, take this time to adjust your new principles to the current state of your business. At some point in our career, many of us will question if what we are doing is still working and aligning with our original intentions. You may need to reinvent your approach to fit the current state of the environment we are working in. Reflect on those essential principles that will influence and possibly determine the success you will have.

What Are Your Basic Principles to Business Success?

1. _____

2. _____

3. _____

4. _____

5. _____

As you identify your basic principles of success and how they apply to your business, consider how those principles can or should apply to developing consistent **customer satisfaction**. In my 20 years in business, I have witnessed many moments of customer dissatisfaction. A good deal of them could have been avoided had there been strategies in place on how to address and identify problems in advance versus dealing with them in a reactive state as they are happening. In many of those circumstances, the employee, manager, or owner is unprepared to address the issue and ends up in a reactive state. As we move into the next phase of our industry, I believe we should be proactive in addressing customers' concerns and aligning our principles of success with how we want our customers to be treated and more importantly, how they expect to be treated. Consider having training scenarios and role-playing situations for your business so everyone on staff is better equipped to handle a dissatisfied customer without disrupting the flow of the business.

Something to always remember when handling a customer's concern is to remove personal feelings from the encounter. Take the moment to first listen closely and take note of the customer's concerns. Instead of an immediate reactive answer, summarize what the customer has said, and let them know that this is how you are understanding what they are telling you. Ask them if that is correct. It is important they know you have heard them and that you want to make sure you are interpreting their concern correctly. After you have received their acknowledgement, let them know the action steps you will take to address the concern, and ask them if they feel that is acceptable. Regardless of whether we are reflecting on the past or planning for the future, the one constant should be to serve our customers with 100 percent dedication and personalization.

Each customer should be handled as an individual with feelings and not just as something that needs fixing. Take a moment to fill out the five actions steps below to see how you are currently handling customer concerns, problems, and complaints. The situations being brought up will always vary, but our action steps on how to handle those should not.

Customer Service Action Steps

1. Listen and relate. Don't talk, just listen. There is power in listening first.

2. Ensure confidence in your service. Be the best at what you offer. Providing confidence will show the customer you are confident you will address their concern.

3. Role play and practice how to address potential customer service concerns and who should handle them. Most issues are unexpected, so handling them efficiently is key.

4. Be clear in communicating with your customer. Ask them if you are understanding their concern correctly.

5. Understand your customers' past and current concerns that may or may not have been addressed. I suggest keeping notes on

each customer profile in case the concerns have been brought up before.

6. Engage in customer score cards or evaluations of you, your service, and your team. This is sometimes difficult for many but necessary if you wish to give your customer a truly great experience.

What Are Your Current Action Steps?

1. _____

2. _____

3. _____

4. _____

5. _____

Action Steps – Action vs. Reaction

To practice how you might act when problems arise, take a few minutes to imagine how a situation might play out and how you would respond. This is a good activity to practice so you can strive to improve personal and team performance in your business or career. This is something we can all do to grow both personally and professionally. The more aware we are of our reactions to challenging situations, the better equipped we are to handle a possible problem or concern efficiently and effectively. Consider printing this page and doing this exercise as often as you need to or as a situation is arising. Practicing our responses helps us formulate the proper reaction when a situation does present itself.

Concern/Problem/Situation: What Was It? What Caused It? How Was It Handled? _____

_____

_____

_____

What Was Your Initial Reaction?

1. _____
2. _____
3. _____
4. _____
5. _____

What Action Did You Take?

1. _____
2. _____
3. _____
4. _____
5. _____

What Are Some Action Steps to Implement? Possible Improve On?

1. _____
2. _____
3. _____
4. _____
5. _____

Customer satisfaction will always be at the forefront of any business or profession. As we maneuver into the next phase of our businesses, we cannot forget that customer satisfaction directly relates to how you and your business is viewed in your surrounding community.

Community connection is vital for any business to be successful. It's often overlooked. It can be the difference in your business being successful or being set up for failure before you even open your doors. Take a moment to think about how you are currently connecting with your community.

Community Connection

Connection within each of our communities is an extremely vital part of our business's success. It only takes one bad experience or review to jeopardize your relationship with your community. Most clients or members of any business usually come from within a five-mile radius of that business. Unless your business is a destination point for others to come to, your community engagement should be heavily focused on that radius. I'm not suggesting you ignore the community outside of that radius, it's just important to identify where your base of clients or members is coming from so you can allocate marketing dollars appropriately. Whether you focus on social media, radio, television, or good old-fashioned mailing, know your community. In my business, we focus heavily on a five-mile radius, but we also get involved in supporting our community as far as 15-plus miles away by organizing 5K races and charity fundraising for Thanksgiving and Christmas. These types of engagements show that you care about being a part of that community. Think of community connection as you would a special friendship or bond you have with your family, showing the community you care and that you want to help in any way you can.

I believe there is no better way to show you are thankful and grateful than community engagement and support. Below you will find some of the ways we support our community, and I invite you to take a moment to write down some things that you are doing or wish to do in yours. Community connection is an essential way to use one of the most important tools to help grow your business – **WORD OF MOUTH!!!** If your community is happy with you, it will be a great resource to increase your revenue dollars by multiplying your marketing efforts and using the community support as a positive resource. If used correctly, it's a simple strategy that can end up being one of the most effective ways to maintain a strong client base. Get involved in the community, and stay involved. Make sure your community can see that you are part of it, not isolated from it.

Our Community Connections

1. Charitable events (live or virtual): 5K, sponsorship, dinner
2. Volunteer opportunities: give-back chances – educational seminar, coaching, mentorships
3. Open house: invite your community in, let them see what you offer and/do
4. Wellness: blood drives, health screenings, recovery days
5. Partnerships: develop a local connection with fellow small businesses – establish options for their staff

Community Connection Ideas: What Are You Doing, or Can You Do?

1. _____

2. _____

3. _____

4. _____

5. _____

Overthinking – Your "Why"

Ask yourself *why* you are doing what you are currently doing, and be 100 percent honest with yourself. Most people can't answer that question quickly or honestly. Until this pandemic hit, a lot of people were operating on autopilot, going through each day without much thought to the future. Tomorrow is never promised, and many operate as if it is. I was one of those people. I left the profession I went to undergraduate school for because I wasn't happy with what I was doing and felt I was going through the motions of life without tapping into what I am most passionate about. My passions were in sports, fitness, and coaching. I recently wrote a book titled *Why Not Me?* I write about discovering your purpose, passion, and drive. Never in a million years did I think I could ever write a book. What emerged from my writing was a sustained message: remember what your why is and stay the course. If you do stray, have a plan to get back on the path that embodies your reasons for doing what you do. Discovering or knowing your "why" sounds like a simple thing until you sit down and take a moment to clarify it.

In our industry, everyone is trying to come up with the next best thing for their business or career, but have a tendency to lose sight of their "why." I believe that as we progress our businesses and maneuver through our daily routines, our "why" seems to become an afterthought. Being an entrepreneur is a phenomenal experience because you can operate independently. It involves risk, yet within the process, one often finds new avenues for creativity and excitement on so many levels. When deciding on developing strategies for your business, it's important to adapt to what the community and marketplace is demanding. Don't lose sight of your "why" in the process. It can be an important piece in helping create clarity. With clarity you can confidently take steps to either enhance or downsize your business and evaluate the strategies you currently have in place. Below are some questions to help identify your "why" and space to write in your action steps.

Identifying Your Why

1. What makes you happy?

   _____

2. What are your core values?

   _____

3. What is it you think you are meant to do?

   _____

4. If money was not a factor, what would you be doing?

   _____

5. Would you do it for free if so?

   _____

6. What are your strengths?

   _____

7. What do you wish to be remembered for and why?

   _____

Services Matter

Are your services still relevant? Is it time to change? It's very important to take inventory of what you are offering and how people are responding to those offerings on a quarterly basis. As we shift into a whole new host of unknowns in today's world, it's vital to have a handle on what's working within your business and what is not. Some offerings may not be relevant because of the pandemic. Perhaps your clientele demographics have changed over the years and you need to get clearer on who your target audience is. I suggest doing an analysis of your current makeup of clients. Calculate the percentages in terms of age groups served and identify the overall breakdown of the population you are serving.

What are your breakdowns?

1. Ages 16-18: _____%
2. Ages 19-22: _____%
3. Ages 23-30: _____%
4. Ages 31-40: _____%
5. Ages 41-50: _____%
6. Ages 51-60: _____%
7. Ages 61-70: _____%
8. Ages 71-80: _____%
9. Ages 81 + _____%

Through this exercise you'll be able to properly identify your target audience, know how to effectively use your marketing dollars, and get clear on what age group makes up a majority of your current client or membership base. This exercise is great to do monthly or however often you deem it necessary. I would suggest doing it at least once a month to see how those age groups adjust over time. The better handle you have on this, the easier it will be to add, remove, or adjust your programming needs. The more you know who you're serving, the easier it becomes to target the right audience when seeking to grow your business, profession, or brand. This information will serve you well in feeling prepared to navigate the evolving business world we are now living in.

What Programs/Services Do You Offer? Ask Yourself, Are They Still Relevant Today?

1. _____
2. _____
3. _____
4. _____
5. _____

What New Programs/Services Can You Offer?

1. _____
2. _____
3. _____
4. _____
5. _____

Specialization – What Sets You Apart?

When you have identified and evaluated your current offerings, services, or activities, it's time to identify what your specialization is and what your company offers that sets you apart from your competitors. I have asked myself this question: why should a client/customer choose my business or use my services? Now more than ever, our businesses should have a distinct specialization or something that nobody else has. I often preach to my staff, and I am sure you have heard it mentioned, that culture matters. It does. Every client or customer should receive the utmost care and respect and expect to be treated to the highest standard no matter where they go. Even if you believe you are having more success than your competitors, it cannot be the reason that separates your business from a competitor.

I can speak from my experience as a franchise owner that I see a trend of more and more specializations and fewer and fewer large one-stop shops. I believe we'll see companies that offer a wide variety of services, downsizing and focusing on the ones that hit a majority of their target client base. My franchise is a smaller fitness franchise, and we have eliminated the larger group classes and shifted to smaller groups and one-on-one training, focusing on servicing the members with a more personalized connection with their coach. We started this shift in our business model just before the pandemic, and we knew our target audience. Preparation matters. We had no idea the pandemic and the effects of lockdowns were coming, but our franchise had previously encouraged us to maintain business exercises that would keep us fully informed about our clientele, preparing us to better serve our clients when we could not meet them in person. What matters is being prepared and doing the things that will help you be ready to act no matter what the situation you may be facing.

Expanding or Downsizing

When you specialize in any type of service or product, it often forces you to decide on whether it's the right time to expand or downsize your business or services offered. It's undoubtedly a tough question. I know from my experience as a franchise owner, I've been challenged many times to grow the brand, expand my services, and hire more team members. Even when everything is going well in your business or career, maintaining a growth mindset requires regular inquiry. Is it the right time? Do I have enough money? What type of expansion? You may also be asking yourself if you should downsize. These are all valid questions to ask yourself. The advice I would give is to weigh all metrics equally. Don't expand or close based on how you wish things were going, but weigh your options using factual data. As a franchise, we have layers of information about who we are serving. We look at surveys on our facilities and services offered, referral programs for client growth, financial analysis reports, and more. If you don't have any of those services, consider joining a professional network group with peers who specialize in areas where you may be weak. One of the best pieces of advice that was given to me by my mentor and friend Todd Durkin was this, "Do what you do best and hire the rest!" Powerful words. After many mistakes, even as a franchisee with phenomenal support, I've learned that if you wish to be successful, there is strength in numbers. I know colleagues who have tried to operate everything and do it all and watched their businesses collapse. Take a moment to do the exercise below, and consider the pros/cons of expanding or downsizing. Your answers may surprise you!

Expanding (Pros):

1. _____

2. _____

3. _____

4. _____

5. _____

Expanding (Cons):

1. _____

2. _____

3. _____

4. _____

5. _____

Downsizing (Pros):

1. _____
2. _____
3. _____
4. _____
5. _____

Downsizing (Cons):

1. _____
2. _____
3. _____
4. _____
5. _____

Franchising vs Private Ownership?

Entrepreneurs, business employees, owners, and coaches face many tough choices. One of the biggest ones I ever faced after leaving my corporate America job was whether I wanted to start a new business concept on my own or take a leap of faith and join the ranks of being a franchisee. I put a lot of time, thought, and money into making this decision, and I encourage you to as well. If you are thinking of leaving your current job or profession and going out on your own, consider making a list of pros and cons to that move. Gather all pertinent information relating to your decision and the direction you wish to go, and lay it all out in front of you side by side. One side will have the positives and negatives of owning your new venture privately and the other will have the positives and negatives of becoming part of a franchise.

I did this exact exercise when I left my corporate America job working as a business analyst. I was miserable. Although the money was great, I was not happy. The time came to decide, so I took months gathering everything I needed to make an educated decision on what direction I was going to take my career in. If I decided from a quick uneducated perspective, I probably would have chosen to open my own private business. I took the time to decide on all the factors in front of me so I could determine what was best for me at the time.

The biggest obstacle for me was financing options. By going the franchise route, it allowed me to join an established and proven business model and get the best possible opportunities to obtain the necessary financing. When starting out on your own, you're often going off projections and not a proven model that's been tested in different demographic scenarios. Fast forward to what I know today, having lived through the experiences of these past 13 years, I wouldn't change a thing. I will say that owning a franchise offers many benefits that owning a business privately does not. One of the big benefits for me is that my clients have access to over 4,000 locations nationally and internationally, something that I could not have offered my clients if I chose to start my own business. In the future, I see the market shifting to many more individuals capitalizing on a brand and franchising it. Conceptually, it makes sense for a variety of reasons, but at the end of the day, the choice that is meant for you as an entrepreneur is ultimately a personal one. Make sure you are armed with all the tools to make the best possible decision for yourself before making any life-changing choices about your business.

Franchising (Pros):

1. _____

2. _____

3. _____

4. _____

5. _____

Franchising (Cons):

1. _____

2. _____

3. _____

4. _____

5. _____

Private Ownership (Pros):

1. _____

2. _____

3. _____

4. _____

5. _____

Private Ownership (Cons):

1. _____

2. _____

3. _____

4. _____

5. _____

To summarize, everything listed below is what I touched on in this chapter. All the points covered were intended to help answer some lingering questions you might have whether you are in the fitness industry or not. Take a moment to write some notes, and go back and identify each point below. As a fitness professional and having a business that was affected tremendously by the pandemic, I really had to take a hard look at what steps I took to get to where I was pre-pandemic and what adjustments I needed to make to remain relevant and in business. In any industry there will always be a bump or two in the road that any business professional will need to overcome. To look to the future and to be successful, remember to always stay involved in your business and industry that you are currently in. Stay educated on upcoming trends or tools so you can identify what may be applicable to you and your business. Keep your finger on the pulse of your business. If you do so, it will help you maneuver and adapt to making the necessary changes in your business in the event of some unforeseen circumstance within or outside of your control. Always be in the mindset that change is inevitable, and you will never be unprepared.

Chapter Items Review

- Basic Principles of Business Success – What is your "It?" Do you live it?
- Customer Satisfaction
- Community Connection
- Overthinking Your "Why"
- Services Matter Now vs. Future
- Specializations – What Sets you Apart?
- Franchising vs Private Ownership? – Pros/Cons
- Action Steps – Acting vs Reacting

David Pohorence

David Pohorence is an experienced personal trainer, business coach and multi-fitness franchise owner. David holds a master's degree in Sports Management from the University of Connecticut and a bachelor's degree in Health Administration from Quinnipiac University. David comes from a large family and is one of seven children. Originally from Connecticut, David currently resides in the Charlotte, NC area with his wife Shannon, daughter, Avery and son, Caleb.

David currently owns three Anytime Fitness Franchises in the North and South Carolina area of Charlotte. As a former athlete, David has always had a passion for fitness, nutrition and of course, business, but when he is not working on those passions to grow as person and a professional, David is focusing on another passion of his—running! He is an avid runner and has recently completed his first half marathon and full marathons. Something he has always lived by is to remember to write down those goals—"a goal not written down is just a dream." During his down time, David enjoys spending time with his family. "Family is everything to me, and so I believe it's important to cherish each and every moment I get to spend with my family outside of work."

David is an Amazon bestselling author and is very excited to share his message and stories in his book *Why Not Me?* His hope is to inspire and motivate others out there who are struggling with their purpose or maybe they have been told they aren't good enough to amount to anything in life. David believes that if this book can help even just one person, all the time, effort and resources put in are more than worth it.

A fun fact about David: many do not know that while in college, he was in the theater group where he performed in two plays and had to sing and dance. It was something way out of his comfort zone, but he enjoyed every moment of it. David encourages everyone to try something new and step outside your comfort zone. While doing that, always remember, Why Not Me? Why Not Now?!

Contact David:

Email: dpoho@msn.com
Instagram: davidpoho94
Facebook: David Pohorence
LinkedIn: David Pohorence

RECOVERY
MATTERS

CHAPTER 12

Recover Your Revenue

By Geoffrey Wade

How many of us coaches spend countless hours with our clients? How many give them fitness tips? Nutrition tips? Spend hours writing up programs and workouts all, for our clients to get stagnant, hurt, bored, or just not really listen to us? What if we could give them the gift of recovery during every session? What if we could help them leave forgetting they worked out and completely feeling like a million bucks? Well, what if I told you recovery is the missing piece to client retention, client experience, and the missing revenue piece you've been missing?

With 25 years in the fitness industry and 11 years as a business owner, I thought I'd still be in business because I was an awesome coach, great with people, and a pretty cool dude. What's true is, I'm still in business because I stepped out of my comfort zone and learned a new tool that I never imagined would change my path, my business, and to be honest, my life. That tool was fascial stretch therapy (FST). It's the simple power of touch, the knowledge of truly understanding the way the body moves and wants to move, and, most importantly, understanding the importance of helping people feel good and move better.

Years ago, I kept feeling like there was a missing piece to everything I was doing with my clients. I kept feeling like there was more to give them, so I would search the internet for something new, something that would truly make a difference. Out of nowhere I came across Fascial Stretch Therapy, a weeklong course taught by a company in Arizona named Stretch to Win.

Now, I'm a Jersey boy who grew up with learning disabilities. I only passed high school because I was a three-sport athlete. The only way I could step on the field or mat was if I passed my classes. I have never been a school person, and two years of college was all I wanted. Training and working out was all I ever knew, so of course I got into the fitness industry. I worked in gyms, coached boot camps in the parks, and traveled everywhere to train and make a buck. I took course after course to hone my skills. The only thing I've ever truly known is if you continue to work hard and push forward, good things will happen. Luckily, with clients' help and being in the right place at the right time, I got the opportunity to open my own training studio, and Outlaw Training and Fitness was born. Sometimes I wonder if that was a good thing! After the first year that feeling of something missing was still there. My clients needed more and really deserved more. That was when I decided to step out of my comfort zone, face my learning capabilities, and challenge myself to sign up for Level 1 of Stretch to Win's Fascial Stretch Therapy course. Now as some of you know, taking one day off from work is a challenge, but taking seven days off is not only a challenge but very scary. Paying for the course, airfare, hotel, and expenses – when they all started to add up, I quickly said no.

A couple of months later, the feeling wouldn't leave, so I went back on the Stretch to Win website, signed up and paid, and said to myself, it's time. Then I got the welcome email from Stretch to Win with everything that needed to be done before I took the course. I had to read three books, take a 100-question test, and pass it! Well, I had to suck it up and do it. I might have – or might not have – taken a couple of times to pass the test. So, after I passed the test, I was in full prep-and-panic mode. Do I know enough? Am I smart enough? Am I out of my league? Well, either way all those answers were going to be answered.

So, off I went to Stretch to Win in Phoenix, Arizona for a five-day hands-on course to learn the ins and outs of fascial stretch therapy. The Day 1 introduction was a quite interesting. It started with one person introducing themselves as the head athletic trainer for the Seattle Seahawks, then a massage therapist for the Seahawks, a physical therapist for the Carolina Panthers, an athletic trainer for the WWE, and, well, you get the point. This personal trainer from southern New Jersey felt like a fish out of water and a little out of my league. Day 1 was a whirlwind as was Day 2. After I got home from Day 2, I really started to question the decision to come out for this course. Putting yourself in elements you're not used to can be a make-or-break experience. Luckily after Day 3, I started to get my sea-legs, and the light bulb went off in my head. I started to understand and grasp the material with more clarity. Five days done and I was officially a fascial stretch therapist.

Now it was time to get back to Jersey and figure out how to implement this new tool into my current business. After five straight days of practicing the techniques, and having them done on my body, I understood the awesome benefits of fascial stretch therapy. I had to show everyone else how beneficial it would be for them. For the first month I stretched every one of my clients as many times as I could, and the feedback was amazing. I knew I had something special and something that would help my clients as well as help my bottom line financially.

After years as a studio gym owner, I was tired of always pursuing new clientele, and I believed this was the answer. Instead of trying to find

10-20 new clients each month, I could stretch 10 or 20 of my current clients at $60 a session, make twice as much as getting a new client, and provide a huge service to my clientele. Clients were feeling better and moving better, and as a business owner, I finally felt like I had a real game plan moving forward, training my clients at a top-notch level and helping them feel better through stretch and recovery. The benefits of stretching became bigger than I ever imagined. My clients were coming in multiple times a week, and the new clientele I was getting were for stretching more than training.

After a full year of adding FST to my toolbox and my business, Outlaw, it was now time to head back to Stretch to Win for Level 2 to see how much further I could take this stretching therapy. To my surprise, five more days of Stretch to Win blew me away even more, so much so that in the airport coming home, I signed up for Level 3, which was three months later. I knew getting my 100 hours of stretching in was not going to be hard to do. My personal schedule when I got back from Level 1 was 90 percent training and 10 percent stretching. That number slowly started to change the more I stretched clients, and after Level 3 it became 20 percent training and 80 percent stretching.

As time went on, new doors started to open, doors I always dreamt of, but I always dreamt they would open due to training. I never imagined it would happen through stretching. In the summer of 2016, I was lucky enough to share FST with my mentor, Todd Durkin. After a few conversations, Todd invited me out to his gym, Fitness Quest 10 in San Diego, to help him train and stretch his NFL football clients. When I got there, I thought it would be a few guys from the New Orleans Saints and the Philadelphia Eagles. However, I wasn't expecting what I walked into.

My morning started at 4 a.m. to catch a 6 a.m. flight from Philadelphia to San Diego. After my five and half hour flight, I took an Uber to Todd's gym. I arrived and Todd's assistant asked me if I was ready to drive over to the field to meet Todd and the guys. So, as I was driving over, I was thinking I'm so hungry, I need a drink of water, and I am not ready to do anything. We arrived at the field and as I walked up, I noticed there were many more guys there than I anticipated. I glanced over to the bench and there was Drew Brees, Chase Daniels, Sam Bradford, Carson Wentz, Darren Sproles, Zach Ertz, Brandin Cooks, Nelson Agholor, and the rest of both the Saints and Eagles offensive skills players. Todd yelled out my name, gave me a big hug, and then yelled out to the guys "Yo, this is G Wade the stretch guy. You guys need anything, he's going to be here for the next couple of days. Take advantage of him being here because he's the best in the biz." Well, no pressure Todd! Thanks, and boom, just like that, hungry, thirsty, and so tired, I was on the turf stretching NFL guys for the rest of the day. I still don't know how I didn't pass out from hunger! Finally, I finished and got back my hotel, took a deep breath, and thought WOW, that really just happened. A little boy who dreamt of working with pro athletes just lived out part of that dream.

The next day was just as much of a whirlwind, except this time I ate first, and knew what I was getting into! I spent the morning training the guys, then spent the afternoon heading over to stretch a couple of guys at their houses. Here I am in a townhouse in Del Mar, California, stretching NFL pro athletes while I can hear the ocean waves crashing and seals chirping. I quickly thought, well I'm definitely not in New Jersey! The last day, which I thought was going to be calm, was another whirlwind. I trained more guys in the morning and then spent the rest of the day stretching 18 guys in a row. When I got back to the hotel that night, the little boy with a dream became the adult who finally felt like he truly belonged.

When I got back to Jersey, I was lucky enough to have done a good enough job that most of the Eagles I had worked with wanted to continue. Seven years later, I still work with many Philadelphia Eagles and local Philly and Jersey NFL players when they are home. My clientele blossomed to more local pro players from the Philadelphia Phillies and the Philadelphia Sixers, and I became the head stretch therapist for the Philadelphia Sixers.

The struggling business owner who was chasing clients finally figured it out. I now had a staff of six with three of my trainers being fascial stretch therapists. We built a new hybrid-style gym that focused on training people properly to perform on the field, office, or home, and then recover to be able to do it again. Our gym used FST, Normatec recovery boots, and percussion guns to give a variety of recovery tools to our clients. Recovery became part of our culture – perform, recover, and repeat. It was now time for Outlaw to evolve as well.

As I started to be part of coaching groups and masterminding, I quickly realized a lot of trainers, studio owners, and gyms were struggling to stay open and figure out that missing piece. And I began thinking that the industry had given me so much, how could I make a difference and give back? I have always believed in leaving more then I take, so I thought about what I could leave. And it hit me how I could package a recovery program to help fitness professionals add recovery to their current business and stop running in the hamster wheel of chasing clients. Bulletproof Stretch and Recovery was born.

The evolution of stretch and recovery has single-handedly helped me keep my business open by adding revenue, improving client retention, and creating a unique client experience. Stretch and recovery has become close to 50 percent of our revenue, and has opened so many new opportunities for Outlaw, and for me personally. That became even more relevant during the COVID-19 pandemic.

The power of touch and purpose as never been more important. The bulk of our business during the pandemic has come from clients just wanting to be taken care of, feel better, relieve their stress, and have someone listen to them. The time on the table with clients has become priceless, and Outlaw's purpose has become even bigger. When I originally opened, I just wanted people to feel better about themselves through fitness, feeling stronger physically and mentally. Now that has evolved into becoming the best version of themselves through moving better with proper training and even better recovery. Feel better, move better, and be better by training to perform and recover, in order to keep performing at your best. That sparked me to make not only myself evolve, but Outlaw evolve as well. The gym named Outlaw Training and Fitness was now changing to Outlaw Performance and Recovery. Not only did I see the importance of change, but I felt it was time to separate from the normal fitness image and focus on something bigger, and I believed that was recovery.

Now that the gym had taken a new step forward, it was time for me to as well. With watching the fitness industry constantly spinning the "one thing," I noticed the constant so-called gurus popping up on my social media claiming to show me how to make millions with their programs. "Turn 20 clients into 100. Make 100k in six months." That non-substance has continually kept this industry spinning – chasing clients and keeping the hamster wheel spinning. The frustration was building and building on my end. The fitness industry has become the Wild Wild West. So instead of getting frustrated, I wanted to give something back to the industry, something real with substance that would help fitness professionals truly add value to their skillset, as well as add value to their clients, something to assist their growth and help their business in the way my growth with recovery has helped me. With that, came the newest iteration of the Outlaw business, Bulletproof Stretch and Recovery and the Bulletproof Recovery Systems.

After months of strategy and trial runs, I put the pieces together in a way that would instantly help fitness professionals cut through the chaos, as well as respect the integrity of FST. So, with the help and blessing of Chris and Ann Fredricks of Stretch to Win (creators of fascial stretch therapy) I created the Bulletproof Recovery Systems Workshop. This two-day hands-on workshop includes teaching a 6-12 minute full-body systematic table-based stretch routine, which is based on the basics of fascial stretch therapy; Percussion Gun 101 and how to use percussion guns; a full-body routine designed to be used safely and effectively for both chair and massage table; a complete guide on how to instantly implement these tools into your current business to create new revenue; and a review of recovery tools that would work best for your business. See Bulletproofstretchandrecovery.com for schedule and more information.

I am so thankful for the gift that Chris and Ann of Stretch to Win have given me. The gift of recovery has changed my journey, added so much more purpose to Outlaw and myself, and given me the opportunity to help so many more people. I never imagined how far stepping out of my comfort zone would take me. To be able to live my dream of owning a training studio and help people through training has now been elevated through fascial stretch therapy and recovery. I have been able to keep the original dream alive, evolve, and continue to take Outlaw and my personal success to new heights.

So, as you're reading this, good luck in everything you do and if you're thinking of stepping out of your comfort zone – TAKE THE STEP! If you're looking to recover lost revenue, it might be as simple as adding a new tool to your current business. Yes, I'm being very biased because that tool might be **recovery**.

Geoffrey Wade

Geoff is a performance and recovery specialist, a certified master sports performance coach, fascial stretch specialist and soft tissue specialist with over 20 years of experience. He is the owner and founder of Outlaw Performance and Recovery located in Southern New Jersey and creator of the Bulletproof Recovery Systems.

He is part of the National Sports Performance Association, and proud member of the Todd Durkin Mastermind Group. Geoff is the stretch specialist for the Philadelphia Sixers and works with athletes from NFL, MLB, NBA, college and high school levels, as well as the general population aiding with overall fitness, flexibility, and recovery to maximize results.

- Certified Master Sports Performance Coach (National Sports Performance Association)
- Certified Fascial Stretch Specialist Level 3 (Stretch to Win Institute)

- Certified Applied Functional Science (Grey Institute)
- Certified Soft Tissue Transformation (Grey Institute)
- Certified Speed and Agility Coach (NSPA)
- Weightlifting Performance Coach (NSPA)
- Program Design Coach (NSPA)
- Sports Nutrition Coach (NSPA)

Chapter 13

Got Pain? You Can Help

How to Start a Successful Business That Disrupts the Current Chronic Pain Healthcare Model

By Travis Perret

Musculoskeletal pain is an epidemic in our society and around the world. According to the World Health Organization:

- Approximately 1.71 billion people have musculoskeletal conditions worldwide.

- Musculoskeletal conditions are the leading contributor to disability worldwide, with low-back pain being the single leading cause of disability in 160 countries.

- Because of population increases and ageing, the number of people with musculoskeletal conditions is rapidly increasing.

- The disability associated with musculoskeletal conditions has been increasing and is projected to continue to increase in the next decades.
  (https://www.who.int/news-room/fact-sheets/detail/musculoskeletal-conditions#:~:text=A%20recent%20analysis%20of%20Global,around%20the%20world%20are%20affected.)

I believe you can create a successful business that helps people who are afflicted with chronic pain feel better and move better. The number of people who have chronic musculoskeletal pain is not a secret. It is one of the top reasons people cancel their gym memberships or quit personal training. Many businesses have tried to help those who have it, but even though they have good intentions their model is not correct.

Most therapies are focused on the symptom area and are not looking enough for the root cause of the problem. Often this is not the fault of the therapist but of the healthcare system. Our current system is reactive and not proactive. I believe that the demand for an alternative holistic approach is growing every year. Society is getting wise to the inadequacies of western medicine with regard to musculoskeletal pain.

I own a business in Kansas City called Exercise Therapy of Kansas City. We have been open for 17 years. I have a degree in Exercise Science. I'm not a doctor, chiropractor, physical therapist, or a certified personal trainer. I have no certifications or letters after my name. Yet for the last 25 years, I've been helping people overcome the limitations of musculoskeletal pain and many times helping them alleviate the pain and preventing surgeries, shots, and pain pills. I have logged tens of thousands of hours working with thousands of clients looking for an alternative holistic way to relieve their chronic pains. I have worked with the whole spectrum of clients from professional athletes to clients in their 90s who are searching for a holistic way to help their chronic back, neck, knee, and hip pain. I have written also a #1 best-selling book titled *Pain Free Life*.

I do not take insurance, and clients are expected to pay up front. I ask my clients to do exercises every day, and if they don't I fire them from the program. My clients pay $250 an hour for alternative health services in one of the most conservative areas in the country. I also offer a full refund if they are not happy with the results.

I believe to really make an impact on the current epidemic of chronic pain, the world needs you to learn how to do what I do – not just the concept of how the therapy works but how I educate clients, how I pay my bills and feed my family. The world needs you to be successful. People need you to learn how to run an alternative-based business in a world dominated by insurance companies, pharmaceutical companies, and millions of dollars spent on not-needed surgeries, shots, and pain pills.

I'm going to tell you how to do it, but first you need to hear my story. You need to hear how I got started, and why I'm so passionate about what I do.

In 1998, I came home for the holidays to spend time with my family. When I walked into the house, the usual hugs and welcome home greetings were abundant except for one person – my dad. He wasn't at the front door with the rest of the family welcoming me home, which was not like my dad. When I inquired where he was, I was told that he was in the living room.

As I walked into the living room, I could hear the TV playing and I saw him sitting in the recliner with his feet up. It puzzled me that he was not up and excited to see me. I knew something was wrong. It looked like he had been living in the recliner. The table next to him was loaded with newspapers, crossword puzzles, and all kinds of things to keep him busy, and most interestingly, a walker was sitting next to his chair.

At the time my dad was only 45 years old, but he looked like a frail old man, not the youthful young man whom I remembered from only the year before when I had last seen him and my family.

My parents were young when they had me, so I enjoyed the life of a young dad. Playing basketball in the driveway, playing catch with the football in the backyard, fishing trips, and family vacations were normal in our family.

What was sitting in front of me at the moment was not my normal funny and happy dad. He cheerfully said hello and welcome home, but I could see the grimace in his every move. I was worried seeing the walker sitting next to him. I thought for sure he had been in some kind of major accident that I wasn't told about. So I asked, "What's going on?"

He said that his back had been acting up and that the pain had gotten so bad he could barely move without excruciating pain. He could barely walk, and when he needed to walk to go to the bathroom, he had to use the walker.

He went on to describe the pain running down his legs and how when he got up from the chair he was humped over like an old man. He couldn't go to work, and could barely sleep at night.

He sounded and looked miserable.

The orthopedic doctor diagnosed him with spondylolisthesis. Basically, that is where the vertebrae in the low back are slipping forward onto the vertebrae under it. This creates a pinching of the nerves running down into the back of the legs.

The doctor was recommending a spinal fusion. They would go in and put in a little plate with some screws to secure the area that was slipping.

All surgeries are invasive no matter what kind, but a spinal fusion is even more so, with studies showing that back surgeries can often fail 40 percent of the time. What does fail mean? Oftentimes, it means it does not improve the situation, maybe it makes the pain worse, or in some cases it can even cause death. (https://www.asahq.org/madeforthismoment/ preparing-for-surgery/procedures/back-surgery/)

At this point I was deeply concerned about him, what he was going through, and what might happen if he got the surgery.

A few things that I need to tell you about my dad and why I thought he was in the predicament. He has had back pain issues for a long time; never this bad, but I remembered when I was in high school he would go to our local chiropractor on a regular basis, sometimes even multiple times a week. So he had been dealing with this issue for many years. The second thing is he is a truck driver, so he sits for many hours during the day.

The third thing and most important is that his hips were not positioned correctly.

I knew this because I had just graduated from University of Kansas with a degree in Exercise Science and was working in California for a holistic therapy company. I was learning all about the importance of looking at the whole body when helping people with chronic pain.

I received a degree in Exercise Science, which is a pre-Physical Therapy degree for those who intend to become a physical therapist. I was also a Division I track & field athlete. I was a decathlete on the University of Kansas track & field team, and as a decathlete who was 180 pounds and needed to throw the shot put, do the pole vault, and do all the other things in the decathlon, I was deeply interested in biomechanics. To do those movements and to compete and be successful at the Division I level, I needed to learn how to do them biomechanically correct.

The importance of this was I was not speaking with my dad just as a loved one who was concerned, but also looking at him as a patient. I was looking at him through my lens of biomechanics and therapy, and not traditional western medicine. It was a very unique situation where my background and interest put me in a position to help a person I loved and cared for very much.

Piecing that all together as he was talking with me, I realized I could help him prevent the surgery, get back on his feet without pain, and basically get his life back. But convincing him that I could help him was a whole different matter.

Who was I? A kid who had just graduated school with not a lot of experience. I wasn't a doctor. I wasn't a physical therapist. But what I was able to do was look at him from a different perspective, a perspective that nobody else was seeing.

After he told me his story, I told him I could help him.

Well that didn't go over so well. He basically laughed and said thanks for the offer but he felt there was no way he could do therapy. He had tried it in the past and it didn't help. It actually made his pain worse.

I explained to him that I felt he actually didn't have a back problem. Yes, he had back pain, but the actual problem was his hips. If we could get his hips to align better, I felt that it would make his back feel better.

Of course, he came back with the doctor said his back was messed up and said the only option was surgery.

I told him I understood all that and why the doctor had told him that, but then I explained how the hip position is so important to the position of his back, and if we could get his hips to move better it would help his back move better.

He said the chiropractor had worked on his hips in the past and it didn't seem to help. So then I explained the concept of getting the muscles to move the hips better so that there was better interaction between the hips and spine, and when it helped it would last longer because we taught the hips to hold the position better.

He finally agreed. I'm not sure if it was because he trusted me or because he was tired of me talking about it, but he agreed as long as I didn't hurt him. So I made a deal that if we did anything that hurt to stop doing it and let me know.

While I was there on vacation, I gave him some basic hip exercises. It was only four or five, but I helped him do them every day while I was there, and sometimes we did them multiple times a day. The day I was to leave he agreed that he wasn't feeling worse and that he would try and do what I told him to do.

The next few weeks we talked on the phone about what he should be doing to get his hips to move better. I would give him some things to try, and he would do them and report back to me. So things felt really good, but other movements would cause some pain. I started putting more extensive routines together based on his input and what he could do.

As we did this, he started to feel better. He would still have ups and downs, but his ups were higher than his downs. I was able to progress him more as he was able to do more, and he just kept feeling better and better.

After about three months, he was 95 percent better!

To this day, 25 years, later he has never had a surgery and he still does a lot of the same exercises I taught him.

Obviously, this was life-changing for him, but it was life-changing for me as well. This was the start of me focusing my passion and career of helping people who had chronic pain through a whole-body biomechanical approach. From that point on, for everybody I worked with, I would try to figure out where they had improper alignment and how specific exercises or movements could get that joint to move better. Instead of focusing on symptom relief, I started to focus on finding the root cause of the pain.

In the early years, some people would be helped faster than others, and I started to see patterns in those that were being helped. I had the fortunate circumstance of working at a clinic where I was working with people in chronic pain every day. I had mentors who were in the same mindset as me and helped guide me in expanding my knowledge and breaking thought patterns barriers often set out by traditional therapy.

With the original intention of working for only a year or two and then going back to school, I worked for that company for seven years, helping them grow their clinic and expand their programs on educating the public about the importance of whole-body health care. I helped train new therapists and created educational programs on how other health practitioners could implement our ideas and help people feel better and move better.

After seven years I moved to Kansas City, which was a lot closer to my family, and opened my own clinic specializing in helping people who have pain. I called it Exercise Therapy of Kansas City. As of this writing, I have been a successful small business for 17 years.

I love having the opportunity to help people every day, oftentimes helping them change their lives. I've also loved the opportunity to grow my business and be my own boss. It has allowed me the free time to do things I don't think I could have done if I worked for a large company. Sure, owning your own business has its ups and downs, but the ups outweigh the downs. And, I can't emphasize this enough: I get to help people every day. I'm not working somewhere where I hate my boss or a job where I'm sitting on a computer all day. I'm not selling widgets that I don't care about. I'm doing something that I am deeply passionate about, and I'm helping people every day.

I love my job!

I believe you can do what I do.

You can own your own business and be your own boss in a successful business where you get to help people every day. Or you can create a program in your current model that helps bring in more revenue while doing what we all love to do, and that is helping people change their lives.

You just need a little help.

When I started my business, I thought that because it was such a great idea, as soon as I opened the doors people would flock in to get help. I learned quickly that in my conservative part of the country, alternative health concepts were not all that popular. It has gotten better over the last 17 years, and I hope that is somewhat due to what we have done in our community.

Trying to convince people my concept was a better way to feel better and move better was difficult. I was competing against years and years of traditional medicine concepts and competing with the monopoly that traditional medicine has had on our health.

Even though my concepts of how to help people made sense, getting clients to actually take the steps to do the work was discouraging, and getting them to pay for it was even harder.

Only a few years after opening my business, I had to close the doors. I had failed. I was in massive credit card debt, had a huge line of credit that was exhausted, and had to tell my parents who loaned me the start-up money that I wasn't able to pay them back and had lost it all.

So, I found a full-time job, but I didn't give up my hope that there was still a way to reach my dreams. I didn't give up my deep-rooted belief that the world needed what I was providing. I was very passionate about helping people, and believed that I could be successful with helping people. I just didn't know how. So, as I worked my day job, I kept seeing clients in the evenings and on the weekends until I could figure out how to make it work.

I knew how to help people, but I was clueless on how to be successful. I had no idea how to run a successful business. After closing the doors, I knew that if I ever wanted to be a successful business owner I would need to learn how to actually *be* a business owner.

So, I took a deep dive into the world of business. I read all the books I could get my hands on such as Dan Kennedy, Dale Carnegie, Simon Sinek, Jim Collins, and many more. I spent tens of thousands of dollars on coaching programs and private coaching. I called people who I knew were successful and bugged them for their secrets.

I then applied what I had learned. Some things worked, but a lot of it didn't.

I figured out that my business was not like other businesses. A cookie-cutter approach did not work. My business is a mix of therapy, personal training, and education. It took a special approach to marketing, sales, and creating processes that work within my therapy and for my clientele.

The Therapy

Assessment

When working on clients in pain, you have to figure out what to do and where to start. This happens in the assessment. At the clinic we have created our own assessment that works great for us. There are programs you can purchase and certifications you can get to help you do this, but ours has been created through 25 years of trial and error.

During the assessment is a great time to start the client education process. We are explaining, in detail, what we see and how it is affecting the client's body and influencing the pain. Educating the client on what is happening to their body and why it is happening helps create client accountability in doing the work to get better.

The first assessment is the postural assessment. This is simply done by taking a photo of all sides of the client behind a plumb line hanging from the ceiling. We print the photo and show them where their alignment is off and what that means about their muscles. Telling a client their hips are off is not the same as showing them their hips are off.

We then perform a gait analysis. We have the client walk back and forth for us. We talk to them about what we see in their movements and how when they are not moving correctly, it could be affecting their pain.

Then we take them through some movement testing, such as bending over to try and touch their toes. We are not looking to see if they can touch their toes but how they are actually biomechanically doing it.

Through all these assessments we are unraveling what is going on and how it could be creating pain.

Functional Anatomy

Functional anatomy is much deeper than the anatomy most people commonly know about the body. It is understanding the deeper structural anatomy: what muscles are the important muscles in changing a client's posture and gait. It is also learning how the whole body connects together, such as how the psoas muscles affect the spine and how the spine affects the shoulder position. You must have a good understanding of functional anatomy and be able to relate that to the client's issues.

The Proper Exercises

Once we have finished the assessment it is time to figure out what movements, positions, and exercises are going to be best to get them to move better and feel better. This is the most important aspect of helping them.

The first thing is to make sure we don't give them anything that makes the symptoms worse. For example, if they can't get on the floor because it hurts, then we don't have them doing anything there. We might be able to build to it down the road when they are feeling better and moving better, but the first thing is to not make the symptom worse.

This might seem like common sense, but I see it all the time. Someone is having a client in pain work through the pain or ignore the pain to strengthen an area. This almost always backfires and creates bigger problems down the road.

The movements and positions we use are designed from years of experience working with clients who have pain. I didn't invent them, but I have learned what to use and when it is best to use it.

Using the proper exercises is key. Learning how to get at the deeper structure muscles that are going to affect the client's dysfunctions is difficult but important.

Client Accountability

Getting the clients to do their exercises and to do them consistently is also important in their process. If the client doesn't do the work then they won't get better. We have put systems in place throughout the therapy to make sure clients are accountable to doing their job of getting better.

It starts with the payment process by having the clients pay up front, which commits them to the program. We then follow up with weekly visits to change the routine and make sure they are moving forward correctly.

It is important to be very clear and up front with the client so they understand that it is up to them to be proactive to get better.

Marketing the Right Way

Not all marketing works

I have tried all kinds of marketing strategies, and many of them just don't seem to work. The goal is to at least get a two-times return on any money we spend on marketing. After spending thousands of dollars on marketing, we currently spend very little. The money we do spend is spent on marketing that we know works, such as advertising for a webinar or doing a Facebook ad for a marketing funnel we have created. We have seen a return, and then feed it a little bit of money to try and reach a bigger audience.

The marketing we have seen the best result with is marketing that costs very little but often takes the most time and most knowledge. Lunch-and-learns at local businesses have been really successful for us. Getting in front of a group of people and educating them about what we do and how it works creates a relationship with them. We call local businesses and ask to speak to their human resources department or the person in the business who sets up lunch-and-learns. We tell them that we are a local business and would like to talk to their associates about ways they can feel better so they are better employees. We often even offer to bring in lunch.

The pandemic really slowed down the ability to do this at businesses, so we pivoted more toward doing a webinar specifically for them. We created three or four different topics they could choose from that we could specifically speak about.

The pitch to the human resource department for a lunch-and-learn or a webinar is about how we can help decrease missed days at work or how we can help decrease workman's compensation issues. Then the actual lunch-and-learn or webinar is focused on the needs of the employees, such as helping them feel better or how we can help them do what they love to do without the limitations of chronic pain.

It is important that when doing a talk you have the proper process in place so that it makes it easier for audience members to reach out to you. Obviously, have your phone number and website available, but also give them something they can take with them so they remember you. Give them a handout with information such as "Five Easy Steps to Decreasing Chronic Pain," and have your phone number, email, and website on it.

Even better yet is to create a marketing funnel. A marketing funnel is a great way to make it easy for those who want to connect with you to do so. Create a landing page where they can get a free copy of the "Five Easy Steps to Decrease Chronic Pain" handout. If they want the free PDF, they have to give you their email address so it can be sent to their email. You can then create an email sequence that sends them an email every few weeks with information about how important posture is to decreasing pain. In these email follow ups, you tell them they can reach out to you with questions or even offer a free consultation.

We use several different marketing funnels to attract the right client. We use free reports, a chapter of a book, and marketing funnels to gain access to a webinar.

The Business Model

If you can't pay the bills by having a successful business, then it doesn't matter how good the therapy is. Being good at what you do is important, but keeping your doors open is also important. So, you must have some good processes in place to keep the business running. I have basically used *E Myth,* a book by Michael Gerber, to determine our processes. I have a list of specific pillars of our business such as front desk, therapy, and accounting. Each is its own department. In the beginning I was doing everything. So, my name was at the head of each department. But as we grew I would hire according to which department I needed to fill. Did I need a receptionist or a therapist? I would then put their name on that list in that department. If some left or got fired, I would put my name in their place on that list until I filled it with someone new.

Keep Your Expenses Down

Another thing I found through experience is to make a concerted effort to keep my expenses down. Expenses can quickly get out of hand on a lot of little things. Every month I go through the accounting and make sure what we are spending money on is really benefiting the business or benefitting the client. I determine if it saves me time so that I can use my time for other important things that will help grow the business such as writing this chapter in this book or writing my own best seller. Maybe it gives value to the client and connects them with us better. I've had people try to sell me new machines or programs that just don't add value to my business.

Get a Mentor

I'm a big fan of finding mentors. I love talking to people who are successful and trying to figure out how I can apply what they did to

175

what I do, even if it is not in the health world. I ask them questions about the pitfalls they had to endure so that maybe I can avoid them. Or if I have an idea, I ask them their thoughts and opinions on it. I try to find people who run a successful business and I try to model what they do. Business is business, and even though our therapy is unique, the business side is still business.

If you are passionate about helping people and want to learn more, feel free to reach out to me through my website: www.exercisetherapykc. com

Travis Perret

Travis Perret owns and operates Exercise Therapy of Kansas City. For 20 years, he has improved the lives of people affected by chronic pain through pain-free postural solutions. Travis is one of the leading experts in the country on the science of corrective exercise and how it affects and improves chronic pain issues.

Travis graduated from the University of Kansas and received his degree in Exercise Science. He was a decathlete on the University of Kansas track & field team. After graduating, he moved to San Diego, California to study the use of exercise and posture in helping those who have chronic pain. In 2004, he moved back to the Midwest and opened Exercise Therapy of Kansas City.

He is the author of the best-selling book *Pain Free Life: Get Back to a Younger More Active You!* He is passionate about motivating people on how they can decrease chronic pain so they can live their life to the fullest, without pain pills, doctors, and surgeries, helping them to remain active as they age and keep doing the things they love to do.

He currently lives in Overland Park, Kansas with his wife and two daughters.

CREATE AN EXPERIENCE AND BUILD COMMUNITY

CHAPTER 14

The Play Paradigm

By Tony and Amanda Johnson

145 pounds. 12 years. Three personal transformations to arrive at unconditional self-acceptance. These data points are core to our experience in the wellness community, and they also tie into the mighty shifts the pandemic brought to the doorstep of the fitness industry.

This book ponders the question, what is next for the fitness industry after the coronavirus pandemic? Upon first consideration of this question, we imagined the process a computer undergoes when infected with a virus. BOOM! Down goes the hard drive. Then the foundation needs restoration, and finally, like a breath of fresh air, the new software gets installed. This process can serve as a metaphor for how the fitness industry can grow and change more lives post-pandemic.

The coronavirus pandemic forever changed the course of the world, not just the fitness community. It truly represented a wipe of our metaphorical hard drives as individuals, families, a nation, and a global society. We all struggled in our own way with the loss of normalcy due to a contagious virus spreading throughout our system of social and political life. The result was that virtually everyone had some degree of pent-up physical and emotional stress without the comforts of many of the outlets we take for granted, and the additional stress of taking on fear, uncertainty, and the like. This resulted in a drastic increase in mental health challenges, addiction issues, domestic violence disputes, divorces, and physical health struggles like disordered sleeping and eating patterns, gut problems, and a rise in nervous system-related problems.

My wife, Amanda, and I believe the fitness industry has done a considerable amount of work to promote, foster, and cultivate thriving communities capable of bringing people together to unite under a common desire to live healthier, more fulfilling lives. However, our 12 years of working in fitness reveal that much more work must be done if we are to lead and inspire societal changes, grow, and retain more clients. We can serve the world in a meaningful way by encouraging millions more people to live healthy and fulfilling lives if we adapt. The pandemic gave us the perfect opportunity to pause and ask ourselves which practices are best kept, which ones we can grow out of, and which ones should be refined.

If the fitness industry is to be the change we want to see in the world, trainers, coaches, and leaders must help people restore their minds and bodies to factory settings by encouraging them to take a holistic approach to health and wellness, prioritizing mental fitness and physical fitness equally. We also argue it is our job to "install new software" by switching up our programming ideas and marketing strategies to put the FUN back in FUNctional fitness. Our job is to be the catalyst and empower a societal shift in how people perceive exercise from something they "have to do" to something they "get to do."

Before we get to the crux of this chapter, you need to have a context for who Tony is and how he shows up in the world to appreciate his perspective and allow it the opportunity to land and stick with you in a meaningful way. To fitness professionals reading, Tony spent much of his life as the person you need to reach to create impact and change the world. Unfortunately, he was one of the 65 percent of people across the globe who didn't exercise, ate whatever he wanted, and didn't have any conscious awareness of how those patterns of behavior affected his health and wellness. In fact, he was what health experts label "morbidly obese," and wore that scarlet letter as his identity for most of his life, even after he lost weight – regardless of what his body fat percentage was at the time. Believe it or not, he looked in the mirror at 8 percent body fat, and the imperfections are what stood out to him most.

Tony hasn't always been a part of the "fitness industry"

In 2010, Tony lost 145 pounds and systematically changed his life by focusing on himself and his health for the first time in his entire life, but that process didn't change his heart or how he identified. Instead, he carried the shame of the harsh words that became weapons, the laughter that

eviscerated his heart and destroyed his self-identity from a young age. The burden of carrying excess physical weight wasn't even the hard part, and neither was losing it. The much more burdensome and laborious task was processing, and shucking the emotional weight stemming from the pain of being horribly mistreated. For decades, Tony carried the looks, stares, and comments from people who projected their own bodily insecurities onto him. He wore the weight of judgment, criticism, self-imposed limiting beliefs, and toxic social comparison at the root of evil. Tony internalized the vanity and obsession with body image – the artificially superimposed photos in the media – including the "weight loss industry," which profits from recidivism, failure, and self-hatred. He wore the baggage of everyone who told him he would never amount to anything because they told him his worth would always be associated with his weight or how he looked. He was just one of the nearly 400 million overweight children and adolescents struggling in shame. The tragic reality is that kids can't reason or cope with any degree of consciousness – so his problems became self-reinforcing. The more hurtful words were directed at him, the more he saw bodies that didn't look like him. The more he was judged, labeled, shamed, and criticized for carrying excess weight, the more he ate and isolated himself. It was a vicious cycle that he felt helpless, powerless, and out of control over. His 12 years in this industry tells him he is far from alone in this dilemma.

Putting the FUN back in fitness saved him.

This brings us to the purpose of writing this chapter and the solutions we advocate at Mindful and Fit Coaching. Our goal is to promote exercise as an embodied experience of play that brings joy and fosters accessibility and community. Exercise gives people the gift of getting out of their heads, off their screens, and into their bodies. We aspire to change public perception of exercise from something people think they HAVE to do to something they GET to do and WANT to do. We believe our community needs to be restored to factory settings by *creating, promoting, and teaching exercise programming from an exploratory and experiential play paradigm. Let's put the FUN back in functional fitness.* But, what does that mean exactly?

Putting the FUN back in functional fitness means getting back to the basics of who we are as tribal, social communities of animals who need movement to survive. After all, we have more significant instances of addiction, overdoses, heart diseases, heart attacks, and strokes than ever before. We also have more judgment, self-shame, and cynicism as people find themselves glued to screens and addicted to their calendars. To encourage people to view exercise as something we GET to do and eventually something everyone WANTS to do, we have to make it fun. As parents of two children under 2, we have been blessed to watch them learn body awareness. They do this through **exploration** and **experiences**. They have a near-reckless joy for learning through trial and error. In some respects, they are learning to interact with the world and move through space without the cynical forms of socially constructed rules that life has a tendency to put on us. Can you imagine how the world might be different if adults took more of this sense of exploration and experience into our own relationships with our bodies? We like to call this a *Paradigm of Play.*

The Paradigm of Play gives clients permission to explore

An exploratory and experiential play paradigm is inspired by how we all learn as children. Every child's brain learns to notice patterns, shapes, and colors, read nonverbal cues, listen, share, cooperate, problem solve, and embrace failure as necessary for growth and development through exploration and experiential play. A Paradigm of Play applies this rationale to older people who may have lost sight of their child-like sense of wonder and curiosity for the world. They don't know what their bodies can do because of fear, judgment, shame, or routines that keep them from moving. Our experience teaches us that inviting people to get out of their heads, away from their schedules and to-do lists, and into their bodies most often becomes a therapeutic and cathartic experience. This is especially true for those of us who chose to believe we were never, or are no longer, capable of doing hard things physically.

A Paradigm of Play also breaks down the need for competition, social comparison, judgment, and shame by promoting embodied exercise and teaching clients to be in a flow state while exercising. Trainers and coaches get to frame exercise as something that encourages clients to celebrate and explore their limitations and restrictions with curiosity and kindness,

rather than punish their bodies through excessive stress and "embracing the suck" or "pushing through the pain." This way of framing exercise makes it less intimidating to new people who may have never considered exercising before or haven't exercised since primary school. People are allowed to meet their bodies where they are, accept their bodies in all of their beauty, and work within the confines of biofeedback to continue to grow and be in the flow. This requires coaches to know and be able to teach mindfulness and strategies that promote present-moment awareness to their clients.

At Mindful and Fit Coaching, we begin and end each exercise program with a meditation that starts by taking deep belly breaths. This invites a calming of the vagus nerve, which is central to releasing stress and inflammation caused by external stimulation. Breath work encourages our clients to release the baggage of their days and get comfy inside their bodies. From there, we ask our clients to set an intention for their workout, and we offer a few to consider if one doesn't emerge naturally for them. Some examples include: being here now, embracing my body with loving kindness, letting my light shine, celebrating what my body can do, and many others. The process of encouraging present-moment awareness is what contributes to a flow state.

The flow state creates focus, makes our thoughts melt away, and gets us high on life.

A flow state is a way of being that encourages an unmitigated focus on the task at hand. In essence, it is the state of being where the rest of the world – our troubles, thoughts, reactions, judgments, appraisals – melts away, allowing our brains to truly just be in the moment and find joy, satisfaction, and fulfillment in what we are doing. Many of the greatest athletes of all time believe and promote that being in flow gets them the most from their exercise programs. This is likely because when we are in flow, we don't need any form of motivation to do or enjoy what we're doing. We just let life flow as it is. After all, resistance comes from our minds. It comes from the stressful stories we tell ourselves when we try to be the fortune-teller who knows, controls, and predicts a future that is never guaranteed to us, and when we play the woulda, coulda, shoulda games in our minds about the past. So, what are the levels of flow state, and what modalities of exercise encourage a flow state?

There are four stages of being in flow: struggle, release, flow, and recovery. Clients will be in over their heads in the struggle stage and might feel out of control. In this stage, the brain emits beta waves, and the body makes cortisol and adrenaline. In addition, they might be experiencing anxiety or stress. Many clients who never give themselves permission to get out of their own heads never leave this stage. Our experience teaches me that many of them are simply told to "suck it up, buttercup." But what if there was a better way to coach people through physical exercise that could give them permission to elevate their state of awareness to the release stage and flow stage so they could have more fun, judge their performance less, and gain all the neurological benefits of doing so? What if there was a way we, as fitness professionals, could help our clients move to the next stage of flow, the release stage?

In the release stage, our students and clients are invited to detach from their stressful stories and experiences to become an observer of them rather than a prisoner to them. This process of dis-identification and detachment invites their brains to release alpha waves and nitric oxide, taking away stress chemicals. What if we could do you one better and say you have the power to allow anyone to experience the "runner's high" from exercise without running? This comes from being in flow, which is the third stage.

In a flow state, clients have an expansion of their natural awareness where the brain is releasing theta and gamma waves. Theta is a meditative state that allows us to gain new insight and process information rapidly. Gamma waves enable different parts of our brain to combine so that our disparate experiences, thoughts, and stories can also coalesce to create new types of mind-body awareness. Our brains actually release more neurochemicals like dopamine, anandamide, norepinephrine, and endorphins, which can help improve our reactions to exercise by causing greater excitement and curiosity to explore what our bodies can do, all while increasing pattern recognition, muscle firing, and timing. Dopamine and anandamide specifically elevate our moods and encourage fear to wash away, and endorphins promote a pleasure response. Needless to say, being in flow makes exercise fun.

The final stage of flow-based exercise is just as important as the previous three, and it is recovery. This happens in rest periods and sleep, where our experience can be integrated, and real learning occurs. So, to actually install new software, we need to rest and recover. This requires fitness professionals to encourage our clients to implement strong boundaries for screen time and create their own evening decompression routine, and teach them how to use meditation and body scans to surrender into a profoundly relaxing and restorative sleep. Once we teach clients how to be in flow, we can integrate it into all types of exercise. But we think the most accessible entry points into this way of being starts with promoting accessible forms of embodied movement.

Our recommendation for putting the FUN in functional fitness training and wellness coaching includes introducing, prioritizing, and implementing more flow-based embodied movement. The specific types we encourage are based on our journeys as people who transformed our lives through embodied movement. Specifically, that includes excergaming, dance, and yoga.

Can you imagine how the world would be different if the fitness community could promote connections between people from all the other areas of the world, cultural backgrounds, sexual orientations, religions, and political beliefs? The gaming community is the only community we can think of that has done this with any remote degree of sophistication.

Eighty million people work together and collaborate toward completing shared missions and goals on Fortnight each month. One hundred eighty million active users compete in League of Legends. Ask any gamer what makes them fixate and spend so much time and energy in their virtual reality games. Most of them will say it represents an escape from their demands in the "real world." So, what is stopping the fitness community from creating content that allows people to connect in an alternate reality and unite around health and fitness games, in conjunction with or as a replacement for shoot-em-up-style programming? Tony will tell you, if he had an opportunity to burn calories and move his body in these ways as a 345-pound person, he might have lost weight earlier.

Did you know the average person burns between 210 and 240 calories from an hour of gameplay? How might that increase if games were created to focus on incorporating more meaningful physical movement? The fitness community can and ought to make and integrate new and innovative technologies to create a fusion between fitness programming, gaming, and e-sports. Doing so would allow our community to grow in terms of who we can serve and how we can serve our clients. This innovative move toward the future also allows content creators and engineers to collaborate with trainers and fitness professionals to create new and innovative programming that can target people of all ages, demographics, and physical ability levels, and serve those who have chronic injuries and need lower impact exercise. The possibilities are endless. For kids' programming, imagine a dance fitness class led by Blippi or Cocomelon characters. For adult programming, imagine a live interactive version of Dance Dance Revolution, or virtual tennis, golf, baseball, or basketball where you can play pick-up games with your friends in China or the UK and/or your sister who lives across the country. You can walk the course and talk between sets, innings, or shots. The realities are limitless – because anything that can be imagined can be created.

Tony's journey began in a dance class. He felt much more comfortable moving my body in a fun way that required setting aside my thoughts and appraisals to focus on the steps and choreography. This is being in flow. Of course, he struggled – his coordination, rhythm, and timing were off initially, but the supportive environment of a bunch of women in the room cheering him on made it so much fun! He began to view exercise not as something I had to do but something I got to and wanted to do. And, after consistent time and practice, he improved. Later he added more forms of embodied movement, like yoga, tai chi, and Pilates. He saved these for last because they are the oldies and the goodies. Most men in western society wouldn't be caught dead in any of these classes, which is hilarious, because many of them need and would benefit from them the most. These are all embodied movement modalities because they require a brain, body, breath connection, and they encourage a flow-state to get the most benefit from them. These are all breath-to-movement practices that encourage people to move from the struggle stage to release and finally to being in flow. What if we told you there was a way you could make any type of exercise flow-based and that I could teach you how? Well, there is! You can do it by teaching clients what we call the SMILE method.

The SMILE Method

Teaching our clients and students to SMILE at themselves and each other is precisely what FUNctional fitness and the Paradigm of Play is all about. The "S" in SMILE stands for Self-Acceptance. When people accept themselves exactly where they are, they can release judgments. Self-acceptance is a process that requires introspection, excavation of formative experiences, and releasing or expressing these experiences

through embodied movement and creating safe spaces for clients to be vulnerable and practice self-disclosure and consciousness-raising in supportive social groups. Trainers and coaches can offer a daily quote, question, intention, or meditation for clients to keep in their heart and mind while training, and can encourage small-group training and require the mandatory exchange of positive energy (smiles, high fives, knuckles, chest bumps) between sets. Self-acceptance also requires modeling love and creating an environment of psychological safety where there is no guilt, shame, or pain.

"M" stands for Monitoring Biofeedback. We think health and fitness professionals have to do more to teach their clients that our bodies are constantly communicating to us and show them how to develop the meta-awareness to notice the specific feedback before it gets to chronic pain. Again, this is a cultural shift the community needs to install as new software. Fitness isn't about pushing beyond your limits – it's about finding your edge and kindly respecting it with awareness.

"I" stands for Identifying Resistance. Resistance is simply the mental and physical cues that get in the way of our progress and development. It might be a muscle spasm or a self-limiting belief. Rather than attaching ourselves to the inevitability of the resistance cue, it is important to honor the source of resistance, question it with kindness and curiosity, and explore various treatment strategies. The overarching purpose for identifying resistance is noticing themes and patterns and knowing when to intervene and when to surrender and wait for the resistance to pass. Mental resistance almost always comes from stressful stories we create in our minds. However, the attachment to those stories creates acute stress and anxiety that has profound deteriorative physical implications for the heart and gut. Teaching students and clients to identify resistance without attaching to it can help them find exercising more fun and beneficial, regardless of the modality.

"L" stands for Lead with Love. As trauma survivors who have been triggered by many hyper-masculine coaches who act like drill sergeants, all fitness professionals must understand what motivates people to find joy and fulfillment in exercise. Sure, some Brahma bull-types like to be screamed at and can be forcefully uplifted by a barking command. But, the truth is most people just want to love and be loved. They want to be told they're doing a great job showing up for themselves. We could teach a whole class on removing the violent metaphors rooted in toxic masculinity, but instead, we'll ask you to encourage your clients with love whenever and wherever possible. Love always wins. Leaders in the industry can and ought to take this gentle nudging to explore ways to invite more love and kindness into their studios, programming, and overall approach to their own fitness practice.

Finally, "E" stands for practicing Equanimity. Equanimity is a state of being. It is a state of mental calmness while exposed to stressful conditions. Once trainers and coaches have created an environment of openness, social support, and consciousness-raising, they can teach equanimity through a simple game I call "NOTICE, PAUSE, PASS, ACCEPT." Ask clients, "Can you NOTICE when your thoughts take you away from your center? Then when that happens, can you PAUSE to take a few breaths and let the judgments PASS by? Finally, if necessary, can you simply ACCEPT you are off in this moment?" One of our favorite sayings to repeat to clients is "some moments you feel like a rock star, some days you're like a roadie, and other days you feel like a rock." The key is accepting where you are in the moment and considering the particular ways you can re-energize and arrive at creative clarity and confidence. Generally, that comes with non-judgmental acceptance and then action to shift your mental state.

And, don't forget to love yourself!

The shortest way to encapsulate my advice to grow your community and attract clients who might never have considered exercise programming before is this: Love yourself, love what you do, and allow that love to

intentionally break down barriers. Get real, get raw, get vulnerable, and shine your light by embracing who you are and the particular ways in which your gifts can change the dogmatism of judgment, shame, and pain reverberating through our society. Do cartwheels, have dance parties, but also show your clients your struggles and how you've channeled your inner strength to allow them to become your strengths. Embrace your own unique and magical human superpowers, which are simple: sociability, kinship, and collective unity over individual pride, egotism, and isolation. Try not to take yourself so seriously, live in your own head, and find your flow. This happens when we show gratitude for everything we are, focus on living in the present moment, and appreciate and accept our bodies and all they do for us to keep us conscious and aware, energetic and excitable, and focused on inspiring the world to become a happier and healthier place to live. So, have FUN making your gym, studio, or online programming an adult playground for people to celebrate the skin they're in and work toward becoming the best version of themselves possible. Don't forget to SMILE!

Tony and Amanda Johnson

Tony and Amanda Johnson own Mindful and Fit Coaching, a family wellness brand with a mission to provide young families with integrated tools and strategies that touch their hearts, heal their hurts, and give them solid footing as they transform their lives from the inside out.

Mindful and Fit Coaching has inspired hundreds of people to pursue optimal health and wellness by offering best practices in mindfulness-based stress reduction, nutrition, and breath-to-movement exercise. Our brand and work have been featured on the Doctors Television Show, in People Magazine, and on several podcasts including The Impact Show by Todd Durkin.

Tony is an author, college professor, personal trainer, and motivational speaker, and Amanda is an author, yoga instructor, and an Ayurvedic chef. Both of us are trained practitioners of meditation and parents to two beautifully unique and miraculous baby girls named Emory and

Ellie. We are inspired to help bring Eastern Philosophical practices to help families live healthy and fulfilling lives.

In order to learn more about our online and in-person offerings, including our self-directed courses, coaching opportunities, and family wellness retreats please visit:

www.mindfulandfit.io

CHAPTER 15

Community is King

By Tricia Hoyt

The Journey that We Did Not See Coming

You know when you have those friends that you can call out of the blue, even if it's been two years since you spoke, and it's like you just spoke with each other yesterday? You listen to each other and give each other advice. When you hang up, you feel better than you did when you started the conversation. You feel you have the holy grail and more hopeful than you had in a long while.

That type of friend rang me after months of the pandemic, and of course, we shared how the new lifestyles were impacting us and our families. After divulging our struggles, suddenly her voice became crackly, and we entered a whole new foreign conversation.

Cecilia loved her alone time, her mornings and pockets of time reflecting and assessing her dreams. She also loved connecting with people, learning from them and being inspired by them. During the pandemic, Zoom became her routine, as it did with much of the world.

She was still able to see people on Zoom, personally and professionally, and carry productive meetings, adding mutual value. Without realizing the trajectory of what was happening viscerally, she did eventually find an awareness of feeling lethargic, apathetic, lack of zest, and a level of depression that was unfamiliar to her. Even though she was doing things she loved every day such as talking to people, seeing people (on Zoom), helping others, and continuing to focus on her own mental, physical, and spiritual wellness, nevertheless, for the first time, she felt unfulfilled. She also noticed this emotion was becoming consistent.

Then, I had my rant. I thought I was fine. After all, collaborating virtually is still a community, right? It's still a part of belonging, being a part of something, and contribution. It wasn't until I got a taste of getting back to training with my fitness family in a live setting, followed by more isolation, that I realized something different was happening. Even with three kids at home with me and all the hugs and cuddles, there was an empty feeling that I could not quite put my finger on. After more research on this very topic, I begin to understand more about what was going on. The awareness has allowed me to have better control of how to fill some of the lackluster lows I was experiencing. And I have learned that in-person human connection is irreplaceable.

As for Cecilia, what you will continue to read is what we reflected on and digested together. We found the topic fascinating, and it opened the door to further research and understanding of this subject matter.

Where We Are Now

According to the World Health Organization, in the first year of the COVID-19 pandemic, global prevalence of anxiety and depression increased by a massive 25 percent, according to a scientific brief released by the World Health Organization (WHO) March 2, 2022.

According to the WHO, mental health includes our emotional, psychological, and social well-being. It affects how we think, feel, and act. It also helps determine how we handle stress, relate to others, and make healthy choices (Strengthening Mental Health Promotionexternal icon Fact sheet no. 220. Geneva, Switzerland: World Health Organization.) Mental health is important at every stage of life, from childhood and adolescence through adulthood.

Although the terms are often used interchangeably, poor mental health and mental illness are not the same. A person can experience poor mental health and not be diagnosed with a mental illness. Likewise, a person diagnosed with a mental illness can experience periods of physical, mental, and social well-being.

Rear View Mirror

In order to get a better picture of what is happening with mental health, I conducted some informal interviews with friends, family, and clients. I found some interesting results, and I am sharing some of their answers below.

Related to wellness, what challenges did you experience during the pandemic and what did the pandemic help you realize?

- *How important that community is to my mental health.*
- *The community enhances the quality of my life.*
- *The fitness community is much-needed to support our health and well-being.*
- *How crucial it is having a "fitness family" to push you when you need it most.*
- *Physical, emotional, mental health is tantamount.*
- *I missed being cheered on and the high-fives.*

- *Motivation and feeling empowered helps to stay committed to a routine.*

- *Hitting rock bottom, fitness-wise, and creating new habits, is what helped me lose 100 pounds. External factors were, for sure, my tribe of supporters that helped hold me accountable.*

- *People need people.*

- *Loss of motivation. Increased anxiety and depression. Loss of huma connection and interaction.*

- *Since the pandemic, wine nights have been much more frequent.*

- *I drank a lot more alcohol and put on significant weight during the pandemic.*

- *In-person training vs. virtual, it is more natural for me to do the extra rep., go the extra mile, hold the pose longer. I feel supported and greater achievement.*

- *Connecting with other people's energy in person, while also moving my body, produces a feeling that virtual Zoom classes cannot emulate.*

- *In person, I received much more individualization throughout the workout. That makes me get a better workout and greater sense of accomplishment. This excites me and creates momentum.*

Can you relate? Don't beat yourself up. The results are not astonishing, especially once you understand what happens psychologically when we are isolated from each other. Most of us did not realize this pre-pandemic because human interaction was the norm and business was as usual. In retrospect, you can see that there is a correlation between human interaction and joy.

What is **joy**? It's a nebulous term that we would all independently answer with a litany of answers. You may have your own meaning, but Wiki says the word "joy" refers to the emotion evoked by well-being, success, or good fortune, and is typically associated with feelings of intense, long-lasting happiness.

According to Aristotle, happiness consists in achieving, through the course of a whole lifetime, all the goods – health, wealth, knowledge, friends, etc. – that lead to the perfection of human nature and to the enrichment of human life.

The emotions of joy and happiness create a physiological response in our body. Clearly, community and connection are a massive contributing factor. Let's break that down in terms of what happens on a scientific level.

Happy Hormones are our Fuel

Let's take a step back and give a broad overview of what brings happiness:

Hormones are chemical messengers to our brains. There are four "happy" hormones that you can remember by using the acronym DOSE.

Dopamine is the "reward" chemical. Dopamine rises when you are doing something pleasurable, such as achieving a goal or completing a task. Also helping people, kindness and volunteering will give you a dopamine boost. To get a dopamine fix, you want to do something that gives you a sense of productivity, especially something that has been on a to do list for a while, and celebrate your "wins," even the small ones. Dr. Varkha Chulani states in his TEDxSIULavale presentation, "A happy person has a purpose to live. Doing and achieving, whether bathing a child or having work accomplishments, will release dopamine."

Oxytocin: I like to call "the magic of touch" hormone. This love hormone is known as the "hug drug." It's released when you have warm physical contact with someone. Elevated oxytocin will leave you with that happy, fuzzy feeling from love, friendship, and deep trust. To get your oxytocin fix, you might cuddle away with a partner, friend, parent, or pet, have deep conversations, kiss, or give compliments. Also, joking, laughing, and connecting over something hilarious releases oxytocin.

Serotonin is best known as the antidepressant, mood-stabilizing chemical. Serotonin is triggered by things we do casually, such as exposure to sunlight, exercise, a good night sleep, etc. Serotonin decreases our worries and stress. To elevate serotonin, expose yourself to the outdoors for at least 10-15 minutes with a walk or picnic, listen to music, meditate, walk in nature, or journal.

Endorphins: You may have heard of the "endorphin high" or "runner's high" that athletes feel when they push their body to the level of discomfort. Endorphins are the body's natural pain-killer, opioid neuropeptides released by our nervous system to help cope with physical pain. They release a euphoric, even light-headed, giddy feeling to cover the pain. Exercise, playing your favorite instrument and composing music, and having a sense of humor all release endorphins and have a significant impact on emotional well-being.

Dr. Chulani suggests working toward stimulating these four chemicals to achieve a happier and healthier life.

Hormones + Habits = Happiness

As health and fitness professionals, we can go the extra mile to enhance our clients' and patients' experiences to get their dose of these happy hormones. Here are six simple steps to implement what we have learned.

Step 1: Have the awareness of what we have collectively experienced in regard to the impact of isolation on a universal level.

Step 2: Do what we can to keep clients and patients continuously plugging into community, preferably live vs. virtually.

Step 3: Make it individualized by asking the right questions.

Step 4: Provide our clients the means to make it a habit to participate in activities that release the happy hormones.

Step 5: Provide accountability through mastermind groups or a dedicated coach.

Step 6: Apply the accelerators that I will share below that serve as happy hormone boosters.

*"Knowledge isn't power, **applied** knowledge is power."*

-DALE CARNEGIE

Roadmap

I am going to share some simple, yet underused, techniques and systems that will absolutely serve your clients and patients.

We must get people in person. Journey Fitness is one of the coaching organizations that is great at this. They implement a "where have you been system" that creates a vibrant community. Many of the Journey Fitness concepts can be applied to any business:

- Each member gets a dedicated coach.
- The coach keeps some tabs on the members to whom they are assigned. Here, you can get creative. Examples include sending weekly individualized check-ins, texts, motivation, follow-up, acknowledgment, etc.
- During class, a pat on the back or a high-five goes a long way. There is good energy transferred in a personal touch.
- Group classes and partner drills create a sense of teamwork, belonging, and value.

- Reward members with a complimentary massage gun session on occasion.

- Every employee is required to know all the members by name. The sweetest sound to people is hearing their own name.

- Offer group or one-on-one sessions to address individuals desire and activities that generate a feeling of joy in them.

What's Next?

Not only is community a significant variable in the happiness equation, but also the fitness community has an opportunity and the responsibility to leverage this knowledge to better serve our clients and patients. If you are a Fit Pro, own a gym or coaching center, or are a health practitioner, this will indeed augment your business to new heights, significantly increase retention, and create loyal customers and patients. The greatest impact will be touching the lives of your clients, which spreads contagiously to their families, co-workers, and their communities. Your application of even just a few recommendations will create greater infectious joy amongst your circle of influence.

> *"To the world you may only be one person,*
> *but to one person you may be the world."*
>
> -DR. SEUSS

Happy Place

Through research, awareness, and creating new habits, my friend Cecilia and I feel we have cracked the code, at least to a degree, for managing happiness. Like anything, there are aspects that are a conscious effort while other activities we have become unconsciously competent at. Life has a degree of uncertainty, so I believe it's crucial to have the tools that allow each of us the utmost joy and happiness while we are here. Cecilia and I have discussions, at least weekly, on this very topic regarding what we are doing to take action. We also belong to Todd Durkin's Mastermind Group, which continuously addresses all the aspects that I have covered. None of us is meant to do it alone, and the routine discussions with a friend, a coach or a mastermind teammate can have a profound impact on your happiness factor.

I wish you all H*3 (H to the 3rd power)!!!

Hormones + Habits = Happiness

Tricia Hoyt

Tricia has been a fitness enthusiast since she was 12 years old which initially was inspired by her mother, brother, and Auntie Yola.

Tricia's research of nutrition and fitness started her on a crusade to figure out how she could put more meat on her bones. In the beginning of this journey, she naturally fell in love with the science, as well as the whole collection of Jane Fonda and Kathy Smith videos and books. The world of fitness and the realm of learning about what the human body is capable of only grew from there. When it came time for college, Tricia graduated from UMass Boston with her Bachelor's in Exercise Physiology. She has been personal training for over 25 years and also conducting an array of body/mind transformation programs, specializing in coaching busy professionals wanting to acquire or re-establish the mind/body health and physiques they once knew.

Tricia's journey as an athletic competitor began as a junior at Del Norte High School in Albuquerque, New Mexico on the track and field and cross-country team. She has competed in fitness competitions on a national level, completed three Boston Marathons, rowed on the UMass Amherst crew team, competed in many triathlons qualifying for Team USA Championships, competed and podiumed in many Spartan Obstacle Course races of all distances, including most recently her first (and not last) Spartan Ultra Beast (placing second in her age group), and competing in various Spartan Deka events.

Tricia is the Co-owner of Journey 333 New Hampshire with one of her best friends and mentors, Janice Donovan. Tricia's platform, YouTube show and podcast is Turn up the Heat, where she celebrates her guests, while having them share how they do a little bit more, set a little higher bar, to get exponential results. She takes her love for body, mind, and spirit with her everywhere she goes. "I came to a point where my own achievements of wellness and fitness in any capacity wasn't enough for me. I'm not fulfilled unless I am bringing others with me on the journey of making fitness fun and a way of life."

Tricia is passionate about meeting people where they are at, helping them become aware of what brings them the most joy in life, and how fitness is a non-negotiable part of this equation. "Fitness (body, mind, and spirit) is in outlet for all the pillars of our lives." Furthermore, Tricia believes you were not meant to do it alone. "We all need coaches and community. The path to finding your fitness will be quicker, more enjoyable, and sustainable, with the greatest efficacy, when you have coaches and community by your side. People need people."

Tricia is raising three daughters who all have inherited a love for keeping the body, mind, and spirit tuned up. Tricia and the girls are excited to help others become better versions of themselves, using the Journey 333 brand and her Turn up the Heat platform, as a vessel to do so.

In addition to helping people Turn up the Heat and at Journey 333, where we "help people add more years to their life and more life to their years," Tricia's greatest joys are raising her daughters, quality time and adventures with her loved ones, travel, the outdoors, camping, fireside chats and the magic in the unexpected impromptu precious moments.

Tricia is available for writing assignments, speaking, and transformational coaching, specializing in working with busy professionals wanting to re-establish their well-being and recreational athletes that want to push their physical and mental limits.

DM Tricia at IG: turnuptheheat66 or Facebook: turnuptheheat66

CHAPTER 16

Love Bombing

By Mary Bushkuhl

We all want to be seen. The more people don't acknowledge you,
the more you don't feel you exist.

It was a warm September day in 1975. The air was crackling with anticipation. Though I knew this day was coming and try as I might to prepare for what was to come...to be brave, independent...too many unknowns stood in my way.

I was 13 years old. My family had moved six times during my life; two of those moves were to foreign countries. Today, I would be moving to a new country, making this my seventh move.

We were living in Libya, Africa, where my father worked for Esso Standard Libya. In the compound where we lived, schooling was offered through the eighth grade. In order to further our education, my parents had to consider boarding school for myself and my siblings.

My seventh move was to Marymount International School in the Eternal City of Rome. Unlike our other moves, I would not have my family there to help me get comfortable, adapt, fit in, or belong. I was an outsider, plopped down in the middle of a community that was already thriving and moving with its own energy. I was scared to death...a lost soul. I didn't know how to do anything on my own, or how things were done in this new culture. I did not feel I belonged there.

Earlier that day, my whole family descended on the campus, and I moved my clothes and few belongings I would need to live at the school. I was an early arrival to the school. If there were other girls moving in, I didn't see them. My roommates were not scheduled to arrive for a couple of days.

After dinner out, my family and I returned to the campus. My family said their last goodbyes. I would not see them until Christmas break. As I stood out on the patio with tears in my eyes, my dad asked if I remembered how to get to my room. With all the confidence I could muster, I told him I did. When they drove off, I turned toward the dormitory and was completely lost. No longer did I have my family as my safe harbor. It felt like I was cast out into an unknown sea. I walked into the dorm, and after making several wrong turns and feeling so lost, I found my room.

I was alone. I didn't feel like I belonged. But I knew my parents believed in me. They knew I would be able to figure out how to fit in, do things on my own. They believed I was courageous, strong, and independent. My parents also trusted in the nuns at the school to guide me, nurture me, and help me to mature into a capable and confident woman.

There was the Mediterranean Sea that separated us, so I couldn't just run home. Heck, I couldn't just pick up the phone and call home. To do that, I would actually have to go to an international call station and reserve an overseas line before I could call home.

What I realized from that experience and each time I have moved since then is that I was always searching for a place to belong. I needed people to believe in me for me to grow, excel, and achieve any goal I set for myself.

In life, we are always looking for a place to belong. We look to the workplace, places of worship, sports, bars, or schools to find where we would fit in.

The common theme in my life has been **belonging** and **believing**. Those two needs have driven me to help others overcome their fears of new situations, environments, or adventures.

Heck, I'm in the health and fitness industry, and when people approach me in my business, I am seeing them at their most vulnerable. People share their hopes, fears, worst of themselves, and the best of themselves in that first meeting with me. They crave someone to believe in them and the desires of improved health they have for themselves. They want to feel safe in their journey, and yearn for a place to belong. They look to me to nurture them and build their self-confidence.

Think about any new situation where you were the outsider trying to figure out what to do to feel like you belonged: your first day of work; the sports team you just joined; your first steps into a new place of worship; an open house at a new business or a social club. What was it that kept you coming back? Yes, you may have shared a common interest or goal, but there was a moment that someone took notice of you, saw your potential and passion, shared a common goal, and pulled you in.

As you navigate the new horizon of the health and fitness industry – heck, with any business – your focus should be on LOVE. How much love can you show for your clients, customers, patients, people you work with, to draw them in? Show them that they matter? Show them that they belong?

It's not the services or products that keep people coming back. It is how you make them feel. They won't remember the exact words you said, but will remember the fire you lit inside them. It is the way they are treated by you and the people who work there. It's the care or lack thereof – your authenticity, your belief in them, and the journey they are on.

Have you ever worked for someone and not been trained on how to do the job, not told what is expected of you? It's like being cast into the ocean without a rudder. You have no idea if you are doing the right thing or if you are headed in the right direction. Without parameters – a mission to accomplish, a vision to realize, and the tools to get you there – you will lose interest, get lost, and quit.

Navigating the new horizon of the health and fitness industry, or any industry after the pandemic, is one where your focus is on creating systems to help your customers feel like they belong to your community, and that you believe in whatever they aspire to be.

Now, how can you up your love game?

Love Bombing 101

What do I mean by "love bombing"?

Find ways to let people know they matter. Develop systems for new clients, members, customers, patients, or co-workers that shower love on them.

When your client, patient, or customer fills out paperwork, why not include a questionnaire to get to know a few things about them? Below are possible interests to note:

- Spouse's or partner's name
- Anniversary date
- Children
- Grandchildren
- Pets
- What or who is your favorite:
  - Flower
  - Athlete
  - Sport
  - Animal
  - Color
  - Drink
  - Candy, dessert, ice cream flavor
  - Holiday
  - Restaurant
  - Fruit
  - Vegetable
  - Hobby
  - Meal
  - TV show
  - Pastime

30 days

What can you do for someone in the first 30 days of joining your business?

I moved to Cheyenne, Wyoming, in early September 2001. I moved for love and for the adventure of a part of the country I knew nothing about.

I remember my first day at the physical therapy/fitness center, September 10, 2001. I had been hired as part of the team. There was no employee training, no job description, and very little engagement with other staff to introduce me around. Everyone had their duties to complete, and there was no one to teach me the ropes.

After that first day, I was ready to quit. There was no sense of belonging or even that I was needed. But I don't identify as a quitter.

On day two, September 11, 2001, I arrived early. It wasn't much later in the morning that the horrific images of 9/11 started appearing on the TVs in the facility. It was in those first moments of this national tragedy that I found a way to belong in this new community. There was a common thread we all shared as Americans from that moment forward. I was able to make connections with the staff, patients, and gym members. And it was in those first weeks of being in that space that I realized I would have to take my past experiences in the health and fitness industry and use them with my co-workers, the patients, and clients to form a community and a sense of belonging.

Little- or No-Cost Love Bombs

- Handwritten thank-you cards with the top three most important things you heard them say they wanted.

- Stickers. At one small fitness center I managed, people kept track of their workouts on workout sheets. Every so often I would acknowledge someone's efforts by placing a sticker on their card. That one small gesture had everyone in the facility scrambling to earn a sticker. It was a delight to see the engagement.

- Video of strategies to help them get started towards reaching their immediate goals — exercises, supplements, recipes, nutrition hacks, or a summary of the appointment and what was discussed.

- Phone calls or in-person follow-ups within 10 days of starting, especially for individuals you would not be seeing often.

- Saying their name often while they are in your business. I worked for Club Corporation of America in the 1980s, and one of their policies for employees was that each of us had to say a member's name at least three times during that day's visit. Remember, the sweetest sound you will ever hear is your own name.

- Quick check-ins when they are in your business. Notice one thing different about them that day: new haircut, their outfit, looking leaner, nice smile, moving better.

- A quick text to give them a shout-out.

Love All Year Long

Birthday

Lisa joined a small group training class within my personal training studio. She was shy and had some physical limitations, but she had an open and adventurous heart. Within the first couple of workouts, with her permission, I had provided modifications to exercises to help her feel successful. The other group participants encouraged her and acknowledged improvements she had made in the short amount of time she had been with us.

Within a couple of weeks of her joining us, her birthday showed up on my calendar. I created a workout that was all about Lisa. The other participants gave her good-natured ribbing because the workout was challenging. And at the end of the workout, with her permission, I took her picture with her workout and posted it on Facebook and Instagram.

Later, Lisa confided in me that she had joined the boot camp for just a month because she didn't know if she could afford to participate each month. That recognition and pulling her into the folds of our community sealed the deal for her. She felt like she belonged to a special community. She continues to strive to be better and encourage others with each workout.

Here are some ways to acknowledge someone's birthday:

- A hand-written birthday card with a personalized message.
- In my small group training, I incorporate their name and age into the workout. Using the letters of their name, I find exercises with that letter, use their age for reps or seconds of work.
- A FB/IG shout-out to the birthday girl/boy with their birthday workout.
- From the list you curated when they filled out paperwork in the beginning, what one thing you can use to make them feel special.

Train-iversary

At the 15-year mark of working together, I gave three clients premium jackets with my business logo. It was an unexpected gift, and one they wear proudly.

When someone has been loyal to your business, how will you acknowledge and thank them for their continued support? Here are some things that have worked for me:

- A hand-written note acknowledging them.
- Special brand swag, such as T-shirts, caps, hoodies, or jackets.
- Swag bag with some of their favorite things – refer to the questionnaire you had them fill out.

- If they are a training client, design a workout with some of their favorite exercises.
- Meet them for coffee or lunch.
- Post social media shout-outs.

What's Your Story?

People who are part of this special community they have joined have extraordinary stories of adversity and triumph that you should mine for, cultivate, and if they agree, share with others.

I've shared peoples' stories by interviewing them and recording a video to share on social media, and writing and sharing on my weekly email.

People often enjoy a good story, with the challenges and struggles, and the overcoming and rising above. Take the time to know the people of your community on a deeper level.

New Year

- Workout Streak Contest. Who has the longest streak in workouts for the month or the year? This can be a year-long event.

Valentine's Day

- Hand out roses to those who come in that day.
- Bake something healthy and have small bags with samples available for them.
- Give out dark chocolate hearts, Kisses, or Dove candy.
- A fun Valentine's card expressing that you love that they are here.
- Fun heart trinkets to attach to their workout bags or purses.

- A two-for-one workout – bring a friend or Valentine to your workout.
- Encourage people to wear Valentine's socks, T-shirts, and boxers to celebrate the day.
- Be creative!

St. Patrick's Day

- Luck of the Irish drawing – this can be for swag, or they draw an exercise out of a hat that is an extra-credit exercise.
- Wear your craziest St. Patty's Day outfit contest.
- Your favorite Green Smoothie Recipe contest.
- Post winners and crazy outfits on social media.

April

- Okay, it may be only my studio that does this, but every April 1st is "Wear Your Boxers to Workout Day." There's an epic story behind this celebration, and one that our community loves to celebrate. Do you have a day like this?
- April 12th is exactly 100 days until the beginning of summer. Is there a 100 Days to Summer Challenge you can launch?

Easter

- Host an outdoor adult Easter Egg Hunt. When I've hosted an Easter Egg Hunt, after hiding the eggs, I provide clues to the first egg. When you find that egg, you perform the exercise written inside the egg, then read the next clue for the next egg. I had several different routes so people weren't following each other.
- Have plastic Easter eggs in a basket for each person to grab one. Choose what you want inside: candy, positive quotes, coupons

for $ off, or fun little trinkets. Have the eggs available the week leading up to Easter weekend.

May

- May the 4th be with you. Star Wars fans unite. Costumes? Star Wars inspired exercises? The stars are the limit.
- Memorial Day board display for the month, where clients can post pictures and stories of honored or remembered veterans.
- Mother's Day. How are you acknowledging the mothers in your community? Flowers, chocolates, photos on social media?

June

- "Right to Bare Arms" workout challenge.
- Father's Day. How are you acknowledging the fathers in your community?
- June 14th is Flag Day. Consider handing out the American flag?
- Summer. The first day of summer can inspire you to create a theme for your workouts, décor, or challenges.

July

- 4th of July. Hand out anything red, white, and blue.
- Fireworks workout. Have a special workout to complete during the week of July 4th.

August

- The Dog Days of Summer. On the last day of the Summer Youth Strength & Conditioning Clinic offered at my studio, we have an epic water gun or water balloon fight on one of the lawns of a local park. With the heat and humidity rising, consider water gun or water balloon fights to cool off at the end of a workout. Outside? Or can you swing an indoor water war?

- Back to School. This is cause for celebration for the parents, at the same time causing dread in their children. Create an uplifting workout with fun music for the parents to celebrate their "freedom." If you have a youth program, can you get them refocused with a challenge to bring out their competitive spirit? The more like a game you make a challenge, the bigger the buy-in. Make the challenge 4-6 weeks long. Have levels to achieve.

September

- Labor Day workout. Can this be a local charity fundraiser?

October

- The month of October starts the last quarter of the year. The last quarter of the year is when workout engagement can drop off because of the holidays. Can you offer a free "Superstar" challenge? Who can accumulate the most workouts from October 1 through December 31 to earn the right to be called a "Superstar"?
- Costume contest?
- Trick or treat for the kids and adults?

November

- Thanksgiving Day workout for clients and their family and friends. Make it a fundraiser and all money raised goes to a local charity.
- Since it's my birthday month, I've offered birthday workout challenges. Train the Trainer fundraiser. Birthday goodies throughout the month. Anything to keep it festive!

- Five-Pound Challenge to begin the day before Thanksgiving and end December 31. The challenge is to stay within five pounds of your starting weight.

December

- Send Christmas, Hanukkah, or holiday cards out to clients.
- New Year's special pricing for loyal customers.
- Special seasonal workouts. Creative names to entice interest in participation.
- Small gifts. One year I gave out a Christmas ornament with Santa and his workout bag to all my personal training clients.

No matter what time of year it is, showing love, offering a sense of belonging, and displaying how much you believe in those who you surround yourself with, will not only boost your business but will reward you with a greater sense of being.

Mary Bushkuhl

Mary Bushkuhl has been working in the health and fitness industry since 1984. After receiving a Master's degree in Exercise Science in 1984, Mary has pursued her passion of helping others discover good health through diet, exercise, stress management, good sleep, and making healthy choices in this chaotic world.

Her fitness career has taken her to Texas, Florida, Oklahoma, and now Wyoming.

Mary loves endurance sports, and has dabbled in triathlons and long-distance running. She also has a passion for good food, and enjoys being in the kitchen creating interesting dishes.

You can reach Mary at mary@marysfitnesscheyenne.com. Or visit her website www.marysfitnesscheyenne.com.

GET OUR
KIDS FIT

CHAPTER 17

The Path to Health and Wellness Starts Early

By Matthew Smith

The path toward health and wellness is a journey that can begin at any age. Whether we are 5, 15, 55, or 75, the journey begins with the same goal – live your best life in health and wellness. This journey can start at a very young age, yet I believe a more direct and focused conversation with our high school students can build lasting foundations for health and wellness-based mindsets.

I've been immersed in the athletic training field for 25 years, and have been a certified athletic trainer for 21 years. My work has afforded me the opportunity to work with NFL players at a mini-camp, D-I college athletes heading to the NFL, and junior college athletes looking to further their career through a transfer. For the last 17 years, I have worked with numerous athletes at the high school level, witnessing athletes that have taken their health and wellness very seriously, willing to do whatever it takes to keep themselves on the field, including injury rehabilitation. I have also seen athletes use their injury as a reason or excuse to avoid the work necessary to get better. Through all my diverse experiences with athletes, from high school to the NFL, I have realized that to reach the top, regardless of what level you are competing at, you have to be willing to put in the work and make all aspects of health and wellness a priority.

The majority of my experience has been at the high school level. I have observed the need for health and wellness education and associated activities increase during my tenure. Many athletes come to high school, and leave high school, with a performance toolbox that is missing the health and wellness information that they could use to be the best athlete that they can be in their respective sport. Some athletes may know that getting plenty of sleep is beneficial, but don't put the proper food in their bodies. Some may hydrate properly, yet ignore the potential benefits of a well-designed strength program. We need to help our youth fill their toolboxes with the proper, updated information about health and wellness and how the information can be used to help them perform at their best. While recovery, sleep, nutrition, and mental health are topics that have received more attention recently, I believe that our high school children, who are our future, have not been given the proper guidance on those topics. For example, I believe that some student-athletes, predominantly male, have been taught about fitness, encouraged to use the weight room, and spoken to about maintaining/increasing their strength for their respective sport. While male athletes have been taught various aspects about fitness, the female population at the high school level has received less attention and instruction. Thankfully I have seen a slight increase in the number of female athletes using the weight room, yet there remains a resistance to using the weight room and the equipment in comparison to their male counterparts. We need to more thoroughly educate all high school students and student-athletes about the benefits of health and wellness and how to integrate all the various components of health (weight room, nutrition, recovery, rehab, sleep, mental health, and mindset) to perform their best in their respective sport and take those tools into their life beyond high school. I believe that if we educate our female students/ athletes on the benefits of using the weight room and following a strength training program, as well as dispel weight-room myths (i.e. you will get big/bulky), we might see more female participation in the weight room. We can show all students/athletes how being strong/flexible/mobile will help them in their life and sport.

Over many years of being on the sidelines, I have watched athletes eat a bag of chips or down an energy drink before a game. I've had coaches tell me that they don't want their teams doing any off-season, or in-season, weight-room sessions because they don't want their players to get hurt. Post-game snacks have consisted of sweets and sodas. Hydration seems to be a concept that is not well grasped by the high school student-athlete. While individually these choices may not appear to acutely hinder performance on the field, we are well aware that these choices and mindset may have an accumulative, and potential long-term impact on the overall health of the athlete. The issues mentioned above are merely a short list of concepts, ideas, and common practices that are currently not being fully addressed, leaving an athlete's performance toolbox limited and often insufficient.

As an athletic trainer at a high school, I have seen both ends of the spectrum in regards to what an athlete may know about health/wellness and what work they are willing to put in to reach a goal. I once had a football athlete who sustained a dislocated shoulder during a pre-season scrimmage. Despite the thought running through his head that his season might be over, he asked if he could go back in the game, after his shoulder had been reduced (put back in the socket). While he didn't return to that game that day, he dedicated the next couple of months to being in the athletic training room almost every day, working diligently on his shoulder rehab. He would ask constructive questions about why we were doing certain activities and why we were waiting to do others. He asked nutrition-related questions, and wanted to know what he could do to get back on the field faster. He was genuinely interested in using all the tools at his disposal to help himself, heal his body, and be at his best so he could return to the field and perform optimally. He did return to the field that season, in a shoulder brace, and was able to play in the last few games of the season at a level close to where he played before the injury.

In contrast, I once witnessed a soccer player sustain what I deemed to be a minor knee injury at practice during the opening weeks of the winter season. She ended up on crutches and missed the first two months of the season. She did not utilize the athletic training room for treatment, and seemed to have little interest in trying to figure out how to heal and move past her injury so that she could get back on the pitch. She did return to the field toward the end of the season, but was not close to the playing level she was at prior to the injury. Would this athlete's outcome have been better if she had been given the proper tools of strength training, weight room use, and recovery, and proper mindset? Would she have been able to return to her pre-injury level, or perhaps even better?

These two athletes exhibit the differences in performance toolboxes and subsequent mindsets. Their stories provide the basis for the idea that we need to help athletes fill up their toolboxes with the proper health and wellness information. These tools will not only help them in their high school athletic career, but potentially serve as a foundation of insight they can build upon throughout their lives.

Through my experiences with student-athletes, I believe we need to start with the incoming freshmen, integrating the various components of health and wellness into the educational framework of their high school experience. I believe we can do a better job of educating them about proper nutrition, hydration, sleep, rehabilitating injuries, recovery, and how their athletic trainer can serve as a knowledgeable source of assistance. They should be taught the basics of health/wellness and how to apply them to their athletic endeavors and in life.

This vital information should be made easily accessible, readily available, and reiterated throughout the students' high school years with the potential of positively affecting the whole student body, not just the athletes. Some high school athletes lean into their natural physical abilities to excel at their respective sport while others may participate in their sport just because a friend is playing. Regardless of why a student chooses to engage in athletics, all of these athletes could benefit from being taught the fundamentals of health and wellness:

- Drink half your body weight in fluid ounces of water per day
- Get eight hours of sleep per night
- Perform rehab for your injuries to assist the healing process
- Exercise to help build strength and stamina
- Eat healthy meals and limit your intake of sweets
- Find an outlet for your stress (reading, writing, yoga, meditation, going for a walk, etc.)
- Keep a positive attitude
- Take time to recover from a hard workout/practice/game

While all the above-mentioned topics may seem simple, obvious, and easy to incorporate into one's daily schedule, reminders and repetition are needed to form habits. These elements of wellness are like teammates; alone they may be capable of doing good things, but together the results can be great. While athletes may not take each topic to heart, or choose to prioritize certain aspects of their health, we need to make sure that we are providing them with the necessary information to build their toolbox, as well as how to fully utilize these tools they have at their disposal. We do a disservice to our athletes when we limit the conversations to weight-room workouts and hydration. Topics like sleep, recovery, and utilizing their athletic trainer to help them rehab their injuries need not just be mentioned in passing, or as a side note in a team huddle, but woven into their experience as student-athletes.

Unfortunately, some coaches are so hyper-focused on improving their players' skills and making the team better that they fall short in addressing an athlete as a whole individual. This is not a slight against sports coaches, but a simple truth that there is so much to incorporate and most often not enough time to work on the x's and o's of their sport while also highlighting all aspects of health and wellness. We, as the athletic trainers/healthcare professionals on staff, should be finding ways to help athletes improve as a whole individual. How can we help bridge the gap between the sport coach, the strength and conditioning coach, the athlete and their family, and the wellness staff on site? Knowing that wellness is like a puzzle with many pieces, there should be a willing collaboration with coaches, sports nutritionists, athletic trainers, and a mental health team to help give the athlete the best possible tools to deal with their sport and subsequent life situations.

Over the course of my career as an athletic trainer at the secondary school level, I have actively kept my finger on the pulse of all the various improvements and changes in the health and wellness industry. Most schools now have someone to help the athletes in the weight room. There has been increased knowledge on how important sleep is for recovery and overall health. We have seen an evolution in surgical interventions and rehabilitation techniques. A light has been shined on the significance of mental/emotional health and the huge role it plays in one's life. Nutrition has taken steps forward in showing the role food can play in how one feels, thinks, acts, recovers, and performs. Yet with all these areas of improvement available for the general public to consume, it seems like the high school student-athlete has been largely neglected and left out of the conversation. I continue to witness kids eating chips, candy, or nothing at all and consuming energy drinks prior to, or at the end of, practice or a game. When asked what they plan to eat after a practice or game, a common response is fast food or that they don't plan on eating anything. The future of the fitness industry begins with our younger generation. While they are still in school and at an impressionable age, we can help guide them down the health and wellness path and offer them the proper tools for their lifelong toolbox. We can help participate in the future of the fitness industry by finding ways to help student-athletes become more well-rounded individuals, creating a ripple effect that creates powerful waves of evolution and change.

The general landscape for student-athletes has continued to stay the same in the years I have been active in high school sports. Although I have helped make a change in the post-game snacks for the football team, I still see chips, cookies, candy, and sodas coming out of the players' bags on the sideline, behind the bench, and in the dugout, or being provided by the parents after a game. While I have always encouraged small benchmarks of progress in one aspect of health (nutrition) for one team (football), and mentioned the idea to a few other teams, there needs to be a broader reach to help the students/athletes understand all the components of health and wellness.

I believe that we can make a difference in the future direction of health and wellness by filling up the toolbox of these young students and athletes. With adequate and updated information about exercise, recovery, nutrition, hydration, sleep, and mental health, we can sow the seeds of wellness at an age of critical development. While that may seem like a tall order, I believe it is valuable information that has the potential to enhance not only a student's athletic life, but a way of living well that they can carry into their future. Now is the time to equip our children with the proper tools to be their best selves in the classroom, in their sport, and in the world at large. Let's work together to help ensure the health and wellness of our future generations.

Let's put together a collaborative team (strength and conditioning coach, wellness counselors, athletic trainers, nutritionists, coaches) to help present this information to our students and athletes. While this project might seem daunting, I believe that together, we can help shape the health and wellness future for our kids. Whether they are the star athlete, the one that plays for fun, the weekend warrior, or the student who prefers an extracurricular club, we can help provide them with the tools (information) to live their best life in a healthy manner.

Matthew Smith

Matthew Smith is a certified athletic trainer with 25 years of experience in the field. While working in a physical therapy clinic, as well as volunteering at a local community college in the athletic training room, he became certified in 2001. In 2005 he became the head athletic trainer at Burlingame High School in Burlingame, California.

Matthew holds a Master's degree in Kinesiology with a concentration in Athletic Training. He is certified by the National Athletic Trainers Association Board of Certification (NATA BOC). He is also certified in the Functional Movement Screen (FMS level 1) and holds an EMT certification.

When he is not treating athletes or covering athletic contests, Matthew enjoys spending time working out, camping, hiking, biking, spending time with family, and reading. He finds great joy in spending time with his wife, Angela, and seeing where adventures take them.

FB: @matthewsmith
IG: @matthewsmithatc05

CHAPTER 18

Here's One for the Girls

By Sarah Stack

We've seen a rise in women's sports across all levels in recent years, from recreational leagues to professional teams. With an increased interest in women's sports comes an increased interest in fitness programs that are specifically targeted for women. Women-only gyms are popping up across the country. Many of these gyms are not specifically focused on weight loss or management, but instead on all aspects of wellness, including mental, physical, and emotional health. As a society, we're putting more focus on women's wellness. As such, we must also turn our attention to teenage girls' wellness.

Fitness training for teenage girls has historically been an underserved market. There are many reasons for this. Over the years, there have been fewer opportunities for girls to play sports than for boys, and participating in childhood sports is a natural place where fitness training and education begins. In recent years, girls' sports have grown in popularity, and now there are arguably just as many opportunities for young girls to play team sports such as soccer, softball, basketball, and flag football as there are for boys of the same age. However, as kids get older, the number of girls who quit playing sports is disproportionately higher than the number of boys who quit. According to research conducted by the Women's Sports Foundation (WSF), founded by Billie Jean King, many girls who have played sports throughout their childhoods quit playing around the age of 14. Additionally, WSF research suggests that 40 percent of teenage girls are not actively participating in sports.[1]

Some of the reasons why girls quit playing sports, as explained by the WSF, include lack of access, social stigma, decrease in the quality of the experience, and lack of role models. Let's unpack some of these reasons. First is lack of access. The WSF states that girls have 1.3 million FEWER opportunities to play sports in high school than boys. Even though Title IX mandates equal participation opportunities for male and female students in both high school and college, male athletes receive $179 million MORE in athletic scholarships than female athletes. Additionally, colleges and universities spend just 24 percent of their athletic operating budgets on female sports, and 16 percent of their recruiting budget on female athletes.[2]

Second is social stigma. High school years are already stressful times for girls with respect to body image and sexuality. As a society we've made tremendous progress in these areas, but stereotypes about perceived sexual preferences remain. According to studies conducted by the WSF, these stereotypes often surface when girls are deciding whether to continue playing sports. Third, generally speaking, there is a contrast in the quality of the sports experiences of girls versus boys. The WSF cites fewer trained professional coaches and less funding for equipment, uniforms, facilities, etc. for girls' athletic programs compared to boys' athletic programs. Finally, there are simply not as many role models for young female athletes as there are for their male counterparts. Such role models could be female professional coaches, trainers, and professional

---

1   https://www.womenssportsfoundation.org/what-we-do/wsf-research/
2   https://www.athleteassessments.com/gender-equality-debate/

athletes. As Athletes Assessments points out, "women make up 40 percent of sportspeople, however as of 2020 they continue to only receive 4 percent of the total sports media coverage in print and broadcast devoted to them. This holds true despite fluctuations during key events like the Olympics or World Cup."[3]

The benefits, specifically for girls, of playing sports throughout the high school years are well documented. They are both physiological and psychological in nature. Physical benefits include increased bone strength and density, increased lean muscle mass, cardiovascular benefits, and aiding in injury prevention. Strength training does not only help build stronger, bigger muscles, but it benefits bones as well. It puts stress on our bones, which then triggers bone-forming cells to react by building new bone.[4] Osteoporosis is typically associated with older women. In fact, 50 percent of women aged 50 or over will break a bone due to osteoporosis[5]. Laying a foundation for strong bones throughout adulthood can begin in childhood. Throughout our lifespan, our bodies continue to break down old bone and replace it with new bone. Until about the age of 25, we are able to make a surplus of new bone. After age 50, however, we break down more old bone than we can make.[6] Regular exercise also strengthens your heart muscle and improves blood circulation, which helps lower your blood pressure, and supports your overall cardiovascular health. High blood pressure can damage arteries, which can lead to heart disease, heart failure, or stroke.[7] Much like osteoporosis, high blood pressure is typically associated with the older population. Just as the foundation for strong

---

3   https://www.athleteassessments.com/gender-equality-debate/

4   https://www.health.harvard.edu/staying-healthy/strength-training-builds-more-than-muscles

5   https://www.hopkinsmedicine.org/health/conditions-and-diseases/osteoporosis/what-you-can-do-now-to-prevent-osteoporosis

6   https://www.hopkinsmedicine.org/health/conditions-and-diseases/osteoporosis/osteoporosis-what-you-need-to-know-as-you-age#:~:text=From%20about%20age%2025%20to,at%20the%20time%20of%20menopause.

7   https://www.cdc.gov/bloodpressure/facts.htm

bones throughout adulthood begins in childhood, the groundwork for later-in-life cardiovascular disease can begin in childhood. Therefore, we have an incredible opportunity during childhood to set our youth up for a healthier adulthood.

Another physical benefit to regular exercise is an increase in lean muscle mass. It's important to build lean muscle mass for many reasons, including combating obesity, building a robust immune system, and aiding in injury prevention through improved coordination and increased muscular strength. The proteins found in lean muscle tissue act as a protein reserve system for times when your body needs to fight off disease or infection.

The mental health benefits for girls who exercise regularly include having a positive body image and self-esteem, building relationships with other girls with similar interests, increased self-confidence, lower rates of depression and suicide, and elevated mood. Regular exercise leads to improved working memory and focus, and better task-switching ability, which not only shows benefits for brain health but also leads to lower stress levels through better brain function.[8] Additionally, being involved in a consistent training regimen helps girls create healthy habits and routines, such as the development of leadership, time management, and organizational skills, and increased self-reliance and self-discipline.

The Center for Disease Control (CDC) recommends that kids ages 6–17 engage in at least 60 minutes of moderate to vigorous physical activity each day. Further, the public health agency recommends that at least three of those days include bone-strengthening exercises such as

---

8   https://www.hopkinsmedicine.org/health/wellness-and-prevention/the-truth-behind-runners-high-and-other-mental-benefits-of-running

running and jumping, and that at least three more days include muscle-building exercises such as climbing and pushups.[9]

Women's professional sports are undoubtedly on the rise. However, one of the main reasons girls give for quitting sports is a lack of role models. As women's sports increase in popularity, so will female professional athletes' visibility, providing more accessible role models for teen girls. Another benefit to the increase in popularity of women's sports is the "trickle-down effect" of more sports and training options for teen girls.

The teenage girl is quite different from the teenage boy, and the issues facing teenage girls are vastly different from the issues facing boys, yet we approach training girls similarly to how we train boys. Let's take a look at some of the more obvious differences between teen girls and boys.

Girls mature, both physically and emotionally, before boys of the same age. On average, girls begin to show the first signs of puberty after their 8th birthdays, while boys don't typically start to show signs of puberty until after their 9th or 10th birthdays.[10] The bodily changes that girls must handle are quite different from what boys experience. While boys' shoulders are broadening and they're gaining muscle, girls' bodies are changing in ways that may be embarrassing for young girls. They start to develop breasts and gain more body fat. They eventually start having a period and have no choice but to handle this uncomfortable and somewhat embarrassing change every month. Navigating a changing body is difficult enough. Add in societal pressures on teen girls, and it's easy to see how they can get overwhelmed and simply retreat.

9   https://www.cdc.gov/physicalactivity/basics/children/
index.htm?CDC_AA_refVal=https%3A%2F%2Fwww.cdc.
gov%2Fphysicalactivity%2Feveryone%2Fguidelines%2Fchildren.html

10   https://kidshealth.org/en/kids/puberty.html#:~:text=Usually%2C%20puberty%20
starts%20between%20ages,9%20and%2015%20in%20boys.

I believe that a training program that is targeted specifically to teenage girls should meet four basic pillars:

1. Mindset work
2. Nutrition guidance and education
3. Training that is fun, empowering, and smart
4. Recovery work

When all four pillars are met, a complete fitness program that maximizes effectiveness for teen girls is achieved. **M**indset, **N**utrition, **T**raining, **R**ecovery – MNTR – all add up to MeNToR. When we meet all four pillars, we are serving as mentors for our teen girl clients, and therefore we must act and think like mentors for these girls.

Mindset

Creating a growth mindset environment is paramount. A growth mindset environment is one that is steeped in positivity and constantly challenges us to look for the opportunities to learn, rather than at the possibility of failure. A growth mindset environment starts at the top, so in a training or gym setting, it starts with the trainer. As the trainer, we must check our own baggage at the door and put ourselves into a coaching frame of mind. Take the time to talk to your clients about their day and what's going on in their lives, such as tryouts, a big test, trouble with friends. Having a growth mindset means adopting the view that we are always growing and learning. None of us have it all figured out, and every situation that we find ourselves in is an opportunity to learn and to grow. When we experience failure and disappointment, we have an opportunity to learn about what might make us more successful next time we attempt a task. If we experience success, we have a chance to help others grow and learn. For example, if a client is nervous about trying out for a team and starting to waver about trying out at all, we must help her see that not making the team doesn't mean failure. It simply provides her with the opportunity for feedback, to learn what she needs to work on and improve. It creates a roadmap of sorts to get her where she wants to be.

Along with fostering a growth mindset environment, we must also normalize introspective thinking and becoming comfortable with our emotions. Journaling is a fantastic way to foster this type of thought. Provide her with some journaling prompts, such as:

- Describe a time when you were brave. What did you learn from that experience?
- What activities make you happy?
- What are some lessons you've learned through sports or fitness?
- What about this next week/month/year are you most looking forward to?

Nutrition

OK, yep, I'm going there with teen girls. We must talk to teen girls about how to properly fuel their bodies. It's us vs. diet culture, and diet culture is winning in terms of funding, access, visibility…pretty much every category but one very important one, the truth! There's one other advantage we have over diet culture: society has majorly underestimated our girls' ability to understand how fueling their bodies actually works, and why it's important to properly fuel our bodies. Here's the best part: our girls want to know this information. We've all heard that the way to change a family's eating habits is by educating the children. When the kids ask for healthier food, parents tend to comply. We need to do more than give our girls one list of healthy foods and another list of unhealthy foods. This day and age of "eat this, not that" is fostering the loss of developing thought processes. We're losing the "whys." Why is a certain food good to eat several hours prior to a workout or a game? Why do we need to eat carbs after an endurance activity? What are glycogen stores and why are they important? Why do we need protein to help build stronger muscles, and which foods provide good sources of protein? Additionally, we must steer clear of talking about calories. Do not talk to teenage girls about calories! Instead, teach them about the three macronutrients: protein, fat, and carbohydrates. If we teach teen girls about those three macros and how to pay attention to them, the calories will take care of themselves. Teaching teens about healthy swaps, adding in more vegetables, healthy snacks, how to read a nutrition label, and what to look for on an ingredient list develops skills that will serve them for life.

Training

As with nutrition, the third pillar, training, should be presented to our clients in a manner that respects their intelligence. Give our girls enough credit to understand their own body's mechanics. Rather than simply programming workouts, let's explain why we're choosing certain moves, and how strengthening specific areas will translate to better performance, not only in sports but also in daily life. Explaining exercise science basics to our clients, such as the basic chemical reaction that creates energy in our muscles or the agonist-antagonist muscle relationship, not only increases her underlying knowledge and understanding of what each workout is designed to accomplish, but also empowers her to learn more about how her body works. Teaching teen girls proper form for basic exercises serves as a foundation for more complex, compound movements, and helps her to know what her body is capable of doing. In addition to learning proper form and exercise science fundamentals, it's also important to get teen girls out of their comfort zones. They are at an age where they're constantly looking over their shoulders, wondering who's saying what about them, or about anyone, for that matter. Heading into a workout during which they'll practice moving their bodies in new and different ways is a great way to let go of some of those inhibitions. Acknowledge that they may feel silly, but that everyone will feel silly together. Point out that by focusing on their own body's movement and how their own body feels, they're not actually noticing what other people are doing or how silly they may look. Along similar lines, include some exercises that are especially empowering or that release tension or frustrations, like ball slams or sandbag tosses. Encourage them to have fun with the workout, and to channel whatever has been on their minds into that medicine ball as they slam it as hard as they can into a wall or the ground.

Let's take a minute to pull together these components of training and consider a bicep curl, for example. A 15-year-old walks up to a dumbbell rack and picks up a set of dumbbells. If she doesn't know what weight dumbbells to select, how to perform a bicep curl correctly, how far apart should she space her feet, or what part of her arm creates the motion that results in a bicep curl… how effective do you think the exercise will be? How will she feel while she's doing the exercise? How will she know not to let momentum take over the motion? How will she know if she selected the appropriate weight for her abilities? How will she prevent the possibility of injuring herself? Then, imagine a 15-year-old girl who has been instructed about how her body works, and what the purpose of a bicep curl is. She takes her time in selecting a set of dumbbells, ensures that her feet are providing a stable base, and pulls her navel to her spine. She pulls her shoulders away from her ears and broadens her back. She makes sure that the part of her arm between her elbow and her shoulder stays stationary and that the rotation for this exercise stays in her elbow. The dumbbells feel good, but she knows she's gained muscular strength because she feels that she can try this exercise with a heavier set of dumbbells. She tries the heavier set, maintaining good form, and completes a few reps. She knows her body, and takes a few seconds to rest so that her muscles can produce the energy it needs to complete a few more good reps. This is knowing your own body, and trusting your knowledge base. This is confidence, and every teenage girl deserves to know this feeling.

Recovery

Recovery can easily get overlooked in a fitness program. Perhaps this is because we, as a society, do not have a complete grasp on what recovery means within the fitness context. Most people know that they should stretch after a workout, but post-workout stretching is just the tip of the recovery iceberg. Recovery is what allows our body to perform at its peak. It incorporates elements such as quality sleep, nutrition, consistent stretching, and foam rolling, to name just a few. Nighttime sleep can be hard to come by during the teen years, for a variety of reasons. The schoolwork and homework loads increase during high school; teens may have an after-school job; the distractions are plentiful and readily available in the palm of their hands in the form of cell phones, tablets, laptops, and any other screened devices. Non-school activities such as sports practices and games, music lessons, and play rehearsals come with a more significant time requirement as kids get older. In an effort to be involved in school, maintain good grades, participate in activities, work a part-time job and have a social life, sleep can get the short end of the stick. However, it's during sleep that muscles actually repair themselves after a workout. Not only is getting enough quality sleep important, but the effects of *not* getting enough quality sleep can be detrimental. Our cortisol levels rise when we do not get enough sleep.[11] High levels of cortisol send the body into "fight or flight mode," which is essentially the body's instinctual way of protecting itself. When in self-preservation

11   https://www.acefitness.org/education-and-resources/lifestyle/blog/7818/7-benefits-of-sleep-for-exercise-recovery/

mode, our bodies use muscle proteins for fuel to preserve fat cells. Additionally, reduced reflex times, cognitive function, and judgment skills due to lack of sleep can lead to injuries and mistakes both in and out of the gym.

We've already discussed the importance of nutrition in a training program, and how nutrition guidance and education should be approached when training teen girls, but it's worth mentioning that nutrition is a significant component to recovery. It's important to teach girls which foods will help to fuel a better workout, and will help replenish and rebuild their muscles after a workout. It's also relevant to discuss the importance of properly hydrating their bodies for workouts, games, and other endurance activities.

It's a well-known fact that stretching is a part of the recovery pillar. Even fitness novices seem to know that they should stretch, but do they know why is it so important? According to the National Academy of Sports Medicine (NASM), the benefits of stretching include improved posture and strength when combined with exercise; increased joint mobility and range of motion, which aids in injury prevention; improved sleep quality, which we already know is a major component of recovery; and improved daily functional movement. Stretching is an essential part of any training program, but many consistent exercisers will freely admit to skipping the stretching and acknowledge that they need to dedicate more time to stretching. This Indicates that they are well aware that they are not incorporating stretching into their fitness routines nearly enough. By making it a non-negotiable part of training programs designed for teen girls, we're creating the habit and instilling stretching as part of the fitness routine at the early stage of these girls' fitness journeys.

Foam rolling is a relative newcomer to the everyday fitness scene. Previously used mostly by physical therapists and by professional athletes and dancers, foam rollers began popping up in gyms within the last 20 years or so. Foam rolling addresses the fascia and is considered a "self-myofascial technique." All of our muscles, connective tissues, nerves, and bones are embedded in fascia, and addressing fascial health is an important part of an overall fitness program. Teaching teen girls some of the basic science behind foam rolling, as well as the do's and don'ts of foam rolling, will set them up for fitness success.

These four pillars of fitness (mindset, nutrition, training, and recovery) should be considered when a coach or trainer is designing a fitness program for any teen girl, regardless of whether she's a competitive athlete or simply interested in moving her body more. Increased training options for teen girls include programs that are athletic in nature, but make fitness and exercise accessible to all girls regardless of their previous experience with sports. Being able to confidently walk into a gym or weight room is a great feeling. Knowing proper form for basic exercises, and knowing how much weight you can safely move, is empowering. Knowing how to fuel your body so that it performs at its best both physically and mentally is invaluable. Connecting the dots among training, nutrition, and mental health is key for today's teen girls. By educating our girls about how their bodies function and how they use the food they eat as fuel, we're empowering them to be able to make informed decisions that will impact their lives. Fitness has the potential to influence a girl's life in many ways, including working to become better at a sport, learning how her body works, as an outlet for frustrations, building community with other like-minded girls who are interested in fitness and exercise, improving sleep, encouraging healthy habits and routines, offering an opportunity for her to see her body as strong and powerful, and building self-confidence that can carry over to all aspects of her life. Girls are different from boys, and the way girls train should reflect and celebrate those differences.

Sarah Stack

Sarah Stack is a personal trainer, group fitness coach, and strength and conditioning coach. She holds a master's degree in Public Administration and certifications in personal training, fitness nutrition, and assisted stretching and flexibility from the American Council on Exercise and the National Academy of Sports Medicine.

Upon earning her master's degree, she worked at the University of New Orleans in an applied social science research center. After becoming a mom, she had the luxury of staying home with her kids for nine years. It was then that she began her career in the fitness industry. She trains clients one-on-one, as well as both small and large group fitness classes. Athletic training and working with teenage girls, helping them gain confidence in any gym setting and educating them about how their bodies work, is where her passion lies.

She is the head strength and conditioning coach at Southshore Performance Training in Metairie, Louisiana, and writes a blog (In the

Game Fitness) about her training philosophy including the four pillars: mindset, nutrition, training, and recovery. She is in the process of building the In the Game Fitness app, which will make her training model available to teenage girls everywhere. Sarah resides in her hometown of New Orleans, Louisiana with her husband of 16 years and their two children: a daughter, and a son.

You can read her blog at www.inthegamefitness.com, and follow her on social media at:

- @sarahstack.fitness on Instagram and TikTok
- @inthegamefitness on Instagram
- In the Game Fitness on Facebook

SPORTS
SPECIALIZATION

CHAPTER 19

Sportifying Fitness for Adults

By Laura Jones

An Athlete, a Team, a Coach

What does having a growing fitness community with extraordinary member retention require? It requires trainers that are coaches, individual members that are athletes, and a fitness community that sees themselves as teammates. The field of play is set for this type of movement. I began to realize this about 15 years ago, when my understanding of fitness started to undergo reconstruction. With the BOSU flat side down, heart pumping, sweat dripping, I pushed the dome down to the 25-yard line. When I glanced up, ready to push the dome back to the end zone, I saw a tall, athletic figure on the other end of the AstroTurf. He was clearly doing QB drills and wearing an orange University of Tennessee visor. "Could that be Peyton Manning?" I thought. Sure enough, it was. I decided to stay cool and told myself, "Just let the man enjoy his training session." So, I refocused on the sisyphean-like task in front of me and completed my intense workout. After my workout, you better believe I took the opportunity to talk to him. Not because he's one of the greatest QBs of all time, but because I had to thank him. He helped me feel like an athlete again. He was the co-owner of the franchise where I was training. D1 Sports Performance Training created access to Division I-level training facilities and coaching for athletes ages 7-100. And when I say athletes, I mean anyone! Anyone who wants to compete physically with themselves and or others by getting better is an athlete. As a former high school national champion and college athlete, current personal trainer, and mother of two, I knew I was getting a taste of the future. This training made me feel more valued and brought purpose to the work I was doing. While I knew I wanted to serve others in the same way, it took me over 10 years and a global pandemic to see an even bigger picture. **"Sportifying" fitness is the future of the fitness industry.**

Sportifying Fitness

It's happening in my gym and in others around the world. Sportifying fitness, the transformational mindset from fitness enthusiast to fitness athlete focused on physical and mental progress...no matter your level, age, or abilities, has become a powerful tool for helping people fall in love with fitness and reconnect to the gym. That's because they've found more than just a place to work out. Trainers are becoming coaches that lead teams of people who've learned to see themselves as athletes. By becoming members of gyms that sportify fitness, former athletes and average Janes and Joes are developing champion-like mindsets, and it's transforming people's lives. It starts with shifting the purpose of exercise by focusing on training to get better, and centers around more measurable, performance-based goals. The client starts wanting to perform better physically, and the trainer focuses on equipping them to get better. With the right type of coaching, these "athletes" learn how to shift their mindset and become more intrinsically motivated. Great coaches are helping their clients buy into the training process while cultivating a community of teammates that cheer one another on.

In the past, gyms may have organically built community, but the world has changed. On the other side of the pandemic, gyms and trainers are seeing deeper needs and responding. They are beginning to focus on building community in intentional and organized ways. Coaches and teammates are welcoming new people into an inclusive group that's rooting for their success. This group is mission-focused, and through shared experiences like training, competing, serving their community, and planning fun events for relaxed recreation, they become a team. These gym owners are offering so much more than a place to work out. They're providing a positive community and a unique opportunity to be a holistically healthier person. With this goal in mind, many gyms are also able to create opportunities for additional revenue through life coaching, nutrition classes, physical recovery, personal development classes, and even weekend retreats.

When a client's mindset shifts from just wanting to *look better* to wanting to *be* better, it's a complete game changer. Lives begin to change and fitness businesses grow. Once clients fall in love with the process of becoming better, their commitment to their long-term health increases. This creates the opportunity to have life-long clients who are faithful to gyms built on higher goals and stronger relationships. Deep down, people want to be inspired and developed. Most people want to be part of a community with shared goals, striving to achieve something that's bigger than themselves. Sportifying fitness has the potential to create this experience for everyone involved. With great coaching and the right team culture, gyms that put this into practice are changing the industry and making the world a better place.

Adults Become Athletes

By definition, an athlete is a person who is trained or skilled in exercises, sports, or games requiring physical strength, agility, and/or stamina. That

255

should qualify all of our clients as athletes. They might start out being motivated to look better in a bathing suit or lower their cholesterol, but by helping them to create goals centered around progressively becoming stronger, more agile, and building their stamina, they start to reconstruct their thinking about fitness. They begin to celebrate what their bodies can do and who they're becoming, not just how they look.

Gyms win by giving their clients baseline physical performance testing and then celebrating every bit of progress they make, including faithfully showing up and working hard. DEKA from the creators of Spartan Race designed their competitions and training with this in mind. DEKA (meaning the number 10 in Greek) is the decathlon of functional fitness, where participants compete in 10 different functional fitness zones. Spartan founder, Joe De Sena created DEKA to inspire the average Jane or Joe to get off the couch and get moving in the gym. Although more seasoned competitors can enter the DEKA Elite Division, they encourage people of all fitness levels to sign up for a DEKA event with the goal of completing all 10 zones and earning their DEKA Mark. Jarod Cogswell says "At DEKA, our mission is to impact 100 million lives through fitness. We provide training with a purpose. Our goal is to not only maximize the physical gifts we have been given, but to also transform our beliefs within ourselves and mindset. Ultimately the end result is self-confidence and becoming the best versions of ourselves. And our global leaderboards give us a tool to objectively measure ourselves individually, as well as, compare where we are on our fitness journeys in relation to one another. The fitness experience becomes naturally sportified through the process and therefore we celebrate even the tiny increments of progress."

Training for DEKA events in her local gym has played a major role in the success of April Lauren's fitness journey. She says that the DEKA community has always been welcoming and inclusive. April is a popular

256

YouTube blogger who has invited the world to watch and learn as she loses 200 pounds. She's completed several DEKA events and earned her DEKA Mark. April says, "By sportifying my weight loss and fitness journey, I have learned to reach beyond the scale. I have the confidence to continue forward. I don't punish myself for what I am not yet. I celebrate what I can do while pushing to be better." She cites the encouragement of her coaches and teammates at I-F.I.T., a DEKA affiliate gym in Fayetteville, North Carolina, for her success with DEKA. While DEKA prides itself on being a "couch-to-competition" event, they have three types of competitions with various levels of running, and they even have a youth and elite division within those events. Other competitions like HYROX, CrossFit, and Spartan Racing have tapped into a similar but more athletically elite population. They've been successful at targeting their market and understand their competitions aren't for beginners. Whether the competitors are beginners, elite athletes, or somewhere in between, gyms have found these events are great tools for attracting new clients, measuring progress, and keeping clients motivated.

Other gym owners have tapped into creative ways of providing baseline testing, goal setting, and friendly competition without using an outside source. Kelly Young is the owner of Kelly's Bootcamp (KBC) in Chantilly, Virginia. She started KBC 13 years ago as an outdoor bootcamp, and has grown her business into a large but tight-knit community of fitness athletes. Kelly attributes her practical financial decisions and being tuned in to the needs of her clients as key components of her gym's success. She developed an annual competition called Winter Challenge in which clients are part of teams that compete against one another for the championship title. Even though the goals of the competition have evolved over the years, the success of the six-week challenge is still measured by changed lives. Members step into leadership roles as they volunteer to lead their team. The team captains essentially become coaches that provide structure, accountability, and support for their team. Teams develop camaraderie and take their progress more seriously because they want the entire team to succeed. At the end of the six weeks, KBC hosts a huge party with an award ceremony and captain recognition, where the top three teams and competitors receive their awards. Best Team Spirit and Leadership awards are given as well. Yes, most participants lose body fat, have more lean muscle mass, and can crank out more pushups at the end of the competition, but the benefits of competing go beyond that. Kelly says, "We've seen Winter Challenge teammates become best friends as a result of this competition. These clients are learning how to be athletes and realizing how to train not just for themselves but for their team. Fun and competitive experiences keep them motivated, excited, and wanting to bring their friends." Kelly cites the Winter Challenge as being one of the most effective ways to maintain member retention.

Because we imitate what we celebrate, fitness communities like Kelly's are beginning to celebrate what members can do and who they are becoming. They are figuring out ways to recognize and encourage their athletes' self-discipline, leadership, and teamwork. In doing so, they put their higher values on display. Learning to keep showing up and training hard becomes the higher value that serves to motivate the athlete, even when he or she doesn't see immediate results. Exercise becomes training with a purpose. Members shift into training like athletes, eating like athletes, and they're realizing they need to recover like athletes if they want to keep progressing. Gym owners are giving their clients tools for lifelong functional fitness, and in doing so, they're creating opportunities for additional revenue. Some are choosing to provide stretch sessions, nutritional coaching, and various types of recovery therapy, all in-house. Because client athletes are in it for the long run, smart gym owners will keep recognizing needs and serving their team accordingly.

Fitness Communities Becoming Teams

For gyms that sportify fitness, setting a culture that creates a sense of team is key. When members buy into the experience, they become the best recruiters. That's what Dustin Webb, owner of Dust2Glory Fitness in Bloomington, Illinois, believes attracts and keeps his new members. Like what's happening at KBC in Virginia, bonds are forming with teammates, and new clients are being invited in.

Shane Coughlin, new to the Dust2Glory team, credits his work buddy Josh Mast for getting him back into fitness. Shane saw how Josh's life was changed by his involvement at the local gym. Being the good friend that he is, Josh kept inviting Shane week after week to join him in a training session. Finally, Shane agreed. He has now completed three DEKA STRONG events (10 zones with zero running), and has shaved 5:40 off his DEKA STRONG Mark. He says he feels like a kid again because of the sportification of DEKA and the fun atmosphere at Dust2Glory Fitness. Shane is now focusing on getting his sons to workouts, knowing that leading by example is often the best approach. Shane got welcomed into a team-training culture and continues to move forward in his fitness journey.

Training and Competing Together

If you've ever been part of a team that sacrificed blood, sweat, and tears to be champions, then you know how deeply connected to your teammates you become. This also happens in gyms that have sportified fitness. Research now shows us what happens on a physiological level when people work out together. Psychologist and author Dr. Kelly McGonigal says that social bonding molecules are released when people exercise together. These chemicals help relieve pain, increase your energy, and help you feel more connected to the people you train with. She also says that being part of a fitness community in which you both receive and offer support builds resilience in the individual and helps them feel capable of facing other challenges outside the gym. Imagine rolling up in the team van to the competition site. You and your teammates approach the competition floor wearing your team swag. You warm-up, say your mantras, and then take turns cheering each other on. Often, these shared experiences carry over into other areas of our lives and we remember that we aren't alone. Luckily, we have more than just anecdotal stories and life experience to bolster our claims. Research now shows that people who train hard together will feel more emotionally connected, especially when they share a common goal.

Serving Together

Dust2Glory's community isn't big, but they are fierce competitors earning some of the top DEKA scores. Dustin believes that strong team-building includes creating a culture of service among teammates. Teams learn to serve each other and their community. Dustin says "I'm in the relationship business and I happen to work in fitness." Dust2Glory has organized multiple fundraisers for teammates battling major health challenges. When Tammy DeGroot, an avid runner, DEKA competitor, and tenured member of D2G realized her breast cancer had returned, the gym rallied around her to create a network of support called #teamscram. Scram is Tammy's nickname. They dedicated two DEKA Strong events in her honor, hosted prayer meetings, and donated over $1,000 of the proceeds to the American Breast Cancer Society. Team efforts to serve inside and outside the group produce invaluable experiences for members and help provide the glue that keeps people together. It's also a great way to invite new people into the community.

Celebrating Together

Many gyms are seeing the value of regular, fun, but low-key hang-out times at local restaurants or bars. You feel like you get to know people on another level when you spend time together outside of the gym. This type of regularity or rhythm communicates the stability of the group and the opportunity to really get to know people if you're interested. Kelly of KBC recently told me, "I've been to members' weddings, baby showers, and even funerals. It's hard to explain the quality of the relationships we are able to build here." This is the result of how intentional Kelly and her team are in keeping the community fun and creating opportunities for deeper connections. Kelly enjoys celebrating members' birthdays and hosting fun events like themed holiday workouts and the gym's anniversary each year. It's true that a desire for fun and something that feels like a tradition is part of our DNA. People want to celebrate, connect, and "ceremonialize" in groups. Members sharing their experiences training, serving, and celebrating together on social media is the best form of free advertising for gyms. When others see the incredible experiences their friends are having in and through fitness, new people will be drawn in.

Imagine how impactful it can be when gyms are full of athletes waiting to welcome their newest teammates in. Instead of coming and going with maybe a few awkward but polite hellos, clients are being greeted by their names, just like "Normmmm" in the iconic sitcom *Cheers*, "Where everybody knows your name, and they're always glad you came." These gyms know the importance of creating a culture that's caught more than taught. They create a high-energy, fun environment so that as soon as you enter into their space, you feel the vibe shift and you know it's time to work hard and have a blast doing it. It's a place where names like Norm turn into nicknames like "Shake and Bake" or "Action Jackson." It's a place where client athletes respect their coaches, themselves, and the people around them. They show up because they look forward to it, and if they don't feel like working out that day, they show up anyway because they know what happens if they don't. They'll be contacted. My clients like to send each other video messages, texts, and sometimes social media posts calling out their teammates when they miss a session or two. That type of accountability is gold. Coaches realize that relationships are what keeps clients loyal, and cultivating that becomes a huge priority.

Trainers Becoming Coaches

When fitness is sportified, gym owners and trainers become coaches. These coaches have a vision that drives their culture and motivates their methodology. And this methodology is not for the faint of heart. Building a team culture that upholds high standards and inspires people to get better requires hard work. It also opens the door to coach people in other areas of life. This is a high calling and should be taken seriously. By the time we're adults, most of us can recognize good leadership. We already know what it's like to have both good and bad coaches, teachers, or bosses. As we were led, we formed conclusions about whether or not they were for us or against us. We had opinions about whether they wanted to lead for the right or wrong reasons. If we were fortunate, we had at least one leader who genuinely cared about us, saw the potential in us, and developed our potential into reality. That's what great coaches do. Regardless of where we're at in life, we all want someone who sees our potential and cares enough to help us take the next step in our growth and development. This is how fitness coaching can fill that leadership void for adults. That's the deeper purpose behind youth sports, right? For those of us who played sports as kids, we later realized that our experience met needs that we didn't know we had. It taught us about life. It made us better humans. Why shouldn't fitness serve a deeper purpose for adults?

Why shouldn't fitness offer experiences that continue to develop us by making us better humans?

In addition to vision and methodology, great coaches need a lot of energy and focus. This type of energy has to come from deep within, and coaches must tap into it every day. With grit and determination, these leaders are running businesses and doing things like setting the high energy level of training sessions, rallying members to get signed up to compete at an event, leading them to do group volunteer hours serving their community, and so much more. They are regularly advocating for their people and challenging them to get out of their comfort zones. That's because they know that growth should never stop. They also know that leaders need leaders. When I understood that training had the power, like sports, to develop the whole person, it reconstructed the way I thought of fitness and who I've become as a trainer. Leading others has kept me motivated to be my best in every area of life. Knowing that I'm accountable not only for the way I lead myself but also for the way I lead others keeps my "mind right." In order to stay healthy, energetic, and focused, coaches should seek out mentors and/or a mastermind groups with members that will bring out the best in them. They know they need to be regularly encouraged and challenged if they want keep the fire in their bellies. Coaches like Dustin Webb, Kelly Young, and I, know this all too well! Even DEKA's Jarod Cogswell relies on a coach so that he can keep leading others. It takes a lot of work, but when fitness coaches understand the impact they can have and see this as their calling, they find the resources they need to keep going.

What gave me the confidence to walk over to Peyton Manning? I believe it came from being cared about, coached, and developed in my youth. That's where I learned that I had something to contribute, that I could be a great teammate, and even become a leader on my team.

When Peyton was between sets, I walked up to him and spoke with gratitude and sincerity. I looked up at him under that orange UT visor and said, "Hey, Peyton. I just want to thank you for what you've done here at D1. Most of us in fitness either feel like 'has-beens' or 'wannabe' athletes. This place has helped me feel like a real athlete again." Right then and there I decided that as a fitness coach, I could do the same thing for other people. I could help people see themselves as athletes. My experience at D1 inspired me to go from personal training to becoming a certified speed, agility, and quickness coach. I went from working with a few athletes to becoming the strength and conditioning coach of a state champion high school football team. Now, almost 15 years later, I enjoy bringing my experience in coaching back into group fitness, personal training, and small group training.

Wherever fitness is being sportified, trainers are stepping up as coaches and people are developing a new passion training. You can expect to find athletes being developed inside and out. You'll also see adults making deeper human connections by becoming teammates. Because this is happening, you can count on more people becoming members of gyms and staying committed to those communities. You might just find those fitness communities making the entire city in which they dwell a better place to live. The field of play is set for this type of fitness movement. All we need to do is get in the game.

Laura Jones

Laura Jones is a certified personal trainer, group fitness trainer, and speed and agility coach with over 20 years of experience. She brings her expertise as a former strength and conditioning coach and competitive high school (two-time national championship team) and college cheerleader at The Citadel into her current training and coaching. She loves working with sports teams and individual athletes to reach their performance goals. Laura sees all of her clients as athletes, including her oldest client, who's 90 years of age. She's also a member of the Todd Durkin Mastermind Group.

Laura has a degree in Youth Ministry and Biblical Studies from Charleston Southern University. She loves people, values community, and passionately pursues her own growth and development. Although Laura is high-energy and enjoys pouring herself into training, writing, speaking, developing people, and creating challenging but functional workouts, she savors slow, quiet mornings with good coffee. She and her husband, Mike, have been married 23 years and they have a son in high school and a son in college.

You can find Laura on IG @laurajones_jsf or email her at ljonesyep@gmail.com.

CHAPTER 20

Getting Lives Up 'n' Running by RUNNING in Organized Races

By Caren Ware

"Run to add days to your LIFE, and you will find
running adds LIFE to your days."

- CAREN WARE

Running is a flint. It sparked purpose in my own life. I use running to stimulate self-growth, attain goals, and acquire fitness. I also use running to ferret out experiences. It gives me the reason to go places and reach adventurous destinations. I have run a remote marathon on every continent, including Antarctica and in places like the Galapagos Islands, the Australian Outback, parts of Alaska, Africa, Europe, Asia, and beyond. I compete in USA Masters Track & Field meets and travel to national and world competitions. This has gifted me healthy, life-enhancing experiences I call gem moments. It has been a positive tutorial also.

Running is a simple, highly accessible means to generate achievable results and evoke positive change. Most bodies can condition into doing it. Like a gas stove, once one fills up a propane tank of layered endurance from running the pilot light stays ON. It ignites energy and gusto, and a courage to go after all kinds of things one would not dream possible. It is easy to apply the lessons gleaned from running to other aspects of life. It teaches how to set goals, not give up, and stick with a pursuit. Running can develop character. It opens confidence to do so many other things.

Gathering an array of heathy commitments and choices to live actively is one of running's best attributes. It can be the uplifting enhancer you are looking for. Running has a way of scaling things, like a mountaineer does a mountain. I was surprised to find running can evoke change, re-direct, and make life better. You will also. Something that seems like it would tire, instead invigorates. Running is like an additive, quite like the boost engines get when you put in fuel supplements.

I discovered the depths of my own tenacity through running, utilizing strengths I never thought possible to cultivate. It has also allowed me to develop connectivity with interesting people in a life journey I have written about called *Finding Fit. I was* a scrappy kid with an arduous childhood who discovered running as the friction to propel upward. And, in that journey of racing around I stacked up countless stories an active direction gave me in tackling life full on. Life got interesting because I was running.

The physical benefits of running are obvious. A volume of medical research agrees running can increase bone density, strengthen heart health, diminish depression, and fight stress. It can help decrease obesity, diabetes, and many other physical issues or ailments. Yet it is the personal benefits I think that are most amazing and possibly overlooked. Running's gain can be as superficial as having fun, feeling good, or becoming connected to a kind of community in a healthy way. It could dive deeper with a sense of accomplishment or a boast of self-assuredness. Or it can be as rescuing as the light needed in dark moments. Running can be the thing that pulls one out of grief, despair, depression, or a premature death. I am convinced running can help so many external and internal aspects that everybody out there should be trying it!

But running by itself isn't as powerful as running combined with going to running events. Here is the key to making it have the best impact. START GOING TO RACES!

I developed equipment and systems to process data to time running races and continue to do so as a timing company (Itzabouttime.com) And, because running has added so much to my life, I started staging what I call the Something for Every Body & Everybody Races (Carenwareevents. com). I use creatively themed runs to encourage people to be outdoors and active together. "Together" is a necessity we often do not realize. My events are a "come all" kind of race, where one can race, run, jog, or walk. And do so surrounded by active-minded people. I make sure the crowd is enjoying custom medals, great shirts, and live entertainment with a party kind of atmosphere. It is a celebration of natural endorphins. And it is a spectrum mix of all levels of fitness. That's a good running event.

A race is the runner's game day, putting the days of training to purpose. I believe community running events provide a natural medicine to our soul. On the back of my event van I have a slogan "We FIT together." Like a grand puzzle of beautiful humans each of us makes up a vital piece of that puzzle. We are uniquely special yet made better by being interconnected. A community-running event allows any BODY to participate and be a part of something nourishing. Finishing is won by all, and it's truly one of the most rewarding aspects of this sport! Whether one races it, paces it, jogs it, or walks it, running can be taken at a personal choice of gait.

Yet, however approached, think of the satisfaction achieved by anyone when a goal is set and accomplished. Under my finish arches there are fist pumps, jumps for joy, victorious hands held over the head. It is a heart tug to see people of all walks, shapes, sizes, and reasons cross over and take those final steps. When they reach for their finisher medal they are adorning self-victory. Just finishing something started is a worthy triumph. If you want to harness something rewarding, go to a race, enjoy it with others, and feel what it feels like to finish. With all these combined benefits, no wonder running races are so popular. Watch them be on them be on the re-rise.

Thankfully, in-person races are returning in force. Many of us collectively now realize the need for it after having it suppressed during the pandemic. The pandemic protocols did target sports. No mass gatherings in stadiums and at running events, and no close contact in places like fitness gyms, yoga studios, and karate centers was, for many of us, like asking to cut off a body part. We were amputated. Across the spectrum of fitness, people's routines were closed in an instant. Stacked on top of the mental, emotional, and financial challenges the pandemic brought on, we were dealing with this severe reduction of our viable outlets for staying fit.

When the country shut down communal sport activities, I had already spent years passionately coaxing people off the couch and into a mindset of eligibility. They were discovering the joy of movement shared with others. We were on a trajectory of continued health when all of us were asked to suddenly curb ourselves and segregate. This set off my alarms, and hopefully yours. I had already started fighting the war on being sedentary with my running events long before the pandemic crisis hit. The United States was experiencing an increase of physical health issues in scary proportions. Without organized running events like the ones I coordinate, what would become of those who shied away, hunkered indoors and stayed inactive during the pandemic? I feared it would have dismal consequences.

But a lot of people got creative with their fitness routines. I followed suit as the sports industry was locked down and sport fitness professionals were knocked down to near zero income. It was mind-blowing and felt crushing. I determined to stay boldly positive and very active, posting vlogs and sending emails out to show others how to work with what they had to keep moving.

I made an outdoor gym out of chairs, benches, and items on my porch. I made running routes in areas not roped off to public access. I created a STAY ACTIVE, STAY HEALTHY, STAY SAFE medal and awarded it to people accomplishing outside activity goals. I channeled my energy into finding ways to continue doing what I was deeply passionate about… getting people moving.

Thankfully, the stay-at-home order made a lot of people realize how gratifying being outside was. It was almost a necessity. I invited people to run a public path, each on a specific time of day like a conveyor belt. I situated my timing system and an operator on private property and timed the person running by on the charted course. We tabulated the times and did a curbside (restaurant style) shirt and finisher medal pick-up. A Zoom-style awards ceremony followed. I called them Together-Apart races. Although these outside races were viewed by some public and government officials as an almost unlawful activity, we were socially distanced, following guidelines and lovingly linked by the tally of times.

At first, many were hesitant to participate in the Together-Apart runs, anxious that they didn't comply with the COVID-19 protocols. I trusted that we could show the world that our races were not only safe, but a creative way to offer a health-enhancing community event in desperate times. Gradually, as the pandemic wore on, people started asking if they could join, expressing their view that the Together-Apart races were a solution to staying active and feeling connected. Although I was pleased to see the number of participants grow, the numbers involved were only a quarter of what event attendance had been prior to the COVID-19 shutdown. I often wondered what was becoming of that other 75 percent.

I knew that the 25 percent participating were not gaining weight, were feeling determined and hopeful, and were less worried about the outcome should they contract COVID-19. They made the decision to prioritize their current physical well-being and work to stay fit while finding this a safe way to do so. I also noticed something interesting.

Many of my 25 percent participants were over the age of 70 – the "at-risk" group. I had six devoted runners and walkers in their 80s and one 90-year-old, Nelly Williams. All were expressing the same desire. They wanted to die living, not hiding in fear. They wanted to keep moving and stay connected because running did miracles for them. It gave them purpose.

"We need to be moving. Knowing we are out here connected in time is a good thread of hope," one elderly man remarked. "We love seeing each other, even if it is at a distance."

These are my heroes. The 90-year-old Nellie, with a wiggle in her hips, her infectious chortle and charming sparkle finished 5K's and one 10K during the pandemic. She claims being active is one of the keys to longevity. Her giddy smile and get-after-it attitude are something we can be inspired by. The elderly couple say they will continue their active pursuits that have cemented a marriage of 65 years.

So, what became of those who did not stay active? That missing 75 percent? The pre-pandemic runners who shelved running during the quarantine reported an average weight gain of 15 to 20 pounds. They saw a wide range of medical conditions flare up, many of them ailments that are known to be exacerbated by stress. Many said they were having a difficult time finding the motivation or willpower to get back in shape. A huge percentage admitted they struggled with depression. It was astounding and disconcerting, and yet it validated my core belief that running is truly life- and health-enhancing. The harsh data being reported by this 75 percent strengthened my desire to encourage people to get back to running or add running as a new venture.

Find a race to attend. Google a distance, a town, a desirable area, and a specific month of the year. A variety of races will pop up. Some are more specific to regions. Others offer specific distances like marathons or 5Ks, and others are more trail based. There are a host of running calendar sites and so many races to choose from, albeit, you may have to travel. But that is part of the fun in it. See if there is a youthful twinge of adrenalin that comes from getting registered for an event and a feeling of delight to gear up for a goal. Discover the pride that comes in having the guts to do it. And the experience that unfolds. If you can't find a race in your area. Start one. You can contact me for a themed race start consultation package. I offer 10 a year. They are great ways to provide community good will and can help fund raise for charity causes.

Know that teaming up will add layers of enjoyment and commitment to your experience, especially if you include a good cause to run for. Group training and being on a team strengthens the bonds of relationship and ensures that there is accountability to stay on course. But not necessary. You can become your own running advocate and reason for running. Enjoy finding the shoes, shorts, shirts, socks, pants, and all the paraphernalia and gear that can go on your back and into your belly during a race. Add your own kind of hand-picked uniform to this newfound sport. Or wear matching singlets with those in your running group. This adds to the feeling of comradery. Gives your fitness purpose.

Organized races have so many benefits. I see them as a healthy, permanent part of our future. By running in them, I promise you will discover benefits you have been missing. Possibly avoiding. Life can switch from sad to happy, lethargic to hope filled, compromised to healthy, lonely to surrounded by an active community. All by adding an activity that puts one foot in front of the other. Requires nothing more than shoes and getting out the door. Hope to see you at running races and encouraging others to do something this healthy!

Caren Ware

Caren Ware's expertise comes from a lifetime of running and being actively outdoors. An elementary school jog-a-thon taught her determination and to fund-raise by running the most laps. She is among the first females to have run competitively in high school and college. Joining her dad on his bucket list to backpack many Sierra Mountain peaks and cross the Grand Canyon rim-to-rim, Caren developed spunk, stamina, and tenacity. She loves to explore remote places and lofty mountain regions across the globe, and combine that with meeting, learning, and embracing the locals. Her mom, being part-Native American Indian and a gifted photographer, taught her to have a heart for cultures and to look into the eyes of people.

Caren Ware has a passion to open the active world of experiences to others. Her desire is that by running, and just being active, all can build up enough confidence and fitness to enjoy places, people, and outdoor activity in a life-enhancing way as she has been able to do. She completed a goal of running a marathon on every continent, as remote as she could get to, doing so in Europe, the Galapagos Islands, Japan, Alaska, the Australian Outback, Africa, and Antarctica. In addition, she has run many marathons in the United States, including the Los Angeles, New York, and Catalina Island Marathons. She has climbed the Grand Tetons in Wyoming and the almost-20,000 feet Mt. Kilimanjaro in Tanzania, Africa. At the time of this publication, she is heading to Nepal and the Mt. Everest Base Camp to run the Everest Marathon. This incredible journey of discovering self, places, and people can be found in her newly released book, *Finding Fit*. (Finding-Fit.com)

Caren Ware ran on track & field teams, specializing in running the 400m hurdles, steeplechase, pentathlons (five events) and heptathlons (seven combined events). She learned how to develop speed, endurance, and agility to be able to run the 100m hurdles, 200m and 800m, and to throw the javelin and shot put, plus compete in the long jump and high jump. She loved the challenge of doing an array of events that taught her to do the ultimate best, and if an event fell short, work harder at the next one, knowing that it is a patient path to cumulate points. She continues to compete worldwide as a USA Master's Track & Field athlete. She holds 14 National Masters Champion titles in the heptathlon, pentathlon, 400m hurdles, steeplechase, triple jump, and high jump, and has placed two times as top-three in Master's Track & Field World Championships.

Caren Ware makes running her profession. She is a USA Track & Field Level II coach. She owns and operates ITZ ABOUT TIME, a professional RFID chip timing company. She stages running events through Caren Ware Events, the Something for Everybody & Every Body races so that everyone from avid athletes to couch potatoes have an invited reason to run. She holds a BS degree in Education/Camp and Recreation Administration from Biola University and a Master's of Public Administration from Cal State San Bernardino. She has been a city recreation coordinator, superintendent, and acting director of many city and county Parks & Recreation programs and is now a chosen entrepreneur and advocate of RUNNING.

Caren Ware has raised her own two active children and helped six inner city youth get off to college. All are graduates. She has housed over 21 Japanese and Tahitian exchange students, and become the American mom to a Romanian J-1 visa worker. Follow her on YOUTUBE Channel Caren.Ware.Events / Events: Carenwareevents.com/ Race Timing: Itzabouttime.com / Contact: carenfasttrack@aol.com / Get your own: GETTING MY LIFE Up n RUNNING manual offered at FINDING-FIT.com / READ: FINDING-FIT.com and be life inspired. We believe she will come home from Everest Basecamp and Nepal adopting a village!

CHAPTER 21

A Stronger Back 9

By Bob Poston

Have you ever walked up to the first tee of a golf course feeling energized, enthusiastic, and optimistic? Perhaps you waited all week, maybe longer, to get out on the course with your friends, co-workers, or maybe your fellow club members, and you feel yourself come alive as you feel the rip of your first tee shot down the fairway. Hours of fun lay ahead of you. Golf has seen tremendous growth in the last two years, and as an outside activity, people flocked to the fresh air and open spaces of golf courses in response to pandemic restrictions. If I told you your golf outing is actually an athletic endeavor, would you be prepared physically and mentally for this event? After many years of examining golf through an athletic lens, I am going to share some information that will help prepare both mind and body for this increasingly popular activity. I hope you will find the following information useful on the course as well as off the course as health and well-being follows us wherever we go. And if you're a trainer or fit pro, I hope you find information in here that will help your clients take their golf game and their health to the next level.

In my early research and training into golf fitness, I found a quote that initially made me laugh. I quickly found myself shaking my head yes, yes, yes! The quote came from a well-known strength coach by the name of Charles Polequin. Coach Polequin mused, "You can't fire a cannon from a canoe." Did you chuckle at that as I did? If you think about it, there is no way a canoe has the foundation to support the load and power of a cannon being fired. Like a canoe, if you don't have a strong foundation, you won't be able to effectively or efficiently execute a golf swing. Having a strong foundation allows one to maintain balance, flexibility, and mobility. When you set up to hit a golf ball, there is a backward and then a forward motion with the golf club to make contact and advance the ball. As you move through that contact point with the ball up to the top of your finishing swing, you just may take a tumble if you are not balanced. The same thing can happen by simply walking down a sidewalk and making a turn to change direction.

A strong core is the absolute key to maintaining your balance and staying stable while standing over the golf ball or pivoting to change directions when in motion. Did you know that your core is much more than your abdominal muscle group? Your core encompasses muscles and connective tissue of the lumbar spine, the hips, and the pelvic floor. It is where all movement is initiated. The inability to stabilize your body leads to unbalanced and awkward movement patterns that can lead to injuries on the golf course and in your activities of daily life (ADLs). What can you do to improve your core? A good place to start is with a few simple movements like hover planks for strength and single leg balance exercises for balance. A quick internet search will show you how to execute these two moves and provide some target goals for how long to hold them.

When discussing critical elements of our physicality, it's vital to include flexibility and mobility. We must possess both to live a healthy, active life, and both are essential in executing a proficient golf swing. I've come across many folks who think flexibility and mobility are the same thing, when in actuality they are quite different. Flexibility is the capability of a muscle, or group of muscles, to lengthen their range of motion (ROM) passively (meaning with assistance). An example would be the use of a strap to assist and lengthen the stretch in your hamstring. Lay on your back, anchor one end of a strap around the foot, and while holding the other end, raise that leg up as high as you can. Using the strap, you can gently increase the stretch by pulling it slowly towards your upper torso. Mobility is the ability of a joint to move through its ROM, dynamically and actively. These are different abilities that work cooperatively. A limitation in flexibility will impact a joint's pain-free ROM. Awareness of both mobility and flexibility during a workout is so important. Something I do to increase my ROM for my golf swing is twisting movements in my upper and lower torso. This allows me to stabilize one part of my body while I actively increase the ROM in the other and to swing more freely on the golf course with less restriction in my low back and hips. I always finish my workouts with total body stretches to increase flexibility and cooldown.

My passion for physical fitness led to my obtaining multiple fitness training certifications and completing a Master's degree in Exercise Science. I have owned and operated my own training centers and have worked with clients that range from fitness enthusiasts to weekend warriors to college athletes. In 2016, I received my Level 1 Titleist Performance Institute (TPI) fitness certification and my Level 2 certification in 2017. This credential has provided me with the skill set needed to coach individuals to be more physically fit to play the game of golf. Utilizing the TPI assessment screens on a client gives me a clear picture of where their ROM limitations are from their neck down to their ankles (I highly recommend seeking out a TPI-certified professional to perform an assessment if you are looking to improve your golf game). Once the assessment is done, and it is clear to me that the limitations are stability-specific, a program is created that focuses on increasing ROM where needed, stabilizing faulty movement patterns, and increasing physical strength. The program consists of functional exercises, strength training, and some power training. The functional movement exercises progress from easiest to most challenging, with difficulty increasing by changing the position of the movement (as in going from a supported pattern to a standing pattern and by changing the load or resistance level).

TPI has created a 4x4 functional exercise matrix that will systematically reinforce stability disfunctions identified in the screening process. The progressions in this matrix move you through four different starting positions: a supine or prone position, a quadruped position, a half-kneeling position, and finally a standing position. This process allows you to gradually progress from the supported (easiest) position to a standing (most challenging) position, first using assisted movements, then exclusively body weight, and finishing with resistance-only (which is the most complex). These progressions are calculated and skillfully designed to move you safely from an identified disfunction to a healthy function. The overarching goal is to make lasting changes so the client can enjoy their golf game as well as the activities of daily life.

One of my favorite components of programming for my golfers is addressing strength. Unlike most sports where you build strength by adding more load, TPI builds a stronger golfer by making the moves more complex. Using what's called the 3x3 strength matrix, complexity is changed by changing your stance. Golf is played standing up, so by switching up the position of your feet during workouts, the plane of motion is changed and greater stability can be gained. Exercises are performed with a split stance, progressing to a squared-up stance (like your golf stance), and then a single leg stance. As your stance changes, the way you carry and hold your weight changes.

After the strength component, we move into power. There is another matrix we progress through called the 4x4 power matrix. Through my training with TPI, I learned there are four main power sources golfers need to focus on in order to increase their strength and speed: vertical thrust, trunk rotary, arm-chopping, and elbow-wrist release. Additionally, there are four methods used to develop this power: absolute strength, explosive speed, speed strength, and opposite side power. Each one of these builds upon the other, but it all starts with a foundation of strength. Once strength is established, you can bring on the speed. Baseline testing will establish what movements you can and cannot execute and clarify what needs to be in place before you can progress through the matrices. I encourage anyone looking to improve their golf performance and overall experience of the game to connect with a TPI fitness coach and go through the assessments that can lead to a better day on the course.

Whether you ride in a cart or walk the course, the endurance needed for a round of golf requires some cardiovascular training. In my early fitness days, the recommendation for cardiovascular training was to move slow and steady a few times a week for 20 to 60 minutes, which is a great place to start if you are currently not doing any cardio. "Slow and steady wins the race" is a bit old school. I believe that you need to move more often and with more intensity to make changes that will benefit you long-term. I don't necessarily want to debate the advantages of aerobic (brisk walk) versus anaerobic (sprinting) training, as there are benefits received from both. Learning to utilize both of these energy systems while training is a big plus to your overall health and fitness. My endurance programming utilizes sprint interval training (SIT) which is a form of high intensity interval training (HIIT). The movements are performed in a 16-station circuit format. All exercises, including the active rest, are performed for 60 seconds. The start of a TPI (programmed) SIT endurance circuit follows. Remember to continue this alternating format for 16 stations.

- Mobility/Stability/Balance 1 – Stork Turns
- Sprint Interval 1 – Jump Squats
- Active Rest 1 – Recovery Walking
- Strength Endurance 1 – Pushups
- Mobility/Stability/Balance 2 - Pelvic Tilts
- Sprint Interval 2 – Turkish Get-ups
- Active Rest 2 – Recovery Walking
- Strength Endurance 2 – Plank up/down

Proper nutrition is required to fuel and support all of the above-mentioned areas of focus. How we fuel our bodies can not only affect how we golf, but also greatly impact our overall state of health. This is a huge topic, one that we'll just briefly touch upon as we continue to examine the various components that come into play when one is gearing up to golf. The first component of nutrition I want to emphasize is water. I'm sure the importance of being hydrated and staying hydrated isn't breaking news to anyone, but did you know that 60 to 70 percent of your body is water? Did you know that your brain is 80 percent water? This means that being dehydrated can adversely affect your mental focus and your ability to concentrate. If you can't focus and concentrate, whether at work or on a golf course, your performance is going to suffer.

Hydration impacts every corner of the body. Water lubricates your joints and is used to transport nutrients and oxygen. The body uses water to flush toxins from vital organs and waste from individual cells. Your skin, the largest organ of the body, needs to be hydrated as well. Golf is generally a warm-weather sport, which means many people are going to sweat. As you sweat, it is essential that you replace that fluid with clear water to maintain the fluid balance in your body. The simplest formula I share with my clients is to get their morning started with a big glass of water and to drink at least half of their body weight in ounces of water throughout the day. If you find yourself noticeably thirsty, that is your body's way of telling you you're already dehydrated.

When it comes to fueling your body for a round of golf, there are some basic nutrition facts to consider. First, I want to remove the word DIET from your vocabulary right away. Too many people associate this word with varying levels of deprivation, which can lead to extreme and often unhealthy food choices. Just look at the first three letters of the word DIET. When you overly restrict your caloric intake to less than what the body requires to support its daily functions, it starts to shut energy requirements down by slowing your metabolism. The last thing we want to experience on the golf course is waning strength and energy. I want you to walk off the 18th green feeling just as energized as you were on the first tee, and in order for that to happen, your bodies need the proper fuel.

Protein is the major source of energy for building muscle, tendons, and ligaments, all of which are required to execute a well-balanced golf swing. Your nutrition plan needs to consist of "complete" proteins, which come from animal sources. My favorites are eggs, chicken, turkey, bison, and fish. You can certainly get some protein from vegetable sources as well, but these are actually "incomplete" proteins. You can do some independent research to gather more information on the pros and cons of both types of proteins.

Carbohydrates are the main energy source for the body. As a food source is broken down and digested, it is converted to glucose or blood sugar. How fast the body converts it to sugar depends on the food itself and where it sits on the glycemic index (GI). The GI is a scale that rates foods based on how they impact your blood sugar levels. The lower the food is on the GI scale, the slower it is converted and the more stable your blood sugar is. High-GI carbohydrates take you up a steep climb, like that first hill of a roller coaster. After hitting its peak, you go down rapidly, experiencing what is known as a blood-sugar crash. We don't want to have our energy zapped before reaching the end of the golf course. Carbohydrates with a GI rating of 55 or lower are the way to go to avoid the roller coaster and subsequent crash.

Regardless of what you may have heard back in the early days of fitness, fat is an absolute necessity for the body and the mind. Fat-soluble vitamins A, D, E, and K all require fat in order to be absorbed and transported throughout the body. There are many valuable functions that fat provides the body. It's important to focus on the types of fat you consume, as some are clearly more beneficial than others. Monounsaturated fats are the healthiest and are found in plant foods like nuts, vegetable oils, and my favorite, avocados. This fat source is prominent in a Mediterranean food plan. Saturated fats play an important role in health as well and can be found in things like butter and eggs. The third fat is polyunsaturated and also has its pros and cons and should not be used for cooking. Common sources for this fat are pumpkin and sunflower seeds and pine nuts. The last thing on fats is to avoid trans-fatty acids – too many health issues to go through.

I believe that no matter how early the tee time, breakfast should be a priority. When putting together a pre-golf meal plan, consider including a high-protein source, a low-to-medium GI index-rated carbohydrate, and a moderate fat. An example of a simple breakfast would be a veggie omelet with a couple of turkey sausage patties. A nice salad with an added protein would be an ideal lunch before heading out for your afternoon round. Fuel shapes performance, so if we want the best possible experience on the course, our food choices matter.

Whether you are new to the game of golf, have been playing for years, or are thinking of getting started, there are many fitness-related factors to consider to ensure a positive and enjoyable experience. My goal is to not only spark an interest in this increasingly popular sport, but to encourage people to connect these dots of sports and fitness into their lives off the course. It's not just about playing a stronger back nine, but having the energy and vitality for everything else you enjoy doing in your life.

I'm happy to keep this conversation going. Feel free to reach out with any questions or inquiries!

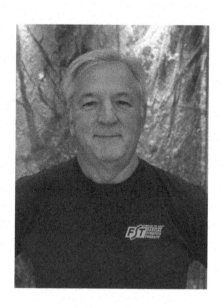

Bob Poston

Bob Poston received his M.S. in Exercise Science and Health Promotion from California University of Pennsylvania. He is the Owner of Poston's Fitness for Life Personal Training in Bridgeville, Delaware. Bob holds fitness training certifications through the International Sports Science Association (ISSA), Titleist Performance Institute (TPI), Training for Warriors (TFW), and has Golf Biomechanics training through the C.H.E.K. Institute of High Performance. Bob is also a Level 1 Stretch to Win Institute Fascial Stretch Therapy practitioner. He is an active member of the IDEA Health and Fitness Association. He holds a Bachelor's degree in Business and has over 35 years of experience in fitness and management.

Bob started his journey with the Todd Durkin Mastermind in 2013 when he attended Todd's 3.5 Day Mentorship and then became a member of the TDMM Institute. He moved to the Platinum Level and became part of TD5, a.k.a. Team Strong, when it was established in 2016. His passion for sharing health and fitness has grown well outside the walls of a physical facility, through his business and his deeper commitment to the TDMM.

www.postonsfitness.com
Postonsfitness@gmail.com
@postonsfitness

NEW WAYS
TO WORK
WITH UNIQUE
POPULATIONS

CHAPTER 22

Keeping Our Focus and Theirs:

Catering to The Needs of Unique Populations

By Janine Loehr

From a very early age, I knew deep down that I loved physical exercise and movement. It began with dance classes in kindergarten. It didn't matter if it was tap, jazz, ballet, or stretching, as long as I was learning and free to move and express myself, I was in my element. My enthusiasm for movement continued in elementary school when I played on the neighborhood community softball team. Through middle school I competed in gymnastics, and in high school I found my way to track & field. It was clear to me that I loved to work out, enjoyed all kinds of physical activity, and really thrived when challenging my mind and body.

When I got to college I joined my first gym, Gold's, in Pawtucket, Rhode Island. It was a very basic setup, with free weights, weight machines, and just a few elliptical machines at the top of the stairs for an added bonus, if you were willing to venture up there. Thinking back, I jumped right in. That first gym experience really resonated with me, and to this day I still love working out with free weights.

When I wasn't training in the gym, I would exercise outside. Every weekend, rain or shine, my friend Angelina Padilla and I would run down the hill from the east side of Providence to downtown. We'd have breakfast in the dorm and run right back up. Providence has many steep hills, so this was not an easy workout! Despite the pleasure I experienced from working out and running, I realized that not everyone enjoyed it the way I did. This realization was a signpost that told me my passions could be harnessed to help other people get healthier, and perhaps with the right guidance and encouragement, I could even inspire others to *enjoy* exercise a little more.

After gaining fitness-related certifications and gathering more and more experience working with many types of people, I was dedicated to learning as much as I could to offer my clients the best possible experience. With each client or class member, it was like piecing together a puzzle as I tried to figure out what would work best with their personality and individual style. This process was and continues to be exciting to me.

I'm now a business owner, coaching and training clients and teaching Pilates classes virtually. I'm also a mom to two amazing teens. What I've discovered is that the people coming into the gyms and studios and virtual training world are a much more diverse population than what we've seen in the past. I believe that we're going to see this trend continue as all kinds of populations come into the training world. As we come out of the pandemic, I think more people realize how important health really is. A focus on health and wellness is expanding as people prioritize fitness and value it in their lives. People *want* to feel better and move with less pain, something regular exercise can help them to achieve. Based on their comfort level socially, physically, and mentally, they are choosing from a variety of options to get healthier, whether it be a big box gym, a small studio, or private training in their home.

As a fitness professional in this ever-expanding space, it's vital to think about how to create opportunities and services to serve the needs of the neurodivergent and aging populations. It is very likely that you will have clients in your gym or virtually that have diverse needs. You may not have realized that you're already working with people in these populations. With the right tools in your toolkit, which many coaches and trainers already possess, you have the ability to reach them. Once you recognize the vast diversity of needs, you can broaden your scope of engagement and add a few new tools to ensure that every client is met where they are and given the best possible fitness experience.

Serving Clients to Encourage Focus

With diagnoses on the rise, there is a high probability that fitness professionals will work with clients on the autism spectrum or those with ADHD/ADD. As a mom with a son in this population, I have direct experience with his unique needs and preferences and the importance of addressing them. Working with my son, I've developed a heightened sensitivity that I have done my best to extend to my clients. With early recognition of a client's specific needs and a compassionate approach, you'll be able to help them reach their greatest potential and goals in the most encouraging and positive way. It's about opening opportunities for people who might not think they fit the mold of someone who works out or is hesitant to join a new space. You can meet them where they are and help them so they can be their best.

Clients with ASD (autism spectrum disorder) are all very different. ASD is a developmental disorder and a condition related to brain development. It affects a person's perception of people and how they socialize with them, so many have problems communicating and interacting socially with others. The main types of conditions are autistic disorder, pervasive developmental disorder not otherwise specified (PDD-

NOS), and Asperger syndrome. The word "spectrum" is used in autism spectrum disorder because it refers to a wide range of symptoms and severity. Some may have more severe effects (nonverbal or inability to speak) and sensitivities which are large obstacles in achieving daily tasks and activities in their daily life. Others are considered "high functioning," and lack attention and the ability to focus. It is very likely that you may encounter clients with the latter.

You may be familiar with the terms ADHD (attention deficit hyperactivity disorder) and ADD (attention deficit disorder). People with ADHD struggle to pay attention, experience hyperactivity, and can be impulsive, while those with ADD lack the ability to sustain attention but aren't hyperactive or impulsive. I have experienced these attributes raising a son with ADHD. People who have these diagnoses can be very focused initially and then appear to stop caring and not follow through. At first they are enthusiastic and all in, and then they get distracted. As their coach or trainer, you'll need to understand that this is not a willpower issue. It is not a lack of discipline. Many of these neurodivergent clients have difficulty compartmentalizing, and it comes down to how their brain processes (executive function). Executive function oversees motivation, organization, and perseverance. These are *all* needed to help any client meet and sustain their health goals. Simply put, for many, if they are not interested, they won't be able to focus and follow through. At the other extreme, if they are interested, they have a tendency to become hyper-focused. To reach these clients, you'll need to find out what interests them as well as unique ways to capture their attention.

Some clients may have the same formal diagnosis, but will vary on how their challenges and issues manifest. We also see many people throwing out terms that define themselves or others when there isn't even a diagnosis. An example of this would be if someone says to you,

"Yeah, I'm a little OCD with this habit." Meanwhile, they haven't been formally diagnosed. Terms are important in how they are used and how they impact our thinking.

As fitness professionals, if you are thinking about anyone that has a diagnosis in a negative light, it has the potential to impact the training and result in fewer benefits. Accept them for who they are, no matter what their obstacles or limitations may be. Take notice of how they pay attention and listen, or not, and why. This will help you determine when to cue, how much is needed, and whether to change or introduce new exercises in order for them to retain what they are learning. It's important to understand their personal challenges and how to present things in order, a step-by-step process. It is not just about program design, but gaining a better understanding of how their brains are wired. How does their brain process information and what motivates them? If your client is willing to be transparent and brave enough to share with you, you'll need to truly listen to what they struggle with. This requires more patience and support beyond a training session with a typical client without these issues.

Observe the Environment

There are many things to take into account that may affect or influence a person on the spectrum or those with ADHD/ADD: music, lighting, décor, the amount of space or people around them, and even uncomfortable clothing. If lights are too bright, music is too loud or not a type they like, or too many people are around, it could be overstimulating or not stimulating enough. They lose interest or get distracted. Sensitivities can range from mild and manageable to quite severe, requiring a keen sensitivity to possible changes that need to be made either on the fly during a session, or overall to the way you approach a training session. When my son was in kindergarten, it seemed like he would avoid a particular room at school for no apparent reason. It wasn't until I looked into this more closely and talked to him that I realized he had a sensitivity to light, especially the color white. The grout lines on the floor in the room at the school were bright white. It's important to pay attention to details that could have an effect on clients or class members that interfere with their session or class.

Simplify and Transition

I have worked with a wide variety of clients, many of whom are highly successful "Type A" personalities. The same strategy can be used with these clients as those with ASD, ADHD, and ADD. I remember one high-achiever client who I gave a circuit of three exercises to. She said, "Oh, just three? I like that. I can remember it easily. It's much better for me." I've found that simplifying their program with fewer transitions makes it easier for them to manage the workout without thinking of all the things they need to remember. I find it helps to break down their program into small parts. This is easier for them to focus on and understand. They may need each of the exercises broken down further into smaller parts to learn them correctly. Work on one thing at a time, keeping it simple, so that eventually they'll be able to do the exercises on their own when they are not in session with you.

It is common for clients to be self-conscious when training and want to do everything correctly, moving their body the right way. But, for neurodiverse clients, who are limited to focusing on one thing at a time, something that may seem second nature like having a conversation while working out, may be extremely difficult for them.

In addition, while neurotypical people are motivated and do things based off of importance, neurodiverse people are driven by what interests them. Their purpose is entirely different.

If you can figure out what they enjoy and what is special to them, this will transform your communication and rapport, and ultimately, their training experience with you.

Serving Aging Clients and Class Members

Exercise doesn't end with aging, it only changes according to each person's unique capabilities.

I've witnessed an older clientele expanding as people become more concerned and educated about wellness and exercise as a preventative way to lead a longer, healthier life. They want to continue to move with ease, maintaining strength, flexibility, and balance for their active lifestyles. They are also looking for a sense of community and social outlet to maintain connections. Regularly scheduled activities hold them accountable and keep their minds active and growing. I noticed this first-hand in the virtual Pilates class I teach. All of the members are 50+ with a majority in their late 60s and early 70s. They truly inspire me as I give my best in each Pilates class. Prior to the pandemic, I had taught this class for four years at the gym. When the height of COVID-19 came and the gym closed, I wanted to continue offering this class. They asked me to teach it virtually, and it was the perfect solution. Most of the general population knew how to use Zoom, but running the class virtually came with a new set of issues to navigate. So together we figured it out, and we tackled technology problems that came up along the way. Now they are all seasoned users and offer advice to others when these tech issues arise.

This aging clientele takes their schedules and exercise routines very seriously. They are highly motivated and really cherish all the benefits fitness activities bring into their lives. My class members always tell me ahead of time when they will be out, reminding me just how much they prioritize these classes and want me to know why they aren't attending that day. At the beginning of Pilates class, they often catch up with each other and share what they've been up to. It's very in depth and personal at times, covering a wide variety of subjects such as weather, surgeries, vacations, and current events. It's both the sense of connection with others and maintaining mobility that keeps them coming each week.

Similar to working with clients who struggle with focus, these older demographics thrive with routine and simplicity. Breaking down workouts and class programs and keeping things at a more manageable pace is important for these clients. Speaking with a clear, audible, and energetic voice can be very helpful for these clients, especially during virtual classes. They may also require shorter sessions or more frequent breaks to have the most enjoyable and beneficial experience. Taking music into consideration, it should add to the value of the session and not detract from it. I remember a particular discussion with a class member when she told me that music with any loud beats really bothered her. Luckily it was a Pilates class and that wasn't a music genre I was using that day. I realized that for some people, the music selection can determine the quality of their experience and even whether or not that particular class member would continue attending. She chose not to attend other classes at the gym for this particular reason.

It's helpful to remember that older populations may have a very unique experience with virtual training and classes as compared to those in younger age ranges. They may experience sight or hearing issues in addition to technical problems with their iPhone, iPad, or computer. Be willing to slow down, repeat what you say, and regularly remind them of things. For a virtual class or training, consider doing a test run or short intro class to show them how to use Zoom before they start the class. This will help get them comfortable with the online space. They want to have exercises that they cannot only do, but keep track of and count on. This helps them focus and gain more confidence as they learn and improve session to session.

As we continue to move beyond the pandemic, many people are struggling with a broad spectrum of mental challenges, beyond the special populations of ASD, ADHD/ADD, and aging. It's wise to consider wearing multiple hats to serve people in the best, most holistic way possible. Contemplate adding a life coach certification to your toolbox if you're a personal trainer. If you're already a life coach, it may be of great benefit to encourage fitness training to your clients, whether it be you or someone you trust and recommend. You don't have to be an expert on all things, just remain flexible and wholeheartedly willing to make changes that are necessary for your clients in these special populations. Get to know them the best you can. Communicate from the heart, listening to them attentively when they share. Take into account the environmental factors such as sound, light, music, and the energetic elements of the space. Simplify and break things down into smaller parts. Adjust your voice, and be willing to repeat or remind as needed.

Most people want to be understood and supported by others. They want to feel good when they wake up, move well throughout the day, and generally lead a healthy life. We have the ability to reach even further into these diverse populations and help them achieve their goals and live their best lives.

Janine Loehr

Janine Loehr is the founder and CEO of Embrace Fitness, located just east of Seattle, where she works with a private clientele and specializes in personal training and nutrition coaching in person and virtually across the United States. She also teaches Pilates virtually and caters to the 50+ age group in specific classes. Janine's purpose is to encourage, motivate, and support people to get stronger by combining mental and physical exercise to live in a healthy, vibrant body, all without needing a gym membership.

Janine grew up in New York. She was always involved in sports, loved fitness, and had a passion for helping others. Prior to her career in fitness, she worked for several years in the corporate technology industry, and now combines her unique life experiences, abilities, and compassion to have a larger impact on other people's lives in their health and wellness.

She is certified personal trainer through the National Academy of Sports Medicine (NASM), and a certified Pilates instructor through the American Council on Exercise. She also holds certifications in TRX and a Todd Durkin IMPACT Coaching Certification Level 1. She holds a Bachelor's degree in Marketing from Johnson & Wales University in Providence, Rhode Island, and also graduated from the Art Institute of Seattle.

Her association with the Todd Durkin Mastermind Group has helped her navigate the fitness industry. As an Institute-level member, she works with 150 of the top fitness professionals in the U.S. and internationally. They strategize on personal and professional development and everything involved in running a fitness business.

She also serves as an intern and community manager for Trish Blackwell's College of Confidence, where she embraces how she has grown and uses what she's learned to give back and help others do the same.

When she is not busy coaching or teaching Pilates, she spends time with her two teenaged children. She stays active through her favorite forms of exercise, which are running, hiking, and cycling near her home. She teaches her clients that building a strong foundation through their in-home workouts will help them continue living at their best, no matter their age.

Janine Loehr, BS, CPT
Owner, Embrace Fitness
www.janineloehr.com
Instagram: @janine.loehr
Facebook: @EmbraceFitnesswithJanine

CHAPTER 23

From COVID Ageism to Aging with Joy like a Pro

By Marion Recktenwald, PhD

*"We need to uncouple our understanding of even the word 'aging',
the connotation of it. Aging isn't about 'old age'. Aging is a series of
interconnected processes that begin to change in the mid-20s. It's about
reproductive maturity. It's about addressing health in a more holistic sense."* [12]

---

12   Milled.com. (2021, September). *Elysium CEO Eric Marcotulli on The Bob
     Johnston podcast.* Elysium Health. Retrieved August 28, 2022, from https://
     milled.com/elysium-health/september-newsletter-our-new-product-launches-
     next-week-UNT-PSV7OB5cismE

Ageism in the Wake of the COVID Pandemic

Close your eyes so you can imagine for just a moment. Then, think about older people in the context of the pandemic.

What do you see?

Do you see words such as "frail", "vulnerable", "at risk", "isolated", "helpless", "alone", "disease" and "death"?

Although similar stereotypes have always been present, they became more frequent and pronounced during the pandemic. Derogatory memes, negative stereotypes, and biased discourses against older adults were featured on the internet, media, and social networks, evincing age-based discrimination in society.[13] One study found that that age-based framing of older adults increased negative stereotyping in the media by seven times compared to more positive familial role-based framing during COVID-19.[14] On the one hand, words such as "fragile", "helpless", "illness", "loneliness" and "death" led to prescriptive ageist attitudes expressed through pity and sympathy toward older adults, taking the form of benevolent or compassionate ageism.[15] On the other hand, language such as "boomer remover" suggested that the lives of older people were not as valuable as the lives of younger people and reflected hostile ageism which also contributed to intergenerational tensions.

---

13   Silva, M. F., Silva, D., Bacurau, A., Francisco, P., Assumpção, D., Neri, A. L., & Borim, F. (2021). Ageism against older adults in the context of the COVID-19 pandemic: an integrative review. *Revista de saude publica, 55*, 4. https://doi.org/10.11606/s1518-8787.2021055003082

14   Ng, R., & Indran, N. (2022). Reframing aging during COVID-19: Familial role-based framing of older adults linked to decreased ageism. *Journal of the American Geriatrics Society, 70(1)*, 60–66. https://doi.org/10.1111/jgs.17532

15   Vervaecke, D., & Meisner, B. A. (2021). Caremongering and Assumptions of Need: The Spread of Compassionate Ageism During COVID-19. *The Gerontologist, 61(2)*, 159–165. https://doi.org/10.1093/geront/gnaa131

What is Ageism?

Robert Butler, an American gerontologist and the first director of the National Institute on Aging, described ageism as entailing biased attitudes toward older people, old age, and the aging process; discriminative social practices against older adults; as well as institutional practices and policies that perpetuate stereotypes against these age groups.[16] The International Council on Active Aging defines ageism as "discrimination against persons because of their age and implies the tendency to regard older people as unworthy and debilitated."[17]

Ageism is not new. It relates to the belief that some people still hold that life follows a simple, almost automatic pattern. We're born, we go through childhood and adolescence, we reach adulthood, then begin our declining years. This "declining years" label has been perpetuated by many negative stereotypes of aging. Unsurprisingly, in many Western cultures, old age has been viewed as a time of fragility, disability, declining function, and physical and mental limitations.

Do you think you are free from such stereotypes? You may want to think twice because we often do not realize how deeply these negative stereotypes are ingrained in us. Have you ever told someone that they didn't look their age? I have had that experience myself. People have said, "Marion, you look really good for your age." In the past, I thought this was a well-meant compliment until I started thinking a bit deeper. While such expressions are indeed meant as compliments, they insinuate that I, as an example, should look frail or appear less healthy because I'm not 45 anymore. Be honest. Have you ever tried to hide your age because you didn't feel as old as those pervasive stereotypes suggested you should?

---

16   Butler, R. N. (1975). Why survive? Being old in America.
17   International Council on Active Aging. (2011, June). *ICAA's Guidelines for effective communication with older adults.* Retrieved August 28, 2022, from https://www.icaa.cc/business/whitepapers/communicationguidelines.pdf

The Dangers of Ageism—We Are What We Believe and Why it Matters

There are numerous ways in which ageism manifests itself in our society. It can sometimes be overt, such as when an employer refuses to hire someone because he or she is too "old."

Ageist discourses, such as those suggesting older people have lived past their usefulness in society, may exert a negative influence in older adults' lives in very practical and concrete manners. Consider discussions, controversy and sometimes actions surrounding fundamental ethical issues, including the right-to-life and professionals' decisions on who lives and who dies. Some health professionals likewise reinforced the emphasis on age as a determining factor of Covid-19 severity, highlighting the knowledge gap on ageism. It may come as a shock that ageism also exists in our healthcare system: A 2015 study found that one in five Americans over 50 reported age-based discrimination in healthcare, and those who reported it had worse outcomes.[18]

And there is one more subtle and rather sinister way that it impacts us. Often, we're not overtly aware of it. When people are exposed to negative messages surrounding aging each day, it's easier for them to believe those messages. When individuals internalize negative stereotypes about aging, it negatively impacts their health and aging/wellbeing, while speeding up the aging process.

According to the World Health Organization, internalization of false beliefs about aging can speed up the aging process. Recent research (actually) shows that older adults with negative attitudes about aging

---

18   Rogers, S. E., Thrasher, A. D., Miao, Y., Boscardin, W. J., & Smith, A. K. (2015). Discrimination in Healthcare Settings is Associated with Disability in Older Adults: Health and Retirement Study, 2008-2012. *Journal of general internal medicine, 30(10)*, 1413–1420. https://doi.org/10.1007/s11606-015-3233-6

may live 7.5 years less than those with positive attitudes.[19] The exact science behind this association is not yet fully understood. One study found that "aging self-stereotypes had a direct impact on physiological function, with negative aging stereotype (subliminal) primes increasing cardiovascular stress."[20]

It can be further surmised that the internationalization of negative stereotypes fueled by anti-aging slogans may perpetuate fear, lower self-confidence, and even contribute to depression.

Those among us who internalize the widespread negative beliefs of aging, may feel little motivated to take life and health into our own hands. These beliefs are often met with thoughts like, "Why should I get off the chair and exercise when chronic diseases and frailty are part of normal aging?"

"The model of aging that people construct influences interpretations of and responses to actual situations when they occur, as well as preparatory actions that people take. Thus, the question of what people foresee for themselves and the process by which they construct and revise this subjective aging trajectory has implications for such issues as healthy behaviors, retirement planning, migration and residential moves, and advance directives, as well as for overall well-being in old age."[21]

Have you heard people say, "I am too old to exercise. At my age we don't have enough energy remaining."? They might not come to our gym and if they did, they might not be motivated or not for long. Imagine how different life could be for so many if every time somebody consciously

19 *Discrimination and Negative Attitudes about Ageing Are Bad for Your Health*, World Health Organization, 26 Sept. 2016, https://www.who.int/news/item/29-09-2016-discrimination-and-negative-attitudes-about-ageing-are-bad-for-your-health.

20 Rylee A. Dionigi, "Stereotypes of Aging: Their Effects on the Health of Older Adults", *Journal of Geriatrics*, vol. 2015, Article ID 954027, 9 pages, 2015.https://doi.org/10.1155/2015/954027

21 Furstenberg A. L. (2002). Trajectories of aging: imagined pathways in later life. *International journal of aging & human development, 55(1)*, 1–24. https://doi.org/10.2190/3H62-78VR-6D9D-PLMH

made an ageist comment, they were met with a resounding chorus of "Why do you think so? Let me show you the science and the practice that will help you to joyfully thrive through the ages with an active body, brain, and mind."

4 Ways to Debunk Ageism

To offset the damage caused by Covid-Ageism and Ageism overall, we need to counter Covid age-based stigmatizations that almost never consider aging as a complex, dynamic, and heterogeneous process, and there was rarely a mention that chronological age does not necessarily equal biological age.[22] In conjunction, we also need to debunk the myth that genes are our destiny.

1) Let's choose our words wisely.

Words make a difference.[23] So let's choose carefully. Whether we work in media, talk to friends or clients, or write blog posts, let's use language to emphasize choice, planning and control among older adults as our later years are a time of possibility and opportunity. Successful aging, active, joyful aging, aging well, healthy longevity are a few of many choices. As an example, I never use the term "old people" or "anti-aging." I am not anti-aging. I am pro age-transformation or pro age-optimization. While a first step, words alone won't do it.

2) Let's reimagine aging through positive life stories.

People love stories, especially positive ones. Whenever appropriate, I share stories such as my former client, Jean. She is a prime example of a

---

22   Silva MF, Silva DSM, Bacurau AGM, Francisco PMSB, Assumpção D, Neri AL, et al. Ageism against older adults in the context of the COVID-19 pandemic: an integrative review. Rev Saude Publica. 2021;55:4. https://doi.org/10.11606/s1518-8787.2021055003082

23   International Council on Active Aging. (2011, June). *ICAA's Guidelines for effective communication with older adults*. Retrieved August 28, 2022, from https://www.icaa.cc/business/whitepapers/communicationguidelines.pdf

life well-lived, and a person who embraced all the aspects of active aging. Jean was fully active and enjoyed every second of life. When she turned 102 and arthritis forced her into a wheelchair, she continued to make the best of her life. Jean took her wheelchair on the road and participated in cultural events, dined with her friends, and continued her fitness classes until she turned 103! Even then, she would still come to me for strength and stretching exercises while dancing in her wheelchair to music. At 104, after a short illness, her heart gave out.

Still stories alone will achieve only so much unless we can back them up with science-based explanations. Do you know people who argue that our genes are our destiny? Some of my clients have wondered whether Jean's joyful long life was simply the result of the good genes she inherited. Indeed, some people may chalk their future up to a "genetic lottery," of sorts. That is, instead of taking proactive steps to prevent chronic illness, it is easier to say, "Whatever happens, happens." After all, we cannot alter our DNA on our own, correct? Many people believe they are part of some sort of gene lottery and how they age will be determined by "good" or "bad" inherited genes.

3) Let's debunk ageism with scientific evidence.

Such comments reflect the believe that aging is not something that happens *to* us. When indeed, it is something that happens *with* us.

I have been successful using similar statements to demonstrate that the myth of a genetic lottery is just that—a myth. Many people are still surprised when learning that most experts in the field currently estimate that only about 25 percent of the variation in human life span is determined by genetics and the remainder by our environment and lifestyle choices.

Given my background and personal experiences, I am as much a passionate researcher and educator as a practitioner. I tend to test the water for interest and to the extent appropriate, support such statement with additional science and evidence. Not everyone of us will want or need to dig as deep into science as I do. I have had good luck explaining that the science of epigenetics shows that our genes, rather than being "static," can be turned "on and off" by our environment and lifestyle habits. Environmental factors can impact gene expression from our time in the mother's womb, throughout childhood, and into our later years. More importantly, epigenetic changes are reversible. Genes combine with the environment to produce complex human traits, our health and how we may age. And that this reality is a major factor that provides us control over our well-being as well as how we age.

Twin studies are always particularly helpful to illustrate and bolster this fact further such as this more general study that proposed that "People whose parents and ancestors have lived longer, tend to live longer and vice versa. At the same time, we know that genetics alone are not the sole cause of aging. Studies looking at identical twins reveal that there is clearly something else going on; identical twins who have identical genes do not always live an identical number of years.[10]

Just recently I had a client who was inclined to let "thing just happen." They have a family member with Alzheimer's, and I pointed them to a study which found that twins who were less physically or socially active, or who had more depressive symptoms, were likelier to bear a greater burden of tau tangles (one of the two major hallmarks of Alzheimer's) than their siblings.[24]

---

24 CHeBA. "Twins Study Indicates Environmental Factors Significant in Alzheimer's Pathology." *Medical Xpress*, Medicalxpress.com, 20 Dec. 2021, https://medicalxpress.com/news/2021-12-twins-environmental-factors-significant-alzheimer.html?utm_source=nwletter&utm_medium=email&utm_campaign=daily-nwletter.

If still not convinced, I might take it a step further: If genes determined how we age, why are so many cancers preventable? Why can lifestyle factors still have a beneficial impact in those who inherited "breast cancer" genes? What about neurodegenerative diseases? The National Institute of Health states adopting healthy lifestyle factors can reduce one's chance of developing Alzheimer's by 60 percent.[25] Experts such as Dr. Dean Sherzai and Dr. Ayesha Sherzai (known as Team Sherzai) note that "Ninety percent of us can avoid ever getting Alzheimer's, and for the rest of us, the 10 percent with strong genetic risk for cognitive decline, the disease can potentially be delayed by ten to fifteen years."[26]

From the understanding that many genes are "plastic," there is a short transition to open our perspective to both the need to play our genetic cards well and to recognize the power we have over our aging process. While some scientists and individuals suggest that aging is a disease that can be stopped altogether, this is not supported by current science. What we know instead is that aging, and particularity premature aging, is a major risk factor for chronic diseases of body and brain.

But there is also lots of good news. In line with many of our genes being "plastic" – so is aging plastic, and modifiable.

It helps to show clients images of trajectories of aging to demonstrate that - depending on our environment and choices we - have the option to increase our chances to staying up high on the aging trajectory to never reach disability and complete loss of independence until a short period at the very end of our life as was the case with my client, Jean.

---

25 *Combination of Healthy Lifestyle Traits May Substantially Reduce Alzheimer's.* National Institutes of Health (NIH), 17 June 2020, https://www.nih.gov/news-events/news-releases/combination-healthy-lifestyle-traits-may-substantially-reduce-alzheimers.

26 Oberst, Lindsay. "Book Shows How 90% of Alzheimer's Cases Are Preventable." *Food Revolution,* 13 Sept. 2017, https://foodrevolution.org/blog/food-and-health/prevent-reverse-alzheimers/.

Alternatively, we can contribute through our choices to a trajectory of accelerated decline and disability.

My friend's Sanjay's father represents a sad example of an accelerated decline. Sanjay's father worked in a very stressful job. While focusing on the need to procure for this family and earn money for his daughters' education, he had little knowledge of the need to take care of his own health and little time to do so. He even decided to delay retirement until age 70 to save extra money for a comfortable retirement and world travels. Unfortunately, a short while after retiring, he developed a rare and rapidly developing and debilitating form of Parkinson's disease that prevented him from doing all the things he wanted to do before, but never had time. This took a toll on the entire family. His wife became the primary caregiver. Sanjay and his sisters were tasked with finding doctors and managing financial records and personal affairs. With nothing to look forward to anymore, Sanjay's mother fell into a deep depression. Her life and hopes for retirement were squashed due to the intensive care her husband desperately needed. Now she is stressed and neglecting her own health. It is incredibly unfortunate, but also, too common. Too many people out there, and possibly some of our clients are waiting to spring into action until diseases develop. They then try adding years to life through medical interventions and pharmaceuticals which often have side effects, are very costly, and can eat up our financial resources and in some cases may even lead to bankruptcy.[27]

If stories of successful or accelerated aging don't suffice to convince our clients to take control over their health and aging there is another scientific fact that may help motivate the.:

---

27   Witters, Dan. "Https://News.gallup.com/Poll/317948/Fear-Bankruptcy-Due-Major-Health-Event.aspx." *Gallup*, 1 Sept. 2020, https://news.gallup.com/poll/317948/fear-bankruptcy-due-major-health-event.aspx.

"Instead of increasing life expectancies by only a few years from curing one disease, delaying aging could increase life expectancies by a few decades. Importantly, those added years would be spent in relatively good health, because instead of only fixing one disease, all of the functional declines and diseases of aging would be targeted simultaneously."[28]

One of the greatest fears people have as they age—second only to cancer—is the propensity to develop dementia or other neurodegenerative diseases. This concern is for good reason. Our brain is our most important organ. Our brain is nothing short of amazing. It is the repository of a lifetime of acquired skills and experiences. It defines who we are, and it processes the world around us. It is the keeper of our memories and the generator of our emotional and physical responses. If we "lose" our brain, we lose who we are, we lose our independence and our life. Here again to calm unnecessary fears I may use twin studies, or stories to demonstrate that genes are not destiny. I may also bring in my favorite graphic to illustrates how the one hand, even in "normal" cognitive aging, the brain ages on the declining trajectory, while on the other hand, it is up to us to move the trajectory again upward in later years, even though the later we start the more time and effort it will require.

28 *Is Targeting Aging the Future of Medicine? Researchers Make the Case.* The Gerontological Society of America, 18AD, https://www.eurekalert.org/news-releases/546285.

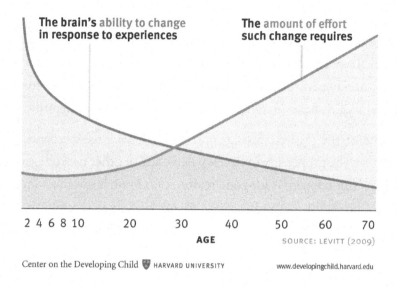

The brain's ability to change in response to experiences

The amount of effort such change requires

2 4 6 8 10   20   30   40   50   60   70

AGE   SOURCE: LEVITT (2009)

Center on the Developing Child ❦ HARVARD UNIVERSITY   www.developingchild.harvard.edu

The pandemic has provided us with scientific evidence that can serve as an additional anchor to motivate our clients to take their life into their hands and get "off the chair. "Although frequently not emphasized enough, we have learned that the risk and severity of the disease not only depends on chronological age but also very much on our biological age[29] and comorbidities such as diabetes and heart disease. These are medical conditions that should be a first hint that your choices and actions, not just the numbers of years you have lit a candle on your birthday cake, play a role in Covid-related risks.

We have since learned that younger people with relevant comorbidities are also at greater risk for infection, severe illness, and death. Thus, pointing the finger solely at the older population as posing a social and economic burden has been factually incorrect.

With direct relevance to the importance of exercise and movement, we learned that Covid patients who regularly exercised before becoming

29   Lauc, G., & Sinclair, D. (2020). Biomarkers of biological age as predictors of COVID-19 disease severity. *Aging, 12(8)*, 6490–6491. https://doi.org/10.18632/aging.103052

sick, were less likely to become hospitalized, admitted to the ICU or die because of their illness.

One study found that "compared to those with low levels of activity, high engagement in physical activity was associated with a 34% lower risk of hospital admission, 41% lower risk of ICU admission, 45% lower risk of requiring ventilation and 42% lower risk of death.

Even those patients engaged in moderate activity had a 13% lower risk of hospital admission, 20% lower risk of ICU admission, 27% lower risk of ventilation and 21% lower risk of death compared with the low-activity group.

The study also revealed that being older, male, and having a diagnosis of hypertension or type 2 diabetes all make poor Covid-19 outcomes more likely — but it added that, for these people, exercising for more than 150 minutes per week could have an even more significant positive effect than in healthy individuals."[30]

4) Let's adopt a holistic whole-person centered fitness and wellness approach

There are a variety of relatively novel concepts, frameworks and paradigms evolving that can help open our perspectives for how to optimize our programs in alignment with current science.

The constitution of the World Health Organization defines health as "A state of complete physical, mental, and social. well-being and not merely the absence of. disease or infirmity."[31]

30   Govender, Dinesh. "COVID-19: Regular Exercise Can Protect You from Severe Illness, New Study Shows." *World Economic Forum,* 28 Feb. 2022, https://www.weforum.org/agenda/2022/02/study-regular-exercise-can-prevent-death-from-covid-19-by-up-to-42/.

31   Hofgastein, Bad. "'Designing the Road to Better Health and Well-Being in Europe' at the 14th European Health Forum Gastein." 7 Oct. 2011, Austria, Austria.

The International Council of Aging (ICAA), promotes seven dimensions of wellness—physical, social, spiritual, intellectual, emotional, vocational, and environmental wellness— as the backbone of active aging.[32]

Interestingly, the United States Army states "takes a holistic approach to fitness by optimizing five dimensions of strength: Physical, Emotional, Social, Spiritual and Family."

According to the National Institute of Health "Whole Person Health" "...involves looking at the whole person—not just separate organs or body systems—and considering multiple factors that promote either health or disease. It means helping and empowering individuals, families, communities, and populations to improve their health in multiple interconnected biological, behavioral, social, and environmental areas. Instead of treating a specific disease, whole person health focuses on restoring health, promoting resilience, and preventing diseases across a lifespan. [33]

While these concepts and frameworks include elements that are that our outside our role as Fitness professionals, may notice social, emotional, mental as aspects, all aspects that we certainly can and ought to program with our trainings.

Here let's focus on what is clearly in our role and it starts with the who we are and a still somewhat narrow understanding of what influences our health and fitness

Thanks to dramatic technological advances and intensified interdisciplinary research, we gain an ever-expanding perspective to this question of who we are and how our health is being shaped. Several

32   *Nine Principles of Active Aging.* International Council on Active Aging, https://www.icaa.cc/activeagingandwellness/principles-on-activeaging-9.htm.

33   https://www.nccih.nih.gov/health/whole-person-health-what-you-need-to-know#:~:text=What%20is%20whole%20person%20health,promote%20either%20health%20or%20disease.

scientific developments lead to a paradigm shift. We are currently at a stage of this shift where we have more of a skeleton rather than having all the answers, including understanding specific mechanisms of the interactions. More research will be needed to build out the skeleton, and as some note, we are in the revolution stage of a paradigm shift. There is a good chance that this paradigm will undergo further challenges (including perhaps a rejection phase prior to consolidation). But what we know now, is sufficient for us to understand that we are not solely body and mind. Instead, we exist with body, brain, mind, and our microbiome interfacing in a dynamic and multidirectional manner.

A new paradigm is in the process of emerging that describes health outcomes and aging as the result of dynamic interactions between our body, brain, mind and our microbiome. To achieve the greatest benefits for our clients and ourselves, we ought to leverage our lifestyle factors within a newly emerging new paradigm that presents our best chances to age joyfully with an active body and brain.

I illustrate these characteristics and implications in other places in greater detail. Here are just a few tidbits of insight that can serve as initial eyeopeners to these realities.

We are not merely our bodies (in terms of cells and organs). Our bodies are made up of trillions upon trillions of collaborating, cooperating and occasionally competing microorganisms. Research has shown that the types and number of these bacteria can have profound implications for human health — affecting everything from body weight to brain function. Did you know that we have as many bacteria as the number of human cells?[34] We have a 50:50 partnership with the bacteria living in our body, and it is not a far-fetched idea to think they call some of the shots.

---

34 Guarner, F., & Malagelada, J. R. (2003). Gut flora in health and disease. *Lancet (London, England)*, 361(9356), 512–519. https://doi.org/10.1016/S0140-6736(03)12489-0

In fact, studies in recent decades revealed that a disrupted microbiome can lead to chronic diseases like autoimmune disease, cancer, obesity, diabetes, anxiety and, as we discussed, Alzheimer's. We should already be amazed that as intelligent as we consider ourselves, humans are partially under the control of single-celled lifeforms.

When it comes of the question where Parkinson's starts, there is a hypothesis that it may start in some cases, in the brain, and in others in our gut. With our microbiome playing a role, it could then move from our gut, over our valgus nerve, to our brain.

The gut-first hypothesis of Parkinson's disease (PD) says that in some patients, misfolded α-synuclein protein first begins to accumulate in the nerves of the enteric nervous system decades before the appearance of neurological symptoms[35]

The gut microbiota is emerging as an important modulator of neurodegenerative diseases, and accumulating evidence has linked gut microbes to Parkinson's disease (PD) symptomatology and pathophysiology. PD is often preceded by gastrointestinal symptoms and alterations of the enteric nervous system accompany the disease.[36]

While our microbiome has a profound impact of every aspect of our health and how we age, this is not to say that we do cannot, in reverse. influence our microbiome. On the contrary, what we eat, when we eat, our mental state, how we sleep and how often we exercise and at what intensities

Many of us use the word "mind" without clearly elaborating what we mean. We often use the word "mind" interchangeably with the word

---

35   Arnold, Carrie. *What Part Does the Gut Play in Parkinson's Disease?* Nature. com, 3 Mar. 2020, https://www.nature.com/articles/d41591-020-00003-3.

36   Romano, S., Savva, G.M., Bedarf, J.R. *et al.* Meta-analysis of the Parkinson's disease gut microbiome suggests alterations linked to intestinal inflammation. *npj Parkinsons Dis.* 7, 27 (2021). https://doi.org/10.1038/s41531-021-00156-z

"brain." In fact, recent sciences proposes that our mind (which I define here as encompassing mental states including thoughts, beliefs, attitudes, and emotion) and our brain, interact dynamically and bidirectionally with each other. Our mental state can have a positive or negative influence on our brain structure and function and consequently also on our bodies and microbiome.

"Every time you have a sad, hopeless, mad, cranky, unkind, judgmental, or helpless thought, your brain immediately releases chemicals that make your body feel awful. Your hands get cold and wet, your muscles get tense, your heart beats faster, and your breathing becomes shallower. Additionally, the activity in your frontal and temporal lobes decreases which negatively affects your judgment, learning, memory."[37]

More importantly, prolonged thoughts and feelings of chronic stress, anxiety, or untreated chronic depression[38] can affect our cognitive abilities as well as literally shrink parts of our brain[39] and thereby contributing to neurodegenerative diseases.

But rather than being the helpless bystander it is in our power and those of our clients, to employ positive thinking techniques and via neuroplasticity, rewire our brain for a healthier brain, mind, and body.[40]

The article, "How does positive thinking affect neuroplasticity?" outlines how positive thinking affects our brain. Synapses (areas connecting neurons) increase, in turn, increasing mental productivity by

---

37 *The Number One Habit To Develop In Order To Feel More Positive.* Amen Clinics, 16 Aug. 2016, https://www.amenclinics.com/blog/number-one-habit-develop-order-feel-positive/.

38 Davey, Melissa. *Chronic Depression Shrinks Brain's Memories and Emotions.* The Guardian, 30 June 2015, https://www.theguardian.com/society/2015/jun/30/chronic-depression-shrinks-brains-memories-and-emotions.

39 Booth, Stephanie. *How Stress Can Shrink Your Brain and 6 Ways to Keep It from Happening.* Health Line, 21 Nov. 2018, https://www.healthline.com/health-news/how-stress-can-shrink-your-brain.

40 *The Number One Habit To Develop In Order To Feel More Positive.* Amen Clinics, 16 Aug. 2016, https://www.amenclinics.com/blog/number-one-habit-develop-order-feel-positive/.

improving cognition. Intensifies ability to pay attention. Improves the ability to think and analyze incoming data.[41]

Almost all of us know from own experience how our mind affects our bodies. One example is the so-called gut-brain axis. Our gastrointestinal tract is sensitive to emotion. Anger, anxiety, sadness, elation — all these feelings (and others) can trigger symptoms in the gut.

If you ever had had a "gut-wrenching" experience, or felt "butterflies" in your stomach, then you know that the so-called gut-brain axis is not a joke. Talking about interface, have you ever had an upset "stomach" making you feel a bit less energetic happy. No wonder, keep in mind that about 90 % of serotonin is in your gut. Science has evolved to suggest that the status of our microbiome may even play a role in depression.

We are also aware of the simple fact that if the brain malfunctions or stops working so does our body. But the reverse namely that our body affects our brain while true is less known. Want to surprise your clients with a few selected facts?

What got sex to do with slowed cognitive aging? The physical act of sex can not only releases stress and promotes sleep it can also support our brain's health. In fact, sex has been linked to the making of new brain cells. People over 50 who had more sex were better able to recall numbers and do basic math.[42]

What have bones got to do with memory? The connection between our body and brain gets more amazing the more we look at it! There is a link, for example, between bones, muscles and brain. Our bones are living things, and every day our body breaks down old bone and

---

41   *Your Brain Thrives On Positivity.* Achieve Medial Center, 29 Nov. 2020, https://www.achievemedicalcenter.com/blog-post/your-brain-thrives-on-positivity.
42   *14 Reasons You Should Have Sex Now.* Webmd.com, 30 Aug. 2020, https://www.webmd.com/sex-relationships/ss/slideshow-have-sex-now?ecd=soc_tw_220415_cons_ss_havesexnow&linkId=100000120231250.

replaces it with new bone. Our bones also contribute to our brain's ability to create new synapses for cognitive reserve. As shown by Eric Kandel and colleagues, when bones are stimulated during training, including walking, they release a hormone called osteocalcin into our blood, which is transported into the brain. There it boosts adult neurogenesis, serotonin, and dopamine. Even more intriguing is a study at Columbia University in which osteocalcin improved the learning ability of younger mice while reversing the memory loss of older one.

What does leg strength have to do with a healthier brain? Older women who have strong legs are likely to fare better when it comes to ageing of the brain, a decade-long study of more than 300 twins suggests. As an example, a twin with more leg strength at the start of the study maintained her mental abilities better and had fewer age-related brain changes than the twin with weaker legs, the study found.[43]

What is our second heart? "That's right, it's your calf muscles! "The second heart is a system of muscles, veins, and valves in the calf and foot that work together to push deoxygenated blood back up to the heart and lungs. Vein valves act as trapdoors that open and close with each muscle contraction to prevent the backflow of blood."[44] And everything that is good for your heart is good for your brain.

What has our brain to do with balance? Yes, we need physical fitness for good balance such as leg strength, leg power, flexibility, and core strength. But that's not everything"

"How do we keep our balance? The inner ear, which senses head motions, is an important part of the intricate system of balance. So is

---

43 Preidt, Robert. *Strong Legs Linked to Strong Mind.* Webmd.com, 11 Nov. 2015, https://www.webmd.com/fitness-exercise/news/20151111/strong-legs-linked-to-strong-mind.

44 *The Circulatory System and the Second Heart.* The Heart Specialists Group, https://www.heartspecialistsgroup.com/the-circulatory-system-and-the-second-heart/.

the body's somatosensory system, which relays the feeling of the ground beneath your feet. And, of course, vision tips you off to obstacles around you. The brain takes in all this information, plans our movements, and carries them out. "Balance is a complex system," Manor says. "Especially as we get older, cognition becomes a big part of it." Keeping the mind fit keeps us mentally sharp and helps us to navigate the ever-shifting obstacle course of the world.[45]

Can exercise benefit neurodegenerative diseases? The following is a graph that shows the results of a study that explored the prevalence of Parkinson's disease if physical activity levels in adults increased. The blue line reflects the currently projected increase. The red line projects the increase if adults increased their activity levels by 20 percent and the green line if they increased them by 80 percent.[46]

There is more to say about the necessary ingredients of exercise for brain health in general and for Parkinson's disease in specific including the role that specific exercises have in leading to higher circulating levels of dopamine and more available dopamine receptors. Suffice to look at the above chart to gain an appreciation of the enormous role that exercise and physical activity play in brain health and brain change.

---

45 https://www.health.harvard.edu/promotions/harvard-health-publications/
better-balance-easy-exercises-to-improve-stability-and-prevent-falls?utm_
source=delivra&utm_medium=email&utm_campaign=HB20210902-
Balance&utm_id=3140045&dlv-emuid=5c73ed9f-a6b1-4c31-b24f-
f96f66891d58&dlv-mlid=3140045

46 Simon, D. K., Tanner, C. M., & Brundin, P. (2020). Parkinson Disease Epidemiology,
Pathology, Genetics, and Pathophysiology. *Clinics in geriatric medicine, 36*(1),
1–12. https://doi.org/10.1016/j.cger.2019.08.002

Program Implications for the Present and Future of Our Fitness Industry

Holistic means appreciation of the interplay between lifestyle factors

Although regular physically fitness is a multi-pill that decreases the risks for virtually all chronic diseases, optimal health and aging is best achieved in conjunction additional healthy lifestyle habits. We recognize 1) that lifestyle factors support or block each other with effects reaching from our DNA to other parts, inside and outside our cells, to our organs, including our most important organ, our brain, 2) that they work best synergistically, 3) that benefits can be additive, with each additional enhanced lifestyle habit adding greater benefit for our health and well-being and to our chance of aging successfully. We won't promise an older obese client significant weight loss based on exercise alone. We understand that weight management needs physical activities, healthy nutrition patterns, restorative sleep, and negative stress management. Overall, we will refer clients to aligned health care providers when appropriate, while offering holistic evidence-based support within scope of practice.

Holistic means programming for a positive state of mind and social interactions

We are not personal trainers who read our emails while letting our clients perform a task. We actively solicit positive engagements. We may bring in smiles and laughter, music for enjoyment, motivation or when needed for relaxation. We may teach classes that allow for engaging social interaction and joy or recommend our clients to do so on their own. If not part of our program, we will suggest that our clients, choose a variety of physical activities from high intensities to so called mind-body exercise as Tai-Chi and Yoga. Our repertoire may include trainings in nature. If not, we will recommend outdoor activities as important ingredients of healthy living and aging.

Holistic means programing for Brain Health and/or Brain Change

One of the greatest fears of the older generation aside from cancer and falls are "losing their mind" and thus control over their life. Recent studies have shown that Baby boomers scored lower on cognitive functioning tests than members of previous generations. Scores began to decline in those born between 1948-1953 and decreased further in those born between 1954-1959[47] - lending additional credence to projected drastic increases of neurodegenerative diseases.

Not all of us need to become a certified Brain Health Trainer[48] or specialized in niches to benefit clients with neurodegenerative disease. However, since cognitive aging starts in our 30s, since neurodegenerative diseases often begin 10 to 20 years before any clinical symptoms (where we can best prevent, arrest, or slow them), it will behoove to all of us to acquire basic knowledge and skill to augment our trainings with of cognitively enhanced exercise techniques.

Holistic "Whole Person "Fitness also means personalization

Our interventions need to be tailored in accordance with functional and cognitive fitness levels of our clients. We know better than attempting to develop a six-month program for an older sedentary individual with one or more chronic diseases while setting the expectation that he/ she will be able to participate in the senior games or climb mount Everest. In fact, many of our interventions need to be tailored to meet the emotional and safety needs of the population fitting such criteria.

---

47 https://neurosciencenews.com/baby-boomer-cognition-16759/?fbclid=IwAR0VN
 A3JYSA_8SyG9oidr5BofL6LFPAfvSCtCDjMp8Dg86rR8Xyjowa-kxw
48 https://functionalaginginstitute.eu/fai-courses-2/

Cutting-edge science proposes that certain types of movements may benefit specific brain regions or cognitive abilities foremost. This type of knowledge helps us currently tailor our intervention. Future science will provide opportunities for even better tailoring interventions to our clients' needs.

We possess preliminary, but sufficiently solid information of the types of exercises that have the greatest chances at benefitting motor and non-motor symptoms of neurogenerative diseases including in their different stages of progression, again highlighting opportunities for o personalization.

Although current science on the role of FITT - Frequency, Intensity, Time, and Type – in exercise for brain health and brain chance is at best preliminary, science continues to evolve. In the future our cognitively enhanced exercise programs will also be based on the knowledge of how incorporating FIIT with our cognitively enhanced exercise interventions.

In the Future.

(And now) We will understand the difference between more mindless exercise (which more correctly speaking should be called brainless exercises) like running a treadmill without further thought, and exercises that will engage our brains in ways to help build cognitive reserve or strengthen our cognitive functions, such as attention and reaction time.

We will understand the fact that no matter whether Parkinson's starts in our gut or in the brain, particular movements at given dosages and intensities increase dopamine amounts and receptor sensitivities. We will know which movements have the best chances to target the motor and symptoms of Parkinson's in ways that can potentially slow the progression of the disease.

We will be able to calibrate and personalize exercise intensities with an understanding that certain intensities can support our microbiome and gut health with an extension being our immune system and overall health, while others are more likely detrimental.

Even if a client comes to us with the goal of building "big muscles," (now and in the future) we may be able squeeze in a question or hint to the client, that focusing on big muscles alone is not necessarily functional fitness and cognitive power. And if such does not work, we can still do a little to support his brain health. Namely, rather than having him do the movements without giving them any thought, we may want to place a heavy emphasis on concentrating on the right form. If nothing else, this will support his attention, which is one of the first brain functions to age.

The fitness industry has many niches requiring in-depth expertise, knowledge, and skill.

Not everyone will, or should become, a Parkinson's fitness specialist or a certified Brain Health Trainer. But it is in our own personal interest, and that of our clients, to help break the ageist stereotypes. It is important to open perspectives to the amazing opportunities we have in shaping our life's course, and to start integrating into our programming what we have learned through technical advancements and novel scientific insights about who we are, what affects our health, and how we can optimize our aging process. When we help our clients reimagine aging, we help them lead more vibrant, active, and joyful lives.

Marion Recktenwald

Marion Recktenwald, PhD, is a researcher, educator, and aging transformation specialist for body and brain with over 15 years of experience.

Marion's mission is to change the current picture of aging and help clients thrive through the ages in their best version possible, no matter their genetic predisposition. By sharing years of deep research, theoretical knowledge, and practical experience, she has helped hundreds of clients optimize their health, prevent premature aging, slow chronic disease of body and brain, and add good years to life.

Marion somewhat involuntarily slipped into her health and wellness career when faced with Lyme disease, celiac disease, and fibromyalgia. She started by pursuing certifications as a personal trainer (National Academy of Sports Medicine), group fitness instructor (Athletics and Fitness Association of America), functional aging specialist (Functional Aging Institute), aqua instructor (Yet Wet), and Zumba instructor.

As fate struck again with Marion's father, aunt, and mother being diagnosed with vascular dementia, Alzheimer's, and Parkinson's, Marion became the Dementia Detective® in theory and practice. She expanded her knowledge and skillset by pursuing certifications as brain health trainer (Functional Aging Institute); PWR!Moves® instructor & PT (PWR!® Parkinson Wellness Recovery); Ageless Grace® educator (Ageless Grace®); distinguished *tai-chi* instructor (Open the Door to *Tai Chi*); and AFA partner in care (Alzheimer's Foundation of America).

Marion's programs offer personalized cognitively enhanced and holistic approaches, which consider that our health and aging are being shaped by dynamic interfacing of our body, mind, brain, and microbiome.

Website: agewithjoy.com
FB: www.facebook.com/AgeWithJoy/?ref=pages_you_manage
TT: twitter.com/agewithjoy
LI: https://www.linkedin.com/in/marionrecktenwald/

CHAPTER 24

Tattered Capes Can Still Fly

By Catherine L. Owens

When you hear the words "fitness," "active lifestyle," or "healthy choices," what comes to mind? For many of us, myself included, our initial thoughts go to someone who is physically fit, with low body fat and lean, sculpted muscles. A person who is consistently engaged in exercise programs and eating a health-conscious diet. How many of us have thought this is what defines and encompasses what health and wellness is?

What if, instead of letting your mind go to the "picture of perfect health" we have been taught to think of, you let your mind go to a picture of what your ideal healthy lifestyle and overall wellness looks like. What are a few simple choices and commitments you can make for yourself today that will help start you down the path of better health, wellness, and overall quality of life.

Health and wellness are not only defined by lean, sculpted bodies, eating a health-conscious diet, being young and in your prime, with no physical limitations or health conditions. The reality is one's overal health and wellness is often determined by many different lifestyle choices that encompass all areas of our lives. We tend to be a reactionary society that waits until there is a concern in our health to start making lifestyle choices that focus on our health and wellness. An example of this is waiting until you have concerns with the health of your heart to start exercising and eating a heart-healthy diet, as opposed to taking a proactive approach in doing the things you can, such as exercise, reducing stress, and healthy eating to help prevent the possibility of heart disease. This chapter is about shifting your mindset and preconceived idea of what you have believed health and wellness should look like, and what limits you from achieving it, to a mindset and belief that you can take control and make choices to live a healthier lifestyle that encompasses all aspects of overall wellness.

In my professional career I have been fortunate to work closely with older adults within the senior living industry. The most common fear clients share is the fear of "getting older" because of the idea that a decline in physical and cognitive ability, loss of independence, the inability to care for oneself, or continue living the lifestyle they enjoy, is a direct result of "getting old." A common question I am asked is, "At what age will I no longer be able to care for myself?" They are surprised when I tell them age can be irrelevant. Health, wellness, and quality of life, at any age, is often directly related to lifestyle choices a person makes, good and bad, and how those lifestyle choices impact their ability to maintain and enjoy a healthy, active lifestyle.

Years ago, I had the pleasure of befriending Margie, a sassy 103-year-old who walked three miles every day, was conscientious about eating a nutritious diet, and other than a little arthritis, was in great health. Margie was still living in her own home, active in her church community, and enjoyed playing bridge and other social activities with her friends. On one occasion she shared with me the tremendous grief she struggled with for her daughter, whom she had recently lost, and her two sons who were living in care communities due to failing health brought on by a lifetime of not focusing on health and well-being. During one of our visits, she asked me, "Why am I outliving my children? It doesn't seem right or fair that my quality of life is so much better than theirs."

In contrast to Margie, I have worked with clients in their 50s and 60s, who like Margie's adult children, were in poor health and had significant medical concerns because of unhealthy lifestyle choices and were experiencing those fears we tend to associate with "Aging Adults."

A decline of physical and cognitive abilities, loss of independence and ability to care for oneself, and the opportunity to continue living a lifestyle we enjoy.

A long-term study by the MacArthur Foundation found that 70 percent of physical aging and approximately 50 percent of mental aging is determined by lifestyle choices we make every day. Imagine the positive impact it could have in your life if you were to shift your mindset from focusing on the fears we have associated with "growing older," to a mindset of incorporating lifestyle choices that enable you to better control and determine how well you age.

There are six key dimensions of wellness as defined by Dr. Bill Hetler, NIW:

- *Emotional:* Showing awareness and acceptance of your feelings, as well as the ability to express them in a healthy way. This includes how positively you feel about yourself and your life, the ability to manage your feelings, coping with stress and realistically assessing your limitations.

- *Physical:* Understanding your body and its relationship to nutrition and physical activity. As you might expect, it involves eating well, and building strength, flexibility, and endurance in safe ways. But it's also about taking responsibility for your health, paying attention to your body's warning signs and seeking medical help when necessary.

- **Intellectual:** Expanding your knowledge and skills through creative, stimulating mental activities. Think about ways you pursue personal interests, develop your intellectual curiosity, stay on top of current issues and ideas, and challenge yourself.

- **Occupational:** Contributing your unique skills and gifts to work that is rewarding and meaningful to you. It can mean working at a job, but it also means developing new skills, volunteering, mentoring, teaching, or coaching others.

- **Spiritual:** Recognizing the search for meaning and purpose, developing an appreciation for life and the world around you, and letting your actions become more consistent with your values and beliefs. Some people follow specific religious practices, while others lean toward a more general pursuit of harmony and self-awareness.

- **Social:** Contributing to your community and environment and recognizing the interdependence of people and nature. This is about making choices to build better personal relationships, a better living space and a better community.

There is no one-size-fits-all for these dimensions of wellness. What one person does to stay physically active and engaged will be completely different from another, due to preference and/or abilities. Spiritual practice will vary greatly for everyone. For some it may be religious practices, meditation, volunteering, or simply enjoying nature. One or more of the dimensions may be easier to focus on than others, simply because of what you enjoy.

The National Institute of Wellness (NIW) puts it this way: "Wellness is an active process through which people become aware of, and make choices toward, a more successful existence."

How you define each dimension may change at different stages of your life. There may be things out of your control, such as physical limitations, medical concerns and conditions, environmental and social factors, and many other things we let ourselves define as limitations or reasons to not live a more active, healthier, and fuller life. And there are always things in your control that you can choose to do to start living a healthier, more active, and better quality of life. Start where YOU are. Start making lifestyle choices that support your overall health and wellness.

One of the most memorable opportunities I have had in my life was the opportunity to volunteer at MDA Summer Camp. This week, held every year for children living with Muscular Dystrophy, was a chance for them to enjoy activities that can often be difficult without the physical support of others. I didn't really know what to expect when I signed up to volunteer, as I had never personally known anyone impacted by or living with it. One thing I was not expecting was the incredible and infectious positive attitude these children continually shared. The children were ages 5-17, and their physical abilities, complications, and limitations caused by Muscular Dystrophy varied greatly from one another depending on the type and stage of progression. Regardless of so many differences among the children, there was always one clear and consistent theme. Instead of focusing on what they *couldn't do* because of their physical limitations, they always focused on what they *could do*, all while knowing that what they could do would change as the disease progressed.

One activity the children enjoyed was playing soccer. Soccer, for the children who could still walk and run, consisted of kicking and chasing a soccer ball on a field of grass, while soccer for the children who had significantly more physical limitations often consisted of pushing and chasing a large rubber exercise ball around a basketball court in their wheelchair. To the children, it didn't matter if they were kicking a soccer ball with their feet on the grass or pushing an exercise ball with their wheelchair on a basketball court. All that mattered was spending the afternoon having fun playing soccer with their friends. Along with teaching me that you can, in fact, play soccer and do the chicken dance in a wheelchair, more importantly, they taught me an incredibly valuable lesson I have been reminded of and had to learn to practice myself as I have been faced with life-changing events and medical diagnoses: to focus on what you *can do* instead of what you *can't do*, to start where you are, even if it is a different starting point from where you were before.

It sounds simple, and yet it can be a hard mindset to maintain when you find yourself faced with challenges and changes in your circumstance and capabilities. I have always been athletic, participated in all types of sports, and was someone who was not only physically active, but I would push myself to continually improve on my performance. Since I was a young girl, I would say, "When I grow up, I want to be Wonder Woman," and always had the shiny red cape somewhere close by. In my mind, she was a strong woman who could do anything. And like her, I wanted to be a strong girl who could do anything. Many would say I was competitive, and the truth is, I was and still am, mostly with myself and the desire to continually strive to do better – sometimes with a misguided belief of what "better" was.

An example of this was when I was on the track team in high school, and my favorite event to race in was the mile. It wasn't that I particularly enjoyed running. It was more to do with it being easy for me, usually placing first in my event. When I was running track, I had the opposite mindset of the children I would later work with at MDA Summer Camp. I would tend to focus on what I couldn't or didn't do. I remember one race when I placed third, which again, was unusual for me, yet I had increased my personal best time by 10 seconds, completing the race with a time of 5:02. Instead of being excited that I just ran a 5:02 mile and setting a new personal best, all I cared about was not breaking the five-minute mark, and not placing first.

Many years later, and a few years after spending time with those incredible children at MDA Summer Camp, I was diagnosed with a rare lung disease that would completely change my physical capabilities. To go from someone who had always pushed themselves physically, to having difficulty just walking up a flight of stairs without being completely short of breath, was a difficult adjustment. If there was ever a time to shift my mindset to being grateful for what I could do, instead of what I couldn't do, that was it. I would soon come to realize and appreciate that although I wasn't running five-minute miles, I still had the ability to stay physically active, even if it looked a little different. The shiny red cape, although a little tattered, could still fly.

When what you can do changes, regardless of what dimension of wellness it is, remember to start where you are, doing what you can to continue making healthy lifestyle choices that will help you maintain your health, wellness, and quality of life to the best of your ability. It may not look like the picture of health you once knew or enjoyed. The important thing is to start picturing what your healthiest self looks like physically, spiritually, intellectually, occupationally, socially, and emotionally in your current stage of your life. Then ask yourself, "What are simple things I can do today to start working toward that picture of health?"

When you are mindful of areas you are doing well and recognize areas you may have opportunities to improve and incorporate lifestyle choices that encompass overall health and wellness, you will have the greatest opportunity to continue living and maintaining a healthy, active, quality life at any age.

Sources:

- *National Institute of Wellness*
- *Successful Aging. John W. Rowe, M.D., & Robert L. Kahn, Ph.D., Dell Publishing, 1998.*

Catherine L. Owens

Catherine L. Owens is the Owner of CLO Consulting and Internationally Award-winning Author of the books *Be Your Own Hero: Senior Living Decisions Simplified* and *Shine On You Crazy Diamond: Even When Your Crown Feels Heavy.*

Catherine is a nationally recognized Senior Living Industry and Aging Well expert who has worked in various roles within the industry including:

Individual, family, and professional consulting, staff training and development, sales and marketing, corporate development and advisory, and community education.

Catherine has been published and featured in national industry journals, is a regular guest on local and national radio shows and speaks to audiences across the country about understanding and navigating senior living decisions.

Catherine is a 2017 recipient of the Tribute to Women and Industry (TWIN) Award which honors women who have excelled in their field and made significant contributions to their industry.

Catherine loves spending time with her family and enjoys kayaking, golfing, and photography.

Website: https://www.catherinelowens.com
LinkedIn: https://www.linkedin.com/in/catherine-l-owens-8ab3778/
Facebook: @catherine.owens.1422
Instagram: @catlowens72

CHAPTER 25

The Power of "Cultural Norms"

By Esta McIntyre

*Might there be a fountain of youth? For it to be so, we must first believe
and act as if it exists. Then we must dive into science and
explore the lives of those who've gone before us.*

Mom was 88 years young when she moved from Florida to California.
Technically she was my mother-in-law, but if I didn't call her "mom,"
she scolded me and let me know that I was her daughter. She would
hear nothing of the term "daughter-in-law." As our family's last surviving
parent, she had been in my life for 50 years. Mom lived through the
aftermath of the worldwide influenza epidemic that killed nearly 20
million people, 500,000 in the U.S. alone. She had weathered the likes
of the Asian Flu, World War II, and the Korean and Vietnam wars, and
had lived through 17 American presidents. Her advice to me when the
COVID-19 epidemic arrived was to keep going. "Stay healthy and it
will pass," she said. I wholeheartedly believed her. After all, she had lived
through numerous tragedies, as did her family and most everyone she
knew. In hindsight, I wish she had taken her own advice.

As the reality of COVID-19 unfolded, we heard rumblings that there was to be a "safer at home" order. I wondered what that could mean, and stayed glued to the news like most small business entrepreneurs. For the past 13 years, my husband and I had owned and operated a successful fitness establishment serving a demographic aged 50 years and older, and we began to fear the impact the pandemic and its associated restrictions would have on our clientele and our livelihood.

On the afternoon of March 19, 2020, our fears were realized. As of midnight, we were told to stay home. Our beloved fitness studio was to be closed beginning the next day, and no one knew for sure exactly how long that would last, although we were told at the time it would take two weeks to "flatten the curve." We knew we had to think fast, so we called every member and instructed them to drive to the studio with the largest vehicle they had. We sent them home with trampolines, balls, bands, weights, and everything that was not nailed down. The very next day we were streaming live Zoom classes. At first it was a hot mess, but we were doing what was necessary to survive. We were determined to continue serving those who had put faith in us, and we dedicated ourselves to the mission of staying healthy and helping others do the same.

Control is one of life's complicated illusions. We think we are capable of manipulating our circumstances. It's only when we learn that our capacity to survive is dependent upon our ability to stay creative, that the solutions to success beyond measure are revealed.

In order to provide solutions for our community to keep moving, creativity was key. We played Wine and Cheese Bingo where we had to act out what was in the winning boxes, with the free square in the center directing players to yell "Set Me Free" at the top of their lungs. We had over 30 participants, and they were all good sports. We figured we all needed a rest, and playing bingo together was a way to inject some fun into a harrowing circumstance.

We were allowed to reopen, but two weeks later we were told to close again. At this point I knew that the fitness landscape would be irreparably damaged, especially for "at-risk populations" like the clients with whom I worked. The very life-giving, health-affirming actions and activities that could keep them alive and well were being taken from them. I couldn't just sit back and let that happen.

I knew there had to be a way to reach our population, even if they were fearful, depressed, and stuck at home. With decades of work-centric living behind them, this was a time when they thought they were supposed to be fully enjoying life. That was the "cultural norm" to which they ascribed and the motivation behind a lifetime of hard work. The government and media had now sent them reeling into a world of dread and anxiety most of us had never before experienced. Forget about enjoying the day, life was now consumed with the preoccupation of survival. As health and fitness professionals with an understanding of how the human immune system functions, we wondered how we could spread the critical message that nutrition and movement could literally save their lives.

Like many around the globe, I prayed, paced, researched, and reached out to others in my field. I cried, over-ate, worried, and panicked while trying to figure out what would come next. I knew it had to involve the virtual world and the use of technology, a discipline many older clients were reticent to adopt. We were determined to overcome those objections and apprehensions in our quest to keep everyone moving. I knew that what had started out of necessity on Zoom needed to expand beyond elementary fitness classes.

Fear can be crippling and ducks rarely get in a row. Once you're reasonably sure you're doing something of value, keep moving. If you're panicking, do it anyway. Don't be timid. Just keep putting one foot in front of the other.

I instinctively leaned on the trusted voices in my life that had helped shape my perspectives on the fitness industry. Years before, I had met several individuals who turned out to be life-changing mentors. The first was Todd Durkin. My initial impression was that Todd's organization was not a good fit, as his team loves exercise, and I simply don't. Most of his members were significantly younger than me, yet there was something about Todd's teaching that I found compelling, helping me to overlook the initial contrast between our two worlds. There is something powerful about associating with like-minded professionals, and after joining Todd's team, I quickly learned so much about myself and the fitness industry. My husband, Scott, and I refer to Todd as the epitome of the man depicted in the book *Man of Steel and Velvet* by <u>Aubrey Andelin</u>. He was simultaneously tough, nurturing, and kind.

Through Todd I met Larry Indiviglia and Vito La Fata. Larry is a wise teacher and avid supporter of our fitness studio and personal endeavors. Vito is a bold New Yorker who holds nothing back when he speaks, one of his most appreciated and admirable qualities. His wife (formerly Anna Renderer) was someone I'd known from afar as the face of PopSugar a company whose exercise content and approach to fitness and wellness had always intrigued me. I figured if Vito was married to Anna, he must have something interesting to add to the conversation. As it turned out, this dynamic duo offered ideas that would change the trajectory of my business and provide me with a deeper mission than I ever thought possible. Vito and Anna had a program that taught me how to alter my business model, enhance my brand, and increase exposure beyond my brick-and-mortar business. My prayers had been answered, and the solutions were becoming clear: I would write and deliver a life-changing online course.

Most of the things we worry about never come to pass. It is the small, seemingly insignificant choices we make – the ones we don't think twice about – that result in life-altering lessons. Don't think, just do.

Scott and I visited the La Fata vineyard where we spent days dissecting the "My Health Studio" brand. Who did we wish to serve? What made us different from everyone else doing what we wanted to do? There were many components to consider. We came up with an outline course, and I undertook the task of writing the first module (of what turned out to be 60 modules). I then offered a one-hour free workshop and charged what was then to be half price, $997. I referred to the course as a beta trial where I guaranteed my clients would get the results they desired, called the participants "Founding Members," and gave them lifetime access (without consulting Vito and Anna). In return for that, I solicited input from these initial participants to improve the course and to post positive findings on social media in an effort to recruit future members.

Thirteen women attended the first Zoom workshop, after which they had two choices – they could buy the program or schedule a consulting call with me. Once the workshop was completed, I retired to my sofa and shared with Scott that it was the worst thing I'd ever done. I was sitting next to my phone, and after three "dings" with messages indicating I had $997 (x 3), I panicked. You would think I'd be happy, but instead doubt and panic settled in. I would now need to conceive of, write, record, and deliver 59 additional modules. I decided that since I was going to be at my desk nearly 24/7, I would personally call the rest of the participants, promising them the sun, moon, and stars to ensure they would participate. Of the 15 who initially showed interest, 13 decided to sign up for the course. They knew they were reading and listening as I was crafting, writing, and recording. We all felt that we were on the cusp of something that was more than a mere diet or exercise plan. A new movement was taking shape.

Never underestimate the power of a group of women with like minds. When females act in one accord, they are fierce and more powerful than the fastest Ferrari and stronger than Wonder Woman, Oprah, and Ruth Bader Ginsberg combined.

Fast forward through two beta tests and 20 exceedingly bright, motivated women later, the course was in full swing. What began as a way for Gen X and Boomer women to shed pounds, gain muscle, and muster the courage to grow some additional confidence became an opportunity to challenge old paradigms. We collectively realized that we were consumed with fitting into a mold that generations (and society as a whole) had created for us. Without initially being conscious of it, we realized we were experiencing ageism.

As I began to study this concept, I realized that everything from television and radio advertising to social media outlets depicted any women over 60 as slow, dull, and hard of hearing. Further, I discovered that Millennials hate Baby Boomers and blame them for our earth's terrible environmental dilemmas, while the Boomers view Millennials as entitled and lazy. The fact is, I detest any negative "ism," whether racism, terrorism, alcoholism, or ageism. I have always lived my life thinking I was capable and energetic. However, I had taken a head-in-the-sand approach to aging. Indeed, as I began to focus on my relationships with younger generations, my problem became increasingly clear; I had simply ignored what was right before my eyes. The time had arrived to take back our power!

Age does not kill us. Disease kills us. Does it not make sense then to run like hell when disease is approaching? Longevity research is robust and ongoing. So why are so many of us masking the symptoms instead of proactively searching for ways to stay healthy and well?

I fully acknowledge that there are mental and physical effects that result from getting older. But I also believe that we should not *deny* the aging process, but work with it lovingly and skillfully as our bodies and minds age. The time has come for us to *defy* the molds arising from society and re*define* the ways in which we move forward through life. Television commercials depict 65-year-old women as having gray hair piled in a bun on top of their heads, with caretakers nearby as their eyesight, hearing, balance, strength and memories have faded. This myopic view is outdated bullshit! Getting older is a blessing to be embraced, a reality that can be met with wisdom, bravery, and the willingness to make the best of each precious day.

As a corrective exercise, nutrition, and wellness coach, it occurred to me that even with the plethora of information available, many won't do what we know to be healthy for us, myself included! In my book *Fitness for Women Who Love to Eat and Hate to Move*, I share my deep love of ice cream and shed light on the addictive power of food. While I had convinced myself that my dependence on this creamy decadence wasn't my fault, the evidence was clearly on my hips. As I navigate through the accumulation of years, it becomes increasingly clear that younger bodies are much more forgiving than aging ones. Does that mean those of us over 50 should throw our hands in the air and give up? Hell no! Although aging culture dictates that our aches and pains may simply be due to breakdowns that occur with aging, it isn't always that black and white. Beyond what we see in the mirror and feel in our jeans, there's a tendency to ignore the havoc many of these food obsessions play with blood sugar, gut health, internal inflammation, and overall well-being. There are often ways to combat many of these common maladies and create the conditions for the body to heal. I remain standing, strong, and vital in my older years with the help of my hand-picked team. We could all benefit from a team of supportive and knowledgeable professionals, capable of guiding us in areas of expertise beyond our personal base of information and helping connect the dots of wellness to achieve our best health.

Great Olympians do not win medals alone. They have teams of specialists that assist them with everything from mindset to muscle building. Why not us? Never be afraid to ask for help. No person should ever go through life solo, and that need is magnified as we age.

It became clear while writing and recording the modules for a course about staying young through the aging process that I would need to gather expertise in areas I knew little to nothing about. I solicited contributions from chiropractors, massage therapists, acupuncturists, Ayurvedic medicine specialists, and physical therapists to discuss shedding pounds and overcoming aches and pains. I worked with aestheticians to teach about caring for aging skin, and interviewed travel agents to suggest places in the world one could visit to increase their sense of adventure. With the help of so many knowledgeable voices, we addressed the value of good nutrition, methodological movement, confidence-building, reigniting excitement, and the significance of building that all-important team. As we traversed each topic, we realized we were building a resource arsenal, one that could be made available to "women of a certain age" to help keep them standing, strong, and contributing to society in ways that may not have been possible had they simply succumbed to the societal and cultural norms.

Aging populations are made to believe they no longer have the knowledge and power to viably contribute to society, when the exact opposite is the case. Stand up and be counted, no matter your age. It's time for Gen X'ers and Boomer women to lock arms and serve humanity. Even if you hurt. Never stop. Regain and hold on to your power.

As I interact with women over 50, I hear their needs, desires, and most of all, their fears. It's worth noting how this amazing group views aging, providing reflections and insights that younger generations would be wise to consider. I've gathered that their needs become more basic as they age. They long for good health, happiness, nice people to spend time with, and less drama. In addition, and high on their lists, is sufficient finances, the ability to travel, and a general feeling of simply being needed. When asked to describe the specifics of what they fear, their answers often include fear of:

- Losing their minds (if you have ever witnessed dementia, you will agree)
- Losing their health (and subsequently their independence)
- Being left alone
- Having no money
- Losing opportunities to a younger, less experienced person
- Getting fat
- Being judged, and
- General uncertainty about the future.

It takes a community to overcome fear. If your fear results in panic, it's important to seek assistance from professionals. Learn to employ techniques such as guided breathing, meditation and prayer to assist. With ongoing support from your customized team, the possibilities are endless.

Fear is the very emotion that convinced mom to stop actively participating in life at the age of 88. It was surprising to me, as she had always loved good food, music, and dance, yet she resigned herself to only participating in occasional family events. Her apprehension dictated that she turn down invitations from acquaintances. She communicated that she felt well enough, but was electing to simply take it easy instead, feeling anxiety about falling if she moved too much. She stopped driving because she thought if she were ever in an accident, she was convinced she'd be blamed due to her age, regardless of whether it was actually her fault. Mom lived in an over-55 community where the club house frequently held a variety of events and activities, all within a short walking distance from her doorstep. Also nearby was a gym and a beautifully maintained pool. She never went. She believed society would forgive her for withdrawing, and when COVID-19 hit, that was further reason for her to stay put. After all, she was 88. Since society defined her as old, she saw herself as such, giving herself permission to mentally and physically check out. Her advice to keep moving that she had given to me earlier, was somehow not applied to her situation. Society's views about aging had left her feeling lonely, anxious, and frozen.

When we believe and buy into the trappings of what is deemed "normal" in our society, we risk robbing ourselves and younger generations of the ability to collaboratively stay well and vital, to solve problems, and to learn from one another. I am not judging those who choose to live in 55- and-over communities, but I have elected not to live in this type of arrangement. I appreciate the availability of health-enhancing activities that these communities work to provide, but for me there is a lack of life diversity and, honestly, too much sameness. I cherish being surrounded by young people. The joy of watching kids run for a school bus or chatting with a neighbor 20 or 30 years my junior provides me with perspective I might otherwise not enjoy.

The ability to participate in life should have nothing to do with chronological age. It should have everything to do with one's ability to execute the daily tasks and activities of life in a way that will not harm themselves or others. Whether or not your body behaves as it did when you were young, you can still contribute to society in positive and amazing ways. Do not let age dictate that it's time to stop. This is the way aging populations should live.

Mom lived to be 94, six years after she largely withdrew from society. As I write this chapter, mom has only been gone less than one month, so her life and contributions are fresh in my mind. I accept that death is part of life, yet watching someone die a little more each day can be a gut-wrenching experience, especially when you believe in your heart that their quality of life can be potentially improved by remaining engaged. In the years between 88 and 94, mom's decline was obvious and steady. Both her balance and her eyesight worsened. Her stamina, flexibility, and strength deteriorated in front of our eyes. She hated what was happening to her, yet never associated it with her decision to stop doing what she loved most, living life.

If you have clients who are over 50 years old, implore them to step up and take back their power. Remember that aging does not kill you but disease does. Encourage them to establish a team who will support them in employing proper nutrition, exercise, and healthy living so they can be their best self at any age. We mustn't allow the media, our families, or any other well-meaning human to influence our progress or convince us we're too old to participate in our own health and well-being. It's time to lock arms with those of like mind and move forward with power and dignity. It's never too late!

Break some rules. The rules keep changing anyway. Aging is not for sissies, so seek help and never, ever give up.

Esta McIntyre

Esta McIntyre is a 66-years-young top-rated health coach, author of the best-selling book *Fitness for Women Who Love to Eat and Hate to Move*, and trusted aging expert known for creating the breakthrough "age-defying" mentorship, *BoomerGenX*, and *Flourish After 50*.

Esta is dedicated to helping ambitious women over 50 live healthier longer by guiding them down a personalized path to aging better.

Her one-of-a-kind approach blends science, wit, and support to get women active, inspired, and excited, so their later years are their best years.

Esta has spent the last 15+ years escorting her clients through the maze of ever-changing fitness and lifestyle data to find what works for them. She received her training from the National Academy of Sports Medicine, Precision Nutrition, MedFit, as well as many other respected accredited institutions. Having been raised in New York City, she takes a no-nonsense approach to staying fit and aging with grace. She combines that with lots of humor, caring, and hope. Once you read her book, you'll have a greater understanding of who Esta McIntyre is.

For additional information visit:

www.EstaMcIntyre.com
www.BoomerGenEx.com
www.FlourishAfter50.com
www.MyHealthStudio.com

CHAPTER 26

Bio-Hacking to an Optimal YOU!

By Amber Kivett, ATC, LAT, CSCS, FMS, FMT

WHAT IS "BIO-HACKING"?

According to the Cambridge dictionary, "bio-hacking" is defined as an attempt to improve the condition of your body and mind using technology, drugs, or other chemical substances such as hormones. Bio-hacking can also be defined as finding a way to more efficiently manipulate human biology, including areas of sleep, nutrition, mental health, strength, and recovery. This gives YOU the option of being in control of your body with options for natural remedies and treatment, so consider this as a positive thing! Think of bio-hacking as an empowering concept that allows one to enhance or improve the efficiency of different aspects of health. It means taking ownership of your body and the aging system, so you can be the BEST version of yourself possible.

Healthcare in the United States is manipulated and directed by Big Pharma, commercial insurance providers, healthcare organizations, hospitals, and the government. Any healthcare organization that accepts commercial or third-party insurance for payment of patient services prioritizes treatment options and medications solely created by the standards set forth by Medicare and Medicaid, and evidence-based medicine, which is often skewed and manipulated by the large shareholders funding the research studies.[49] According to the Commonwealth Fund Research Project, the United States has the worst healthcare system overall among 11 high-income countries, even though it spends the highest proportion of its gross domestic product on health care. The U.S. ranks last on access to care, administrative efficiency, equity, and healthcare outcomes, but second on measures of care process.[50] Considering that the current healthcare system is in crisis, it's important to start exploring new options for preventative medicine and treatment options for chronic illness, disease, and pain management outside the traditional recommendations of doctors and other healthcare specialists.

If you explore some of the happiest and healthiest nations in the world, the concept of mental and physical health is more focused on preventative wellness and is much different from that of our toxic capitalist tendencies to maximize profits from sick citizens. These countries offer solutions that are ancient dating back hundreds of years ago to the Ice Age. You'll find there are many natural therapies that have the ability to correct and cure the root cause of virtually ALL diseases and conditions known to mankind. Many of these natural therapies are available to perform at home, in a clinic, in a gym, or a wellness center, and have minimal, if any, side effects.

BIO-HACKING IN EUROPEAN COUNTRIES

In Turkey, they use Turkish baths to enhance spiritual and religious purification, focusing on cleansing and purifying the mind, body, and

---

49 Brezis M. Big pharma and health care: unsolvable conflict of interests between private enterprise and public health. Isr J Psychiatry Relat Sci. 2008;45(2):83-9; discussion 90-4. PMID: 18982834.
50 Eric C. Schneider et al., Mirror, Mirror 2021 — Reflecting Poorly: Health Care in the U.S. Compared to Other High-Income Countries (Commonwealth Fund, Aug. 2021). https://doi.org/10.26099/01dv-h208

spirit. The detox process involves saunas, exfoliation, steam, and cold-water showers to eliminate bacteria and encourage a deep, invigorating cleanse. Like many practices, it's important to heal and recharge the mind, body, and spirit full circle, while providing a calming, serene environment to facilitate relaxation, stress relief, and improving blood flow.

Greek medicine, also known as Hippocratic medicine, dates back to the Ice Age as a way to cure the root cause of the disease, rather than the illness itself. Hippocrates, known as the "Father of Medicine"[51] is said to be the most notable Greek figure in ancient medicine, dating back to 700 B.C.E., and has influenced medicine as many still know and practice today. He created the concept of "a healthy mind in a healthy body," and used practical, natural solutions to heal the mind and body. Similar to traditional Chinese medicine, there is an emphasis on the five elements fire, earth, water, air, and space, and correlating that to humors of bile, phlegm, blood, and organs. In reviewing the true history of traditional Chinese medicine, there is speculation that much of Chinese medicine is an adaptation of Greek medicine.[52] Alexander the Great built a massive empire in Greece and expanded his influence into the Middle East, building the city of Alexandria in Egypt as a gathering place for learning and education in Greek methodologies and medicine. In modern, alternative medicine, there are many forms of therapy that are historically documented with evidence in Greece and Egypt dating back to 3400 B.C., including acupuncture, cupping, and vibration therapies to create a balanced flow of *qi* (pronounced "chee") within the body.

In Finland, saunas are a way of life and are known for easing sore muscles, improving blood circulation, relaxing the mind and lowering

51   Kleisiaris CF, Sfakianakis C, Papathanasiou IV. Health care practices in ancient Greece: The Hippocratic ideal. J Med Ethics Hist Med. 2014 Mar 15;7:6. PMID: 25512827.

52   Prioreschi P. *A History of Medicine* Omaha, NE: Horatius Press 2 1996 176, 514.

stress hormones, decreasing systemic inflammation, and detoxing the body of impurities.

Italians refer to a philosophy known as *il dolce far niente*, which means "the sweetness of doing nothing." The idea is to find pleasure and calmness when you slow down and remove distractions, and appreciate the simplicity of being present in the moment. Life in the digital world as we know it today is very toxic mentally and physically, and presents many barriers to enjoying happiness in everyday living.

Perhaps you would crave a forest bath in Switzerland? Forest bathing originated as a term in the 1980s by the Japanese, and involves spending time outdoors in nature to soak up the natural sunlight and exchange ionic energy stored in natural landscapes. The purpose is to offer an eco-antidote to tech-boom burnout and to inspire people to consciously connect with and protect the country's forests. You can expect to smell and breathe natural aromas from airborne essential oils stemming from native plants and trees that provide a natural immunity boost. You can immerse yourself into the awes of wonder, visualizing the textures and details of your surroundings, while listening to the soothing sounds of living creatures and water sources that calm the mind and spirit.

ANTI-AGING, BIO-HACKING, AND FASCIA

After reviewing many types of therapies that are part of everyday life in happy, healthy, and wealthy European communities, let's revisit how it relates to modern-day America and what bio-hacking options are available to you! Bio-hacking has the power to eliminate pain from an injury or auto-immune disease, boost brain function, improve athletic performance, reduce anxiety and/or ADHD, and rejuvenate your mind, body, and spirit to a "younger" version of you as you age forward. Each year, as you blow out the candles on a birthday cake or you engage in new opportunities in your life, one thing is definitely happening…you are getting older, and at some point, your body will start to show it with aging, sagging skin, wrinkles, tension, pain, stiffness, lack of sex drive, brain fog, and a body running on a low battery of energy. What if you could recharge your body and slow down or reverse the effects of aging?

If regaining youthfulness is the sweetest luxury, anti-aging bio-hacking is the best currency to buy it.

The secret to anti-aging bio-hacking is consistency and patience! Remember, bio-hacking for anti-aging outcomes is a scientific method that is dependent on each person as an individual, and no two human beings are the same! When it comes to each person, the fascia, which is made up of elastin and collagen, is the governing system of the human body. Fascia gives the body freedom of movement, freedom from pain, and freedom to live life at optimal levels. If you can figure out how to pamper your fascia by "hacking" into the elaborate sensory-rich system to repair it, then you can manage your entire body! As we age, our fascia carries more tension and toxicity, and transmits ten times more pain than that of any nerve or muscle in the human body. There are several things that destroy fascia. At the top of the list include taking medications and supplements, electing for any surgery, moving too much in a dominant movement pattern, lack of movement as a whole, dehydration, foreign chemicals in the body, and excess levels of stress. Every single living cellular structure in the human body is covered by or surrounded by fascia. The older we get, the harder it is to manipulate and revitalize it. Nonetheless, there are therapies and ways to "pamper" your fascia to a newer, younger YOU! Nutrition is the center of all recovery, but we will leave that for a book in itself!

MEDITATION, GRATITUDE, AND MINDFULNESS

One of the greatest secrets to staying young is reducing stress and clearing the mind! As you have learned, most therapies in European cultures involve calming the mind, reducing stress, and recharging the body regularly. The modern-day digital world stimulates our brain to work harder, and induces more stress hormones and brain remapping. It requires our body to remain in the sympathetic nervous system much longer than what the human body was created for! If you aren't able to seek balance between the sympathetic and parasympathetic nervous systems, then your body becomes more inflamed, leaving a much higher concentration of stress hormones and fatigue. Do you wonder why anxiety and ADHD are much more common now than ever before... why mental health is such an epidemic right now? A simple way to clear your mind and recharge your "happy hormones" while lowering your stress hormones is to journal, meditate, or relax with quiet time. Whether it's the first moment in your morning, mid-day, or before you go to bed, simply take out a piece of paper and write down words and phrases, draw pictures, or just put down what resonates with you at that moment. I like to perform this task at night when enjoying a BEDGASM!

BEDGASM: OK…it's not what you might be thinking!!! Bedgasm is described as the euphoric feeling that you experience when you climb into bed at the end of a long day and wonder how you made it through the day as you remember it. It's truly a miracle every day that you get to experience a Bedgasm!

ACTION PLAN: You can start with answering any or all of the following questions:

1. What is the funniest thing you witnessed today?
2. What acts of kindness did you do, experience yourself, or see today in others?
3. What are three things you are grateful for today?…think simple.
4. What do you need to do better tomorrow?
5. What didn't go right today, and how does it affect me?

6. What is something I've learned today?

7. My FAVORITE moment of today is...

8. Tomorrow I'm looking forward to...

9. What did you do today that makes you happy?

10. What excites you when you think about it?

BLOOD FLOW RESTRICTION BANDS TRAINING

Blood-flow restriction (BFR) training involves using a band, similar to a tourniquet, or a blood pressure cuff on your arms and legs, to partially restrict blood flow while working out. By limiting the blood flow during the workout, you can work out at a higher intensity with less stress or resistance on the limb but still benefit from muscle growth, testosterone and growth hormone release, nitric oxide release, and a wide range of health benefits in as little as 10 minutes a day. The goal is to apply enough pressure to completely restrict the venous blood flow, which is blood leaving the muscle, while allowing arterial blood flow, which is blood going into the muscle. When done correctly, blood ends up pooling in the muscle beyond the cuff/band, creating a hypoxic environment in which the tissue is deprived of oxygen. This lack of oxygen is said to increase growth hormones, muscle hypertrophy, and muscle strength.

Hypoxic training is not a new trend. If you've ever heard of someone training at altitude for a competition or race, the principle behind BFR is very similar in that the body is forced to compensate due to the lack of oxygen. The biggest benefit of BFR is that muscle gains can be attained without the stress of high loads of weight or resistance on the joints and keeps inflammatory levels and stress hormones to a minimum. Simple, low-load exercises can produce a muscle burn similar to traditional heavier weight training. With traditional exercise, you need to lift 70-85 percent of your one repetition maximum to achieve increased strength or muscle growth. With BFR, we can produce similar results at only 20-35 percent of the one-rep max. BFR technology was established in Japan over 40 years ago, and has been used by medical professionals, professional athletes, and therapists for several decades. In the last few years, new innovative equipment has evolved making this type of training much cheaper and accessible not only for the medical community but also for consumers at home. There are now BFR bands available for safe use at home without medical supervision, making it possible and more cost-effective for people to experience incredible results at home, more often, with minimal effort! Research proves profound changes in weight management, more accelerated recovery post-surgery, reduction in chronic pain, hyper-athletic development, and human performance with less training, reverses osteoporosis, improves the symptoms of auto-immune diseases, diabetes, lymphedema, chronic disease, hypertension, reduces anxiety and depression, increases energy and metabolism, and has the power to reverse and slow the aging process!

ACTION PLAN: To learn more about the studies, the methods, and the results for BFR training, or to order a set of the safest BFR bands for home use on the market, use the link below for more information. https://amberk.b3sciences.com

GROUNDING, ALSO KNOWN AS BAREFOOT TRAINING

Barefoot training and/or grounding is referred to as "earthing," which is walking barefoot in contact with the earth, including grass, sand, or dirt. An eight-week study showed improved benefits in sleep habits, lowered cortisol stress hormones, decreased chronic inflammation, decreased anxiety, and improved wound healing.[53] The human body has several

---

53   Oschman JL, Chevalier G, Brown R. The effects of grounding (earthing) on inflammation, the immune response, wound healing, and prevention and treatment of chronic inflammatory and autoimmune diseases. *J Inflamm Res.* 2015;8:83-96. Published 2015 Mar 24. doi:10.2147/JIR.S69656

electrical components, and the earth is an electricity-rich environment. When your skin makes contact with the earth, there is a transfer of energy correcting polarity balances throughout the body. Eighty percent of the neuroreceptors that provide your brain with feedback on the body's awareness in space only exist on the skin on the bottom of your feet. When you provide enrichment by walking barefoot on earth's surfaces, the brain "rewires" to enhance overall movement and emotional relief. There are 29 muscles and over 100 ligaments in the feet, and 25 percent of the bones in the human body are located in the feet. If you can strengthen and enhance your feet, your overall foundation and bodily alignment improve, as does your vitality and quality of life!

ACTION PLAN: Simply sit, stand, or walk with your bare feet on the grass, dirt, or concrete outside for at least 15 minutes a day. If you can't go outside, check out NABOSO grounding mats made for indoors at <u>www.barefootstrong.com</u>.

WHOLE-BODY VIBRATION PLATFORMS

In the world of proprioception and neurosensory facilitation, whole-body vibration (WBV) is one of the best-kept secrets for bio-hacking into the nervous system and the fascia! The idea of using vibration dates back to the ancient Greeks, but the technology was discovered by scientists working on the Russian Space Station in the early 1980s to keep bodyweight and muscle tone on astronauts in space. It is also believed that Russian Olympic athletes used WBV for performance enhancement techniques in the 1980s before the United States started adopting the science with NASA. WBV comes in many forms, including lateral, linear, oscillation, and pulsation vibration, and is experienced most often barefoot while standing on a platform. The vibration enters through the feet and stimulates up to 90 percent of the body's muscle fibers to contract and relax 10-50 times per second involuntarily, which serves a plethora of benefits including weight loss; increased blood flow; cellular reproduction; cellulite reduction, improved fat metabolism; greater levels of detox through the skin and organs; improved lymphatic dynamics; increased muscle tone and hypertrophy; decreased anxiety; decreased stress hormones; increased release of the hormones dopamine, oxytocin, serotonin, and endorphins; decreased pain levels; decreased inflammation; and much more. For those with osteoporosis and low bone density, just 15 minutes per day on the platform produces favorable results in a short time. A recent research study showed a significant improvement in the gut microbiome by 17-fold and lowered inflammation. Another recent study proved that WBV could reverse the symptoms of type 2 diabetes, lowering blood glucose levels and improving symptoms, including insulin regulation, frequent urination, and excessive thirst. Research has also proven recently that vibration platforms provide a long-term habitual treatment option for pain reduction in auto-immune diseases, including fibromyalgia, MS, Crohn's disease, diabetic peripheral neuropathy, osteoporosis, and other painful conditions.[54] You can spend as little as $150 or as much as $25,000, but ALL platforms will provide a therapeutic, cellular benefit, regardless of the price.

ACTION PLAN: Once you buy a WBV platform to use at home, simply stand on it for 10-30 minutes per day and experience your body change INSTANTLY each time you use it.

To order a LifePro WBV platform at a discounted price, use the following link and the discount code "AMBER10." The Rumblex Series is the most favored for quick, optimal results! http://lifeprofitness.com/ amber

---

54   Newhart S, Pearson A, Salas E, Jones C, Hulla R, Gatchel R. Whole Body Vibration: Potential Benefits in the Management of Pain and Physical Function. Pract Pain Manag. 2019;19(1).

You can try one of these 21-Day Challenges to get comfortable with your platform. https://www.youtube.com/playlist?list=PLekNZxPduqdcczAeLtwEqtQU3ZBWVO3kW

LifePro 21-Ways in 21-Days to a Better You. https://youtube.com/playlist?list=PLekNZxPduqdfuZkeZm3AVQQ7RYmA0FgrG

RED LIGHT and INFRARED LIGHT THERAPY

Red light therapy (RLT) and infrared light therapy (ILT) are both forms of phototherapy that deliver energy to cells by applying a range of visible and invisible wavelengths of light. It is an FDA-approved treatment for acne, muscle and joint pain, arthritis, compromised blood flow, stubborn belly fat loss, wound healing, minimizing fine lines and wrinkles, stem cell regeneration, oxygenation of soft tissues, and reversing hair loss. Several other benefits include increasing testosterone production, decreasing anxiety, enhancing brain function, and relieving arthritis. Many medical professionals have described RLT and ILT as the "miracle pill in a bottle" that fixes almost everything, but it's not a pill…it's in the form of light therapy. There are over 50,000 research studies on how RLT and ILT can benefit the human body on a cellular level down to the mitochondria.[55] NASA originally began experimenting with RLT on plant growth in space and then to help heal wounds in astronauts. RLT is thought to work by acting on the "power plant" in your body's cells called mitochondria. With more energy, other cells can do their work more efficiently, such as repairing skin; boosting new cell growth and enhancing skin rejuvenation, collagen, and elastin production; increasing fibroblasts; increasing elasticity in connective tissue and fascia; reducing inflammation; reducing stretch marks, and improving skin infections. RLT comes in many forms including flashlights/torches, masks, helmets, wall panels, beds, domes, belts, and more. Full-spectrum light therapy including, RLT and ILT lighting, is now offered in saunas for residential use. The idea of using light therapy is to expose as much skin as possible to the source, so that you can experience a more "global" response to the body's cells,

---

55   Avci, P., Gupta, A., Sadasivam, M., Vecchio, D., Pam, Z., Pam, N., & Hamblin, M. R. (2013). Low-level laser (light) therapy (LLLT) in skin: stimulating, healing, restoring. *Seminars in cutaneous medicine and surgery, 32*(1), 41–52.

rather than focusing on one small area. However, studies do prove that you can use a smaller device and treat a more concentrated area in just three minutes, three times a day, for three weeks for a 30 percent improvement in cellular health and skin texture.

ACTION PLAN: If you are interested in trying light therapy for the first time, you can try a smaller device using the 3-3-3 rule, which is three minutes per day, three times per day, for three weeks in a concentrated area. You can try a larger device for 10-30 minutes per day to treat a larger percentage of cells in the body for a global health benefit. Consult with your physician or healthcare professional for more guidance, if needed.

If you are interested in buying a reliable home-use red light therapy device, feel free to use the following link and promo code "AMBER10" for a discounted rate today. http://lifeprofitness.com/amber

OTHER FORMS OF BIO-HACKING FOR ANTI-AGING

Although we could write an entire book on bio-hacking for anti-aging benefits, this section is intended to inspire you with some options to do at home for optimal living throughout the year! Sometimes combining several therapies together, or rotating different therapies throughout the year, can facilitate your mind, body, and spirit to transform and manifest to greater levels of performance. Every individual has different needs and therefore might prefer a different approach, but all options are evidence- and research-based and produce profound changes for the greater good of living.

1. Massage gun application (http://lifeprofitness.com/amber)
2. Micro-current electrical stimulation ((https://www.dolphinmps.com/?wpam_id=84)
3. Therapeutic massage
4. Cupping therapy (www.kksmagik.com)

5. Fascial stretching, mobility circuits, and stretching labs

6. Vagal nerve stimulation (https://www.dolphinmps.com/?wpam_id=84)

7. Microneedling and dermarolling

8. Stem cell therapy and platelet-rich plasma (PRP) therapy

9. Infrared PEMF therapy

10. Cryotherapy and cryoplunge tubs

If you are interested in or have questions on how you can use "bio-hacking" or any of these mentioned therapies to benefit your life, please don't hesitate to reach out to www.kksmagik.com or support@kksmagik.com for more information. I'm living in my mid-40s, and I feel better now than ever in my adult life using a combination of all of these therapies.

Amber Kivett, ATC, LAT, CSCS, FMS, FMT

Amber Kivett is an award-winning national presenter recognized by a number of publications, including *Forbes, Popsugar, Prevention, Natural Awakenings, LiveStrong, Healthline, and many others.* She is also a #1 Amazon bestselling co-author of the book Dear Her. She serves as the Head of Health and Wellness and global spokesmodel for LifePro LLC world-class recovery tools. She is also a professional ambassador for B³ BFR Sciences and Dr. Mike DeBord. She has received several endorsements from celebrities, professional athletes, world-class coaches, elite athletes, and the general population globally for her work with Kivett Instant Pain Relief Systems ("KIPRS"). She is often referred to by many as the «Gatekeeper of Dreams," "Magic Hands," and the "Magic Lady." She recently launched her own trademarked brand of "MAGIK" cupping therapy products for consumers and clients to use independently on their own with professional instruction. She has been featured for her expertise on podcasts, including the Todd Durkin *IMPACT Show, Talk Healthy Today* by Lisa Davis, *Stop Chasing Pain* by Perry Nickelston, DC, and

370

many others. Amber has also been featured as a fitness expert on Fox59 News. Amber is a Platinum member of the Todd Durkin Mastermind Team and serves on the health and wellness advisory board for LifePro Fitness LLC. Amber is the recipient of the 2021 Jack LaLanne"Pass It Forward award given by Endless Rope and the Todd Durkin Mastermind Team for the giving and sharing of herself to others for the greater good of improving lives globally. She is also a two-time recipient of the IDEA World Inspirational Medal.

Amber is the founder and president of Kivett Kinetic Solutions LLC, a 4000-square-foot world-class facility located in Monrovia, Indiana. Kivett Kinetic Solutions LLC has been in business since 2008, delivering "MAGIK" to clients by inspiring, motivating, and educating them to become the BEST version of themselves possible in mind, body, and spirit! Kivett Kinetic Solutions LLC offers services in sports medicine, sports performance, fitness/wellness, life coaching, self-defense, and clinical massage/bodywork. Amber accepts referrals from sports medicine and pain management specialists, primary care physicians, chiropractic physicians, podiatrists, dentists, physical therapists, training coaches, and other specialists. Clients travel from near and far to "Experience the MAGIK" from Amber's gift of INSTANT pain relief in just 1-3 visits, with a 90% success rate. Amber suffered from eight spinal injuries, a head injury, fibromyalgia, and several other injuries as a result of a motor vehicle accident in 2005. After winning a two-year battle of learning to walk again and rehabilitating herself back to a functional lifestyle, she began the journey of living each new day with the divine purpose of transforming lives, delivering greatness, mentoring others, and changing the world one person at a time!

Amber graduated from Purdue University with a Bachelor's degree, majoring in athletic training concentration and exercise science in

2002. She is certified in over 20 specialties, including multiple fitness certifications, orthopedic technology, eastern medicine modalities including cupping and acupuncture, speed/agility/strength coaching, BFR training, mechanical vibration technology, instrument-assisted soft tissue manipulation (IASTM or "scraping"), mental coaching, fitness, and large group instruction. She has created her own certification courses in percussion massage gun application techniques and KIPRS (Kivett Instant Pain Relief Systems). Amber serves in leadership as a featured presenter with the National Athletic Trainers' Association (NATA), the Indiana Athletic Trainers' Association (IATA), and the Business of Athletic Training (BoAT) Academy for her expertise as a certified athletic trainer in the private practice sports medicine setting, with the support of several physicians and specialists.

When Amber is not delivering "MAGIK" and inspiring others to be the BEST they can be, she LOVES spending time with her daughter Zoey, her husband, Adam, her dog, Jewel, and her closest family and friends.

"GREATNESS is NOT measured by what we have, but is experienced by what we give and share of ourselves to others. The more you give and share of your gifts to others, the more it comes full circle when you least expect it."
-Amber Kivett

Contact Information

5727 W McClure Road Monrovia, IN 46157
Cell: 317-446-7971
Email: support@kksmagik.com
kivettkineticsolutions@gmail.com
Website: www.kksmagik.com

SOCIAL MEDIA HANDLES

https://www.kksmagik.com/home
https://www.facebook.com/amber.hardinkivett/
https://www.facebook.com/kksmagik/
https://www.instagram.com/kksmagik/
https://twitter.com/kksmagik
https://www.youtube.com/c/AmberKivett
https://www.linkedin.com/in/amber-kivett-3a968568

LOOKING
AHEAD

CHAPTER 27

The Fitness Industry Needs to Keep Moving

By Kelly Young

The full impact of the pandemic on people's lives remains to be seen, but it is clear from my vantage point that there's been a significant shift in priorities, especially regarding health, fitness, and overall happiness. The fitness industry must constantly reinvent itself to meet the demands of savvy consumers, with information at their fingertips and ever-evolving priorities. Unfortunately, many of them have also been burned by industry claims, long-term contracts, and "take-your-money-and-run" style tactics.

The health and fitness industry need to shift its messaging away from the idea of rapid transformation and begin to speak to an overall improvement in feeling good both physically and mentally. Health and wellness are much more than just being fit. It is a sense of general well-being and belonging to a community. There are countless benefits of regular exercise, including increased energy, quality sleep, solid muscles and bones, and reduced risk of chronic disease, but there are also numerous mental health benefits that often get less attention in the fitness industry. As the public discourse on mental wellness expands, the fitness industry must join the conversation to promote the promise it holds for a happier, balanced life. According to a study by the American Osteopathic Association, researchers found working out in a group lowers stress by 26 percent and significantly improves one's quality of life. If fitness professionals and the industry as a whole can coach the benefits of exercise beyond weight loss, students begin to value activity at a higher level and have more motivating factors to keep going.

The future success of our industry rests on our ability to convey the long-term benefits of consistent fitness to customers' whole health – physical and mental. Today's consumers are more focused on feeling better mentally than how they look. Because those motivations are deeper than just improving physical appearance, it may give wellness habits more staying power[56].

This is excellent news for the fitness industry, as consistency is essential to long-term health success. While the benefits of movement are many, people should worry less about the outcome of exercise and more about establishing the routine when getting started. In addition, fitness professionals could do a better job of coaching students about the critical importance of just showing up, and reward them with recognition for doing so. Examples of rewards could be as simple as a status symbol after a certain number of workouts or a shout-out from the trainer or coach after a student has been consistent for a certain period of time. It's all about creating the habit of regular exercise. Jim Ryin says, "Motivation is what gets you started. Habit is what keeps you going."

I believe the key to client consistency is creating adaptable experiments rooted in connection.

---

56   According to the 2022 Wellness Index Fitness Report

Why Connection is Critical

One of the greatest factors in fostering consistency is the power of connection. Humans *need* to feel that we belong, and can suffer greatly when that feeling is absent. The more a student feels a part of things, the more likely they will have long-term success in staying consistent. Feeling like your attendance matters to others is crucial to keeping the fires of motivation stoked. If we are part of a community of people who value exercise and do so consistently, we are much more likely to keep going when life gets hectic, we lose motivation, or other life events need to be tended to.

Only a small percentage of the population is self-motivated enough to work out consistently, independently, and without any external source for coaching and accountability. Over the last 20+ years, I have witnessed the impact community has on someone's likelihood of sticking with an exercise program and ultimately adopting a healthier lifestyle outside the gym. The more members connect with the coaches and each other or participate in special events and activities outside the workouts, the more likely they are to sustain long-term success. These clients also boast the most significant results.

People will do more for others than they will do for themselves, and so if a person knows that their attendance matters or that a friend counts on them to be there, they are more likely to be consistent. The common denominator among our long-term students is that they have a buddy or a group of people they feel connected to when they come to work out. Our culture fosters an environment where students learn each other's names, count reps, and cheer each other on. They share in the experience of coming together to get better. We have traditions such as birthday pushups and team challenges that bring people together in ways outside of traditional exercise.

"One of the things I love about group fitness, outdoor classes, and Inergy Circuits is that there's always something different. We often end up in groups, and I usually get to know someone just a little bit better each time," says Meg Phillips, founding member of Kelly's Bootcamp & Inergy.

Meg agrees that members of group fitness programs are less likely to skip workouts. People will join a workout program because they want to lose weight or get in shape, but what keeps them coming back is feeling like they are a part of something bigger than themselves. We offer an annual winter challenge that is very popular amongst our clients and often produces significant results. We have discovered over the years that although people may gain back some of the body fat that they lose, they retain the connections they made, which seems to have more of an overall significant impact on their health.

"In January of 2014, I joined a bunch of crazy people working out in a frigid, empty parking lot. Despite my water bottle freezing solid, I was hooked on Kelly's Boot Camp! KBC has helped me to achieve many fitness goals and has generated some unexpected outcomes as well. Through KBC, I've been able to donate time, money, and food to charities near and far throughout the year. I taught KBC kid's classes with a science inspired twist. I pushed a Gator up and down a long driveway with my friend Melissa when we couldn't attend class one Saturday morning. Best of all are the relationships I've formed. I feel much more a part of my community now! I love running into Bootcampers in the grocery store and when I'm picking up my kids from school. When my husband started doing Bootcamp in June of 2014, I can honestly say that it brought out the best in our relationship. It was fun having something to talk about other than the kids and work. We now had a common interest that was also good for both of us!" -Client Anne Crimson

Consistency Beyond Connection

Variety is key when the goal is to serve a diverse population and see people through their difficult moments in life. One way the fitness industry can help people be consistent is by offering programming to accommodate students entering at any level or coming back from an injury or illness. If all classes or programs are high-intensity, some students will get discouraged and fall off the wagon when they need to modify. Offering a sampling of exercise options improves adherence and helps to avoid a plateau, injury, and general boredom. It is also helpful to have less intimidating offerings for students who are new to training. Beginners-level classes and programs help to create a more welcoming environment, based on the comforting idea that we all start somewhere and work to build ourselves up over time.

A hybrid model of in-person and virtual training will help students stay consistent, by giving them an accessible option when traveling, home with a sick kid, or too time-crunched to come into the facility. Some students may like the convenience of working at home and will want that as an ongoing option. If a fitness studio or club wants to expand their reach and meet the members' needs, they need to offer high-quality live stream and prerecorded workout options, while making sure to pay attention to the members participating in those choices. The goal of a fitness community is to be a fitness solution for members and provide ample opportunities to help members be successful.

Another element of sustained consistency is that participants need to enjoy some aspect of the experience. Enjoyment might arise from the instructor making them feel good about themselves. Maybe they really like the music being played or the way they feel when they finish. It is highly improbable that people will stick with a program if they do not enjoy some aspect of it. I believe that people need more fun in their life, especially after the unprecedented challenges of the last few years. Fun is critical to resilience, happiness, and mental and physical health.[57]

Our new tagline, "the best part of your day," reminds our members that their workout is something they can and will enjoy. When trying to help people establish the habit of exercise, we ask them to be extremely realistic and give thought to what they like to do and what time they are most likely to show up. We ask that they start with two to three scheduled workout times. When people start our program and come every day, they usually stop altogether within a few months. Starting slow and building upon your success is one of the keys to long-term success.

"Process is infinitely more important than the product. Had you held up a picture of a fitness model the first time we met and suggested that should be my result, I would have become overwhelmed and walked out. Instead, you demonstrated the exercises that would become staples in my workouts. Though I could barely complete those five moves, you assured me that over time I would improve. The real magic is in the learning process. What works for me will be different from what might work for someone else."
- Debbie Weigand (KBC Member)

Accountability as a Gift

We offer accountability programs throughout the year with different levels of participation (some virtual and others in person) to re-energize and excite our members. For example, as a 2020 holiday gift, we delivered a custom-made road map journal to all of our members – to document their weekly wins and set goals during the pandemic. The road map journal is a tangible book to write in that participating students completed during the monthly call. It also included a calendar of our offerings and programs to help members plan ahead. We hosted monthly

---

57   According to Catherine Price, author of "The Power of Fun: How to Feel Alive Again"

coaching calls as part of the gift to connect in a safe space, share struggles, and practice gratitude together. This coaching call was designed to help members stay accountable and schedule a time and place to set and share monthly goals. The writing created clarity, and we were able to problem-solve and workshop some of the common theme struggles. This particular accountability allowed us to connect outside of workouts and proved to be incredibly effective for our community as a whole.

In our workout community, when we notice attendance dropping or certain members mentioning that they're struggling with mindset or feeling stuck, we reach out in different ways to offer help. When their attendance drops, we send an email message stating that we know it is a tough time for many and that people are really struggling. We ask if there's anything we can do to help get them back on track, and suggest they reach out when the need arises for some additional support. It often surprises us the number of people that respond. The check-ins help people get back on track in part because we give them a small, specific suggestion and remind them that the smallest amount of exercise can keep them in the game. In some cases, we have started programs in response to what our members were struggling with at the moment.

For example, in 2022, we created our first year-long program in response to members who wanted support keeping off the weight they had lost during our winter challenge. Every aspect of this program was designed with the needs and wants of our current members in mind. The DW program includes first-of-the-month check-ins (flexibility in times across the first three days of the month), simple text messages with individual coaching, and staying connected on a group-message platform that is engaging and inspiring. We even named the program after a current member who created a prototype for the program the year before.

Member Carol Elliot said this on why she joined the DW program. "Every year, it seems harder and harder to lose weight. I turned 60 this year, and I am soon retiring. I want a new me, and I want to stop losing weight over and over again. I need to figure out what works and stick with it. Being a part of a group, being accountable and seeing the numbers monthly, I hope to gain knowledge and power that will guide my decisions and lead me to a healthier me."

Another member, Meg Brinker, had this to say about why she joined the DW program. "I thrive on connection, and I crave community. I'm cleaning up this year and creating healthy long-term, accountable, measurable, reviewed-often habits. I'm ridding myself of toxins, whether it be in the form of people, habits, or food. Surrounding myself with like-minded people that prioritize health, prioritize balance, and are examples of good happy living is what I need. I also want the monthly check-in and support system. I want to stop saying, 'I'll get healthy when or I'll start when.' With this program I receive a monthly check-in, clarity on where I'm headed, and a reminder that I am in control."

Christina Bartz felt the DW Challenge helped her develop consistency and had this to say. "I think the best way I can speak to this is the current DW Challenge. I'm definitely motivated to complete challenges because it gives me a goal line. With the DW Challenge the goal line is a year out, and check-in points are monthly. This is keeping me focused on the long haul and not getting frustrated when I don't see numbers moving the way I want them to. Instead, I focus on being locked in on small shifts in mindset (discipline vs. motivation), nutrition as a lifestyle vs. short-term restriction, focused workouts vs. coasting through, and just doing 'whatever' fits in for the day. I love these mindset shifts that the year-long DW Challenge is supporting."

Adaptability with Purpose

Being an adaptable and reliable fitness professional builds trust. Trust is absolutely essential, as fitness consumers are often on the defensive when it comes to their ability to stick with a workout program. The fitness professionals who genuinely care about their clients' long-term health, and are able to express that, are going to experience success with their clientele. Connecting in meaningful ways to clients allows you to adapt to their current situation and create programming based on their unique set of needs.

Being adaptable also means incorporating technology that matches your culture. For example, we use MyZone (a fitness tracking device that measures all workouts and individual efforts). MyZone has developed a reward system around consistency. Status is built up over time and drops if you do not earn at least 1,300 effort points for any given month. The level shows up on your tile while you are working out, and we always make a point to give shout-outs to members who level up. Another feature of MyZone is that it allows those working out remotely to have their heart rate show up in real-time during a class. This is a game-changer for participants and coaches.

Kristi McKeag, a virtual participant who lives out of town said, "MyZone has allowed us to participate in MEP (MyZone effort points) challenges and to be held accountable every month! It's easy to put off a workout, but when you are looking at a month as a whole (or a challenge), you want to stay committed and focused."

While making adaptations is essential in the fitness industry, paying attention to what is working and feeding that success is also necessary. When we had to shut down our studio and were limited to 10 people in our outdoor sessions, we wanted our members to continue taking classes that they loved at times they were used to, with the instructors to whom they felt connected. We maintained all of our offerings and went from having two early morning classes to one. We also offered additional classes at the 7 a.m. time slot because that became a popular option with fewer people tied up by commutes or getting ready for work and school. We never looked for ways to cancel. It was all about serving the community and showing our participants how important we considered their workout times. It was paramount for us to let them know we cared and that we *believed* in consistency as the foundation of a healthy lifestyle and fitness routine.

Consistency, connection, and adaptability will be the keys to ensuring people with health-related goals achieve the long-term success they seek. Fitness related businesses will no longer be a place where people simply join, but a place where they belong. Individuals are looking for more than just a workout, and those establishments that can adapt to their needs, connect to their why, and help them value the process as much as their results will thrive. There has never been a greater emphasis on health and well-being, and the pandemic has taught us that people who recognize the need to connect and stay motivated will subsequently see results. I believe that the fitness businesses that cater to mental and physical health demands will appeal to more consumers and have greater staying power. Career satisfaction will be greater than ever as fitness professionals will genuinely help people with all aspects of their health, ensuring a more significant impact for all.

Kelly Young

Kelly Young is a passionate health and fitness professional, entrepreneur, and dedicated leader who values consistent efforts, serving her community, and being on a mission to get stronger both physically and mentally. As a certified personal trainer through the National Academy of Sports Medicine, and with a Master's in Public Health, she has enjoyed a long and rewarding career of helping people make incredible, lifelong transformations. She is the founder of Kelly's Bootcamp & Inergy. Both were voted Best of Northern Virginia for indoor and outdoor training.

Kelly takes her role as a fitness professional very seriously and believes that she has a gift when it comes to bringing out the best in her clients and team of trainers, helping them to see how powerful the benefits of fitness can genuinely be.

She encourages people to think positively while challenging them to push the limits of what they believe is possible – hence her slogan, "Get What You Came For."

CHAPTER 28

The Time is NOW!

By Todd Durkin, MA, CSCS

In 2015, I had an opportunity to become a partner in a brand-new fitness platform called Fitblok. It provided real workouts, live-streaming and on demand, in every field of fitness, worldwide. It was an "open" platform where any trainer who wanted to deliver programs or workouts, could do so. Being able to have personal trainers, group-exercise instructors, yoga instructors, sport-specific coaches, or meditation practitioners offer their workouts "online" allowed people to bring fitness into their homes and allowed "clients/members" to train with trainers from all over the world.

Of course, this happened well before 2020 when the pandemic forced the fitness industry to quickly shift to online workouts in order to serve our clients and keep our businesses running. Now online training is normal, but back in 2015, Fitblok was a new concept. While some say it was "cutting-edge," I would just say it was "before its time." Despite our best intentions and the desire to make it work, we couldn't get enough clients to buy-in to the value of having workouts at their fingertips.

My business partner and I knew its potential, but unfortunately, the world wasn't quite ready for it. After close to 7-figures invested in it and little traction, it failed. It just didn't move the needle...YET. If we had waited a few more years, I truly believe Fitblok would have been an extremely successful endeavor...and I'd be writing this chapter from a hut in Bora Bora. ☺

The point is that timing is important in new ventures. And the "timing" for a lot of new opportunities might be "right" just about now.

I'm sharing this story because innovation in the fitness industry isn't new. People often come up with great ideas. Sometimes they take off, and sometimes they don't.

Just think about this.... although Fitblok never took off on its own, it certainly laid a strong foundation for the platforms that followed, and it opened the door to a new way of thinking about fitness. If Fitblok hadn't revealed the possibilities, I wonder what would have happened when the fitness industry had to pivot so quickly during the pandemic.

We are at a point now where we need to continue to innovate and come up with new ideas. The pandemic and what has followed have left so many people empty, tired, and exhausted. Mental health is being challenged at levels we've never seen before as people are depressed and more "lost" than ever.

Many people seem to be searching for something to help them feel better...but are coming up short in finding happiness, prosperity, and most importantly, FULFILLMENT.

As down as the world seems to be, though, I believe that rock bottom is the perfect foundation to build back up. To help people think, feel, and do better, we need to give them the opposite of "doom and gloom." We need to inundate them with energy, vitality, positivity, optimism, faith, hope, and love! The only cure for darkness is to "be the light!"

How does health and fitness play into that concept?

In *every* way!

The fitness industry offers the tools that everyone needs to feel better. By addressing the mind, body and spirit through training, nutrition, mindset, soulset, and heartset, the fitness industry is the ideal place for people to find what they are searching for. In a world that so desperately needs hope, motivation, and a "getting your mind right" mentality, trainers, coaches, and life transformers have a unique opportunity to step up and be their best as they continue to serve people to be their best.

Of course, there are *a lot* of ways to achieve this and there are *a lot* of ways that "What's Next" in our world is required. I've spent a long time thinking about this and imagining what we need in our industry. Paying attention to where the needs are in the world and thinking about how fitness responds, I've created a list of areas where I think innovation will happen. And this provides OPPORTUNITY for those whose passions, purpose and gifts best align with these ideas.

Before I share that, though, let's first look at what is *not* going to continue to grow going forward.

What's Not...

*Large box gyms that do *not* focus on driving culture, customer relationships, and results. If it's just a big "box gym" with a lot of equipment and little "life," it will soon join the ranks of the dead.

Here's why I think these types of large "box-gym" facilities that don't cater to culture, customer relations, and results will miss the mark in the future...they don't meet people where they are right now. They don't provide stimulation or connection. They don't provide the experience that people are craving. People want to be stimulated in all areas. They want their senses to be awakened so they feel more connection. These types of gyms are not set up to address those needs.

391

However, there are many areas where I think growth can and will happen, and I've created a list of ten categories to share with you. Although this is not intended as an exhaustive list, I believe that many of the shifts and growth areas ahead of us will fall into one of these ten areas:

What's Next...

1. 1-1 Customized Training for "Transformation"

Wait...what? You thought 1-on-1 training was "old-school" and dead? Au contraire!

Because of the depths of despair of many people, I believe that for those coaches and trainers who want to specialize in customized 1-1 training, there is tremendous opportunity to truly help improve people's physical and mental health. The fact that people are "sicker" and more unhealthy than ever before only raises the opportunity to help even more. I believe this training will encompass detailed programs and workouts, nutrition, and have an intense amount of accountability for clients as well.

Now here is the kicker: I believe this can be "live" or "online" but the training-rate needs to be at a premium. It's going to go beyond the current rate of just paying for "1-1 Training." It must incorporate a rate that better reflects the time for the programming, the actual workouts, the accountability that will occur through daily/weekly texts or emails, and the "24-7" ongoing support to pour into a handful of clients.

With this, a trainer does not need to have 30-40 clients to survive or thrive. One may want to work with a handful of 10-15 clients, offer a highly customized experience, and charge them a rate that is about 2-3x what they would invest in "just" training.

Who this is best for:

*Trainers who love 1-1 training, want to offer a higher touch-point experience for their clients, want to make more money, and want to provide an opportunity/experience for their clients to get even better results.

*Clients who have specific health needs, struggle with adherence and motivation, and need increased accountability.

How it can be delivered: Both Live and Online

Timing for this opportunity: NOW!

2. Recovery (on all levels)

Recovery will be one of the greatest areas of growth because people *need* it more than ever! Whether it's hands-on massage therapy, bodywork, stretching, FST, Bullet-Proof Stretching, KKS (Kivett Kinetic Solutions Magik), infrared saunas, cupping, float tanks, soft-tissue work, acupuncture, or other, recovery *is* the name of the game. People need it whether they are working out intensely and need to amplify recovery or are feeling stressed or burned out and need more work on the "parasympathetic" nervous system to activate healing.

I first started proposing "Recovery" latch-ons to brick & mortar studios in 2019. Little did I know that prediction would not only come true, but I believe it's where the greatest opportunity now lies.

At Fitness Quest 10, we have had massage therapy and bodywork services since we opened in 2000, and now our facility, including our lobby, is filled with recovery modalities (many listed below).

Depending on if you choose to incorporate "recovery" modalities into your existing fitness offerings or offer a stand-alone brick & mortar "recovery" model, you might delve into additional modalities such as:

- Infrared saunas (ie. HealthMate)

- Percussive massage guns (i.e. Hypervolt, Theragun, LifePro, or other brands)

- Normatec compression boots and sleeves

- Hyperice Lounge Chairs

- Cryotherapy

- Ice baths

- Nutrition supplements around recovery including everything from glutamine and creatine to BP-157 and Sermorelin. (See www.ToddDurkin.com/Supplements for my complete list of supplements for recovery, healing, and performance.)

Little did I know in 1995 when I went to massage therapy school, or in the year 1999 when I did my graduate thesis work on touch-therapy (*The Physiological and Psychological Effects of Massage Therapy on Stress & Anxiety*), what a role it would play two decades later following a pandemic. But if there is ever a time that touch-therapy, massage, bodywork, and all the aforementioned modalities and services can keep people well, it's right NOW!!!

3. Brick & Mortar Studios Offering a Hybrid of Offerings

Wait, you think I'm crazy? Despite the instability of the economy and rising inflation, if the pandemic taught us one thing…it's that people *need* connection and a community. Many people thrive in going to an actual brick & mortar gym that has great energy, awesome trainers and staff, and a strong community.

While people shifted to "online workouts" during the pandemic (and yes, that still is a trend), many people missed their studios or gyms and the people they worked out with doing pushups, pullups, squats, lunges, kettlebell swings, "Arm Farm" …and even burpees. There is nothing like the soul coming alive as every corpuscle in the body feels the reverberation of great music, smiles, people, high-fives, and even hugs and handshakes!

Who this is best for:

* Anyone who likes or needs to be around people.

* People who feel stuck or in a rut and want to come to "life."

* Those who thrive in small-groups, large-groups, and being around other people.

* People who want more *connection* in life and enjoy being part of a positive community.

Timing for this opportunity: NOW!

Tips & Recommendations:

1. Connection, connection, connection! People need to re-connect. Because of this, keep focus on creating community, and offer programs that help people interact, get to know each other, and have fun.

2. Additionally, if you are a brick & mortar owner, don't be afraid to raise your rates. In order to retain or attract quality staff, you need to pay them a competitive wage. In order to offer "first-class" programming and world-class experiences, it takes increased revenue.

   Note: Many people don't raise rates in fear of the clients won't pay your rates. If you don't make a profit, you don't have a business. If you don't have a business, you can't change lives.

4. Technology & Apps

Technology has impacted us greatly in the last few years. To think about where we were even three years ago and the companies that have popped out of nowhere and have achieved astronomical growth is mind-blowing. Think about businesses like Peleton, Zoom, Bridge Athletics, Hyperice, Whoop Bands, Oura Rings, Myzone, and even Fitblok. (Oh shoot, I forgot that failed. Darned!)

Who this is best for:

* Trainers, coaches, or instructors looking to scale their message or program.

What could you do to leverage technology?

- Create a program(s) that encapsulates your best skill sets, put it on a technology platform to stream, and market it to the avatar you would like to target.

- Become an affiliate to existing technology platforms that your clients/members could benefit from.

- Create a technology that solves the problem of the consumers you work with as it relates to health, fitness, obesity, sports performance, stress, mindset, biometric tracking, nutrition, or whatever else you are *most* passionate about.

Timing for this opportunity: NOW!

Tips/Mindset:

Think about how you can best use or leverage technology that can help you scale what you do. Or think about how you can create a technology that can help solve your clients' problems.

Assume that if your clients have this problem, there are thousands, if not millions, of people with similar problems. How can *you* be the one to offer the best solution to that problem?

5. Yin Activities

The terms "yin" and "yang" are based in ancient Chinese philosophy, and they explain the duality of life. The concept states that opposing forces can be complimentary and interconnected. Yang is bright, action-taking energy while Yin is softer, more receptive energy.

"Yang" activities consist of things like H.I.I.T training, CrossFit, sprint work or metabolic conditioning.

"Yin" activities consist of practices like yoga, Pilates, F.R.C. (Functional Range Conditioning), ELDOA, tai-chi, meditation, and breathwork.

These practices allow us to slow down and tap into our parasympathetic nervous system. This slows down heart rate, respiration rate, and blood pressure.

In an already "stressed-out" world that demands that we are always "on the go," practicing activities that allow us to tap more into "Yin" energy will help us recover and rejuvenate even more.

The million-dollar question is: How are you doing this? How are you helping your clients balance out all of their Yang practices with more Yin activities?

Who this is best for:

- Anyone who has high stress in their life, their sympathetic nervous system is over-active or runs on adrenaline, and just needs to relax more.
- People with hypertension, anxiety, or who enjoy gentler activities.
- A client who has an orthopedic condition, needs gentler activity, or needs to focus on mobility and flexibility.

What can you do to incorporate more "Yin" activities into your practice, personally and professionally?

- Align and collaborate with a practitioner of one of these disciplines.
- Use an existing app like "Calm", "Headspace", or "Pray" to help you with guided meditation, breathwork, or prayer.

Timing for this opportunity: NOW!

Tips:

If you love "yang" workouts and have predominately used running and lifting weights as part of your program, be sure to incorporate "Yin" activities into your program to maximize results. Your body AND your mind will thank you!

6. Life Coaching

At the beginning of the pandemic in 2020, I offered my first "IMPACT Life Coaching" certification program for trainers. Thirty-seven people were certified in that program which taught coaching skills to those looking to help clients beyond fitness training.

I believe there is a great opportunity right now for life coaches to help people physically, mentally, professionally, relationally, and with their LIFE goals overall. And whether someone gets an **"IMPACT Life Coaching"** certification or any other life-coaching program, the future is bright.

As we grapple with the changes that are happening in the world around us, I believe coaching is a valuable solution. John Zenger in his book, *The Extraordinary Coach,* points out that coaching is about growing and developing people. The focus of coaching is looking toward the future by focusing on performance and growing future capabilities. It is collaborative, action-oriented, and it provides much-needed accountability.

One of the things I hear from fit-pros and trainers is they either get burnt-out on just "training," or they would like additional revenue streams that align with their passion and purpose to be a difference-maker on the planet. Hence, they want to create more IMPACT with their gifts.

My prediction is that we will see more trainers and fit-pros adding "Life Coach" to their resume. This will allow them to grow and scale their businesses, increase revenue, and ultimately help more people be the best version of themselves on ALL levels, personally and professionally.

Who this is best for:

- A trainer who has 7+ years of experience with training and is looking to expand their service or offerings.
- A trainer who has come from a different industry and has some "life wisdom" and experience under their belt in the corporate world.
- A trainer who is burnt-out on training but would love to serve people in a "coaching" capacity in a different way.
- A trainer who wants to scale their IMPACT!

What can you do to incorporate "life-coaching" into your professional offerings?

- Get certified!

Timing for this opportunity: NOW! It often takes 3-12 months to attain a life-coaching certification.

Tips/Resources:

- If you would like more information on "IMPACT Life Coaching," visit www.todddurkin.com to get all the details on the program.

** Note: Mindset coaching?

In my book, *Get Your Mind Right*, I share ten keys to improving your mindset. In fact, I don't just say "Get your mind right," I do my best to live it every day. That's because I understand the power that is housed within the six inches between our ears. I recognize that if we don't have the right mindset, things are not going to work out well. As we've lived through the past few years of uncertainty, and as it continues into the foreseeable future, I know that helping people improve their mindset is a key to changing their life. For that reason, I believe that more and more people will offer ways to address mindset in the health and fitness industry.

I think part of "life-coaching" will be to incorporate "mindset" as well. It's such an important part of living and working today and our mind ultimately helps determine our peace, contentment, happiness, and fulfillment.

** The Power of a Coach

As someone who has created and runs several coaching programs (The Todd Durkin Mastermind for Trainers and Fit-Pros, The God-Sized Dreams Coaching Program, and IMPACT Coaching), I am confident that "coaching" is going to be ever-more-popular in the years to come. The power of coaching is exponential because you can't put a price-tag on the value of having the right coach and mentor in your life. While we all need a coach ourselves, there exists tremendous opportunity to deepen your "coaching" expertise in all areas of life today.

7. Retreats, Events, and Experiential Experiences

In March 2020, the world shut down as we quarantined to prevent the spread of the coronavirus. Ughhh. I get a sense of PTSD just writing that!

For several weeks, and in many cases, months, people all over the world were sequestered in their homes. Virtually everything came to a halt, and people felt very disconnected from each other. The result was that people came to appreciate travel and connection even more. That is why I think experiential experiences are a key component of the future of our industry…and this world. We need it!

People want to travel again.

People want and NEED to connect.

People want to heal and get back to living.

People want to experience LIFE again.

How can you do this?

- **Host retreats.** These can be small and have 8, 12, or 20 people. Or they can be "larger" with even more. Either way, people want their body, mind, and soul nourished during these Retreats. These can be held at exclusive resorts, hotels, or even at your own studio or gym. Craft up something special that fits your soul.

  As someone who has hosted 50+ retreats and attended dozens, I know the value that a "retreat" offers to its participants.

  As someone who has not hosted any major retreats in the last 2.5 years because of the pandemic (until our "THE SHIFT RETREAT" in late October 2022), I can't wait to get going again and lead and be part of more retreat experiences.

- **Host events or challenges.** An "event" can be done to gather your community and celebrate fitness, cuisine/nutrition, and life. Or it can be a fitness-challenge, ranging from medium-intensity to extremely challenging. Some great examples I have seen in the last year alone are DEKA-Fit events, Spartan runs, the Senior Games, the Death Race, The Project, or even the Squire Program, a "rite of passage experience for teenage boys and their dads."

What can you do to incorporate these into your business?

- Attend retreats, live events, and conferences again.
- Lead a retreat or live event at your business or in your community.
- Create an "experience" at your event. This means incorporate workouts, hiking, outdoor activities, and tantalizing challenges that will push you outside your comfort zone.

Timing for this opportunity: NOW!

Tips:

- If you want to host your own event or retreat, "reverse engineer" from when you want to host it. Start with putting a date down of *when* you are going to have it, and then work backwards to execute the logistics.
- Ask your clients what they would love to do and choose ONE to do in the next 6-months.
- Attend a live retreat for your own, and watch how it catapults your own momentum in hosting one.

8. Sports-Specific Training & Youth/Kids Fitness Programs

I almost hate to lump these two together but I am going to for several reasons. The big one is that most of the "sports specific training" I'm talking about involves kids/teens. But not all "youth/kids' fitness" involves sports-training. Let me explain.

Sports-Specific Training:

There has been a trend in the past decade or so to provide more specialized programming for sports. I think this trend is going to continue. As athletes continue to improve, we are going to find more and more specialized training programs designed to help athletes get to the next level.

When you look at the millions of dollars that pro athletes earn and now even the "N.I.L" deals that college athletes can earn beyond their scholarships, we are talking about thousands, hundreds of thousands, and even millions of dollars. To say that there is a lot of money in sport is an UNDER-statement. Unfortunately, it trickles down all the way to youth sports and over-zealous parents who believe their young 8-year old pitcher is the next 1st-round draft choice.

The bottom line is that there are tremendous opportunities for trainers, coaches, stretch therapists, mindset coaches, nutritionists, and others who can help young athletes excel in their sports at the youth, high-school, and college levels.

Examples of the type of training or opportunities that exist:

- Speed training for youth athletes.
- Quarterback training for youth and high-school QB's.
- Pitcher training for boys & girls looking to maximize their velocity and results.
- Hitter training for baseball and softball players.
- Lacrosse specific training for the boy or girl looking to be a great lax player.

- Mindset coaching to augment your strength & conditioning program.

The list goes on and on. It comes down to your expertise. How can you help young athletes succeed?

Youth/Kids' Fitness Training:

Let's not forget that all kids are *not* athletes. Nor do all kids want to be athletes. As a matter of fact, when you look at the statistics that over 20% of kids are obese (ages 2-19), it's disheartening. Because of the combined effects of less physical activity, poor nutrition, and increased screen time (watching television, video games, and social media), the trends are all moving in the *wrong* direction.

Something NEEDS to be done.

To my knowledge, the "game-changing" program for kids who are non-athletes who need to move more, eat better, and get healthier, does NOT YET exist.

Who is it going to be?

What is it going to be?

When you talk about "What's Next?", this might be the biggest kahuna of ALL of them. And the most IMPACTFUL one. I'm seeing a program for kids (non-athletes) that incorporates movement for 15-20+ minutes a day, nutrition accountability, short daily mindset messages that are 2-5 minutes long and delivered through the phone, and inspirational messages reminding kids about "who they are" to get into their psyche.

Hmmmm....

Anyone interested in collaborating on this??

Let's GOOO!!! Let's help these kids and athletes be the best they can be. And this means on ALL levels.

Example:

During the pandemic, I created a 4-week program called "Get Yoked" which I offered to kids and their parents to address this issue. We sold thousands of them. It was an extremely successful program because it gave them a focus, a purpose each day, and it addressed mind, body and spirit so that they felt better.

I think we need MORE of these kinds of programs for our kids. We need to show our kids how to take control of their own health and fitness and give them opportunities to connect with themselves and with others as well.

What can you do to incorporate "sport-specific training" or "youth/kids fitness" into your business?

* Choose what you are going to focus on.
* Choose if you are going to use technology to scale it online or offer it in your studio. Or both.
* Ask parents how you can *best* help their kids.

Timing for this opportunity: NOW!

** Note:

Not all "sports-specific training" is around kids. Between the rise of pickleball, the popularity of golf, and lifestyle sports such as snow-skiing and water-skiing, the opportunities are endless.

A great example is my friend, Jennifer Lockwood. She is an expert ski instructor with the highest credentials for skiing. She is also a personal trainer. She created her online "Peak Ski Conditioning" program for adults several years ago and serves people who want to get in great shape for an upcoming ski season.

Her work has not only helped people prepare properly for skiing, she has since signed endorsement deals with companies such as Nordica, who recognize her expertise, devotion to her craft of fitness and skiing, and her ability to communicate through video. You can learn more about her program at www.peakskiconditioning.com.

9. Bio-Hacking & Functional Aging and Medicine

This is an exciting area that I see continuing to grow. The research they are doing in biohacking is truly cutting edge! We all want to live longer, healthier, happier lives and the studies they are doing, and products and services that are being offered, are helping us to do that. I see this as one of the fastest and most interesting areas of growth in the future of health, vitality, fitness, and aging.

Here are five things that I'm doing to not only help "recovery" but also "biohack" my system. These are all things I have done or am currently doing to maximize my health, healing, vitality, or energy. All of these hacks are ones I have used in my own healing from a recent knee "clean-up" surgery. (Listen to my Todd Durkin IMPACT SHOW podcast #263 to hear my complete healing routine.)

These are my "Top 5" biohacks:

1. **Blood Flow Restriction (BFR)**
2. **Red Light Therapy**
3. **Infrared Sauna**
4. **Peptides (ie. BP-157 and Sermorelin)**
5. **Stem-cells**

Let's discuss each briefly and I can give you some additional resources on each at the end of the entire section…

a. Blood-Flow Restriction

"BFR" has been a hack I've been using for about a year now. The purpose of it is to optimize the release of growth hormone, IGF-1, and nitric oxide while working out. The premise is to put your "BFR bands" around your upper arms and upper legs and inflate them to a pressure high enough to maintain arterial blood flow, while restricting venous return. And then using a lighter weight/higher rep methodology with the BFR bands while exercising which allows the lactate-threshold to be reached similarly to performing an intense bout of exercise with heavy weights. This creates the onslaught of the aforementioned hormones, which is a powerful way to get all the physical and mental effects of training without stressing your joints with heavy weights or excessive volume.

Additionally, "BDNF" or brain-derived neurotropic factor, is released which is a protein that stimulates cellular growth and repair in the brain and nervous system. As Dr. Mike DeBord, founder of B3 Sciences, states, "BFR generates an incredible hormonal and metabolic response that leads to enhanced strength, athletic performance, and definitely faster recovery and rehabilitation times."

Needless to say, I have used "BFR Training" as part of my regimen now after two of my knee surgeries and a flare-up of a back injury. I wanted to continue training during all of this but couldn't quite use the weights I desired. By using "BFR," I was able to stimulate the same type of results and get the "euphoria" of training within about 20-minutes of BFR training.

(See Resources below for my preferred brand/recommendations)

b. Red-Light Therapy

I've been using a "Joovv Wall" for several years now, and it's an "easy" way to infuse recovery into your own bedroom or gym. Red-Light therapy is great for cellular regeneration and ATP synthesis. It stimulates mitochondria (the "powerhouse" of the cell), and it has anti-inflammatory effects. Ten to twenty minutes per night is a great way to counter the "blue-light" we are exposed to all day through phones, computers, and screens.

(See Resources below for my preferred brand/recommendations)

c. Infrared Sauna

I've been loving my infrared sauna for 15-years now. Literally. I put my first two infrared saunas into Fitness Quest 10 in 2007. I've long advocated for the benefits of the infrared sauna to rid your body of toxins, assist with recovery, increase circulation due to the deeper penetration of the infrared heat wave (vs. a conventional heat wave), and help in healing.

If I can get in my infrared sauna 2-3x per week for 15-20 minutes, and it's at about 140-degrees or above, life is better!

(See Resources below for my preferred brand/recommendations)

d. Peptide Therapy

Peptides are short chains of amino acids that act as building blocks of proteins, such as collagen, elastin, and keratin. Peptide therapy is *also* used to optimize the production and secretion of growth hormone levels, which rapidly decline as we age. Growth hormone levels affect age management, pain management, weight management and even general wellness.

There are many types of "peptides," but the two types of peptides that have been prescribed to me by my doctor are:

1. **BP-157.** This is a peptide that helps alleviate joint pain, improve joint stability, and boost recovery from injuries. It helps vascular flow to tendons and ligaments. It also stimulates the repair of neurons in the brain and stimulates growth hormone. This is good for cell regeneration, wound healing, and muscle growth. The important thing to remember here is that high-intensity exercise is still the best way to stimulate HGH. However, because it's hard to do when you're hurt or injured, you may also want to use the BFR bands while exercising.

2. **Sermorelin.** This peptide helps the body's natural production of growth hormone levels. Research has proven that sermorelin therapy helps the body burn fat and increase energy, vitality, strength, endurance, and wound healing. You can take capsules or inject it into your abdomen, hips, thigh, or upper arm.

I have used both of these peptides following my surgeries and back pain episodes to maximize healing.

(See Resources below for my preferred brand/recommendations)

e. Stem Cells

Now this is next-level bio-hacking, and I've been using it since 2018 when I flew to London, England, to receive my first infusion of "EV's" (extra-cellular vesicles). I received my second infusion of stem cells in 2020. And my latest infusion of stem cells was just in August 2022, three weeks after my "knee clean-up" surgery.

What happens with the type of "E.V. stem-cell treatment" that I'm receiving?

Stem cells are taken from you in a minor procedure and harvested. The EV's are separated from a patient's stem cells, harvested from a small sample of fat or blood, and then multiplied in the laboratory. The EV's are then placed in a normal saline for infusion back into the patient, delivering a cell-free therapy which is many times more effective than a standard stem cell transplant, and far safer as well.

Why this type of stem cell treatment?

One infusion gives you literally billions of your own EV's (Typical stem cell transplants will give you maybe 300,000 EV's at best).

Some of the best benefits include:

- Cell-free stem therapy stimulates repair mechanisms
- Promotes healthy tissue regrowth
- Helps modulate scar tissue from old injuries
- There is a strong anti-inflammatory effect within days of an infusion

There are many types of stem cell treatments available. They can range in price from $5,000 to $50,000. The great news is that prices are coming down on the various forms of stem cell treatments, and they will be used in many different treatment protocols in the years ahead.

Even now, besides those in orthopedic pain, they are being used by M.S. patients, diabetes patients, people with serious liver disease and other serious conditions involving inflammation.

Here is the company I've used, along with many of my athletes, in my stem cell treatments: www.wellbeingint.com

My Biohack Resources/Links/Affiliations

(While you don't need to use what/who I have used, I have put a lot of time into researching the best brands in each of the areas and am sharing my chosen brands with you.)

- **Blood Flow Restriction (BFR):**
  Web Link: https://td.b3sciences.com/
- **Red Light Therapy (Joovv Wall):**
  Web Link: https://lddy.no/1cj56 (this affiliate link gives you $50.00 off your order)
- **Infrared Sauna (Healthmate):**
  Web Link: https://mailchi.mp/healthmatesauna/impact
- **Peptides (ie. BP-157 and Sermorelin):**
  Web Link: https://katalystwellness.com/?utm_source=todddurkin
- **Stem Cells:**
  Web Link: www.wellbeingint.com

With any of this, I am a big believer in having an allopathic doctor (MD) work with you, as well as a naturopathic doctor (ND). And whether you work with an MD at an "anti-aging" clinic or a naturopathic doctor at his/her practice, it can go a long way in "quarterbacking your health" to optimal levels.

Personally, I have used both an MD and an ND for over 5 years. This allows me to monitor my bloodwork, be pro-active in staving off some of the deleterious effects of stress and keeps my energy and focus as consistent and high as possible.

10. What do YOU think is the "Next Thing" in health and fitness?

While this is open-ended, I don't pretend to know it all. I do believe that "COLLABORATION IS KING." And if there is ever a time to collaborate and come together as an industry, it is right now!!

So, I'd love to hear from you.

You have heard from 27 of my highly respected friends and colleagues. I LOVE what they had to say and believe they are on the cusp of proliferating their own IMPACT.

Now I want to hear from you.

What do you think?

Which of these "predictions" or "trends" most resonate with you?

Which ones are you going to TAKE ACTION on?

The worst thing you can do is nothing.

The feeling of being stuck in a quagmire of mediocrity or uncertainty is not fulfilling. After a while, you feel as if your purpose is diminished and your passions aren't being filled-up.

My hope, my encouragement, my plea is that TODAY you think about "WHAT'S NEXT" for you.

Thank you for letting me share my heart and soul. All of it.

I opened this book with a lot of questions that I have been asking myself over the past couple years.

And on the pages in-between here, my fellow authors and collaborators have given you A LOT to think about.

But let me close by asking you a few more questions:

1. What are your Top 3-5 gifts that you must share more and that the world deserves more of?

2. What project/program are you working on these days that gives you the MOST life? How can you do more of "it" and what can you do to push it "further down the field?"

3. If there was only "one" thing that you MUST do more of, what is it?

4. If you knew that you could not fail and you only had 5 years of life left, what is the "one" thing you MUST do, otherwise you may regret not taking the chance?

5. After reading this book, "WHAT'S NEXT" for you?

That's it my friends. "What's Next?"

My hope and intention is that this book is a catalyst for your next iteration. As you reset, refresh, recharge, and maybe even reinvent yourself in this new "season" we are entering, may you tap into your true full potential, be led by your deepest passions and divine purpose, and have the audacity and courage to go out on a limb and be a trend setter.

After all, that's where IMPACT is created.

I'll see you "out there."

Much love...and tons of IMPACT!

Todd Durkin, MA, CSCS
Founder, Fitness Quest 10 & Todd Durkin Enterprises
Author, Speaker, Podcaster...COACH!
The Todd Durkin IMPACT Show Podcast

Todd Durkin

Todd Durkin, MA, CSCS, is an internationally recognized performance coach, trainer, keynote speaker, author, and life-transformer who motivates, educates, and inspires people worldwide. He trains NFL, MLB, & MMA athletes at his award-winning gym he founded 22-years ago, Fitness Quest 10 (San Diego, CA). He is a 2-time Trainer of the Year, a best-selling author, a recipient of the Jack LaLanne Award, and the 2018 Canadian Fitness Professionals International Presenter of the Year. He was a finalist on the NBC & Netflix show called STRONG.

Through Todd Durkin Enterprises, Todd and his team provide motivational keynotes, workshops, and events worldwide. Todd has keynoted or hosted workshops to brand leaders like Under Armour, Morgan Stanley, Principal Financial, Wells Fargo, Bank of America, Henderson Inc., The Ken Blanchard Companies, YPO, Bath & Body Works, Cal-a-Vie Resort & Spa, the Golden Door, IMG, USMA, UCSD, UBS Warburg, Quest Ventures, Kaiser Permanente, Benedictine University and The College of William & Mary. His passion, energy, and uncanny ability to inspire a crowd has led to countless standing ovations.

If your company is looking for a keynote program to inspire its team and leaders, look no further.

Todd is also the founder of Todd Durkin Mastermind, a best-in-class life business & life-coaching program for passionate fitness professionals. Todd and his team of Mastermind coaches deliver world-class content and coaching in the areas of business, leadership, business, marketing, personal growth, and "in the trenches" content to help individuals grow personally & professionally.

Additionally, Todd coaches people in his "God-Sized Dreams" Coaching program, who are looking for high-performance coaching to excel personally, professionally, and spiritually as well.

Todd also loves to podcast. His **Todd Durkin IMPACT SHOW** podcast inspires millions of people to live their best life NOW. With over 270-episodes shared around the globe and millions of episodes downloaded, it definitely is a podcast you want to subscribe to today!

One of the ventures Todd is most passionate about is The Durkin IMPACT Foundation (501-c-3), which has donated more than $300,000 to families and kids in-need. Todd loves getting people's minds right, motivating them to be the best version of themselves, and ultimately, inspiring people to lead a life worth telling a story about.

Todd has been married to his wife Melanie for 21-years. She has been a full-time professor at Southwestern College in San Diego for 23-years in the Exercise Science Department. They have 3 kids: Luke (19), Brady (17), and McKenna (14). They also have a 7-year-old golden retriever (Jersey Dog).

CONNECT WITH TODD

Website:

www.ToddDurkin.com

Social Media:

  ToddDurkinFQ10

   ToddDurkin

FREE Weekly Messages:

Additionally, please sign-up for Todd's FREE motivational & inspirational weekly messages and videos that he will text you to your phone. Simply text him at (619)304.2216 and text him "WhatsNext" or ask him any question you may have on the book or on your health, fitness, performance...or mindset.

And yes, it REALLY is him that will text you back!!

By signing-up today, you will receive exclusive content and messages and be in his "inner-circle" of communication & motivation.

Text "WhatsNext" to (619)304.2216 NOW!!!

INVITE TODD DURKIN
TO SPEAK TODAY

Todd Durkin is a dynamic keynote speaker who loves inspiring those seeking high performance and maximum success in their life. He has spoken all over the world to a wide array of audiences in a multitude of industries.

As one committed to creating a massive impact, Todd has a passion to instill a championship mindset in people of all ages, levels, and sectors. He has a knack for tapping into people's mindsets and heart-sets to help them reach their full potential personally and professionally. His passion, contagious positive energy, and ability to connect with all audiences allow him to routinely receive standing ovations and rave reviews.

If you, your business, your conference, your college or university, or your organization would be interested in having Todd speak, please contact him via phone at (858) 271-1171 or through his website at www. todddurkin.com.

TUNE IN TO
TODD'S PODCAST

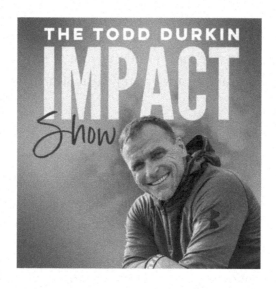

The Todd Durkin IMPACT Show is designed to motivate
and inspire you to live a life full of passion, purpose,
and IMPACT.
It's guaranteed to **Get Your Mind Right**!

The IMPACT Show is for anyone who seeks high performance
in business, sports, leadership, or life.

Available Wherever You Get Your Podcasts

Proceeds from this book will be donated to

The Durkin IMPACT foundation was started in 2012 by Todd and his wife Melanie, when his hometown of Brick, New Jersey, was destroyed by Hurricane Sandy. We knew we had to do something to help the people in Brick who were struggling as a result of the hurricane.

Ten years later, The Durkin IMPACT Foundation not only helps those in need but also awards college scholarships to high school athletes from both Brick Township High (BTHS), Scripps Ranch High School (SRHS), and a few other schools chosen at random each year. Each scholarship ranges from $500 to $1,500 and to date we've awarded more than $250,000 in scholarships.

OUR MISSION

The Durkin **IMPACT** Foundation is a 501(c)(3) that was founded in 2012 on the heels of Hurricane Sandy devastating my home area of the Jersey Shore.

Our Mission: The Durkin **IMPACT** Foundation was established to motivate, educate, and inspire people to be their best, to foster a spirit of giving back and paying forward, and to create a positive IMPACT in the world.

Now our **IMPACT** Foundation is raising money for scholarships to non-privileged, under-served student-athletes going to college who exemplify the qualities, traits, work ethic, and attitude of an "**IMPACT**" person. In addition, our funding priorities help those in need who are affected by natural disasters, childhood obesity, and diseases such as heart disease, disability, and cancer.

OUR FUNDING PRIORITIES

The IMPACT Foundation Founders, Todd and Melanie Durkin, along with the Board of Trustees respond to the needs of people affected by natural disasters, childhood obesity, those with diseases such as heart disease & diabetes, and educational & athletic opportunities for those in need. We are dedicated to funding five (5) significant program areas of interest within the following *general* annual distribution and allocation percentages:

- Natural disaster relief (those that have lost homes, been displaced, out of work, etc.)   30%
- Medical   20%
- Educational   20%
- Athletic   20%
- Environment   10%

Note: From time to time, the Trust may make awards to organizations and institutions that have made no formal request, which we have recognized for exemplary work, and/or show significant promise in one or more of these five areas, and whose continuing work and mission would be more fully enhanced and supported by this funding.

For more information, or to make a donation, go to:

https://todddurkin.com/impact-foundation/

WANT TO BE A PUBLISHED AUTHOR?

Scriptor Publishing Group offers services including writing, publishing, marketing, and consulting to take your book…

From Dream to Published!

Go to <u>www.scriptorpublishinggroup.com</u>
to get started!

Or check us out on social media:

@ScriptorPublishingGroup